THE DYNAMICS OF
RELIGIOUS CONVERSION

THE DYNAMICS OF RELIGIOUS CONVERSION

V. BAILEY GILLESPIE

Religious Education Press
Birmingham, Alabama

Library of Congress Cataloging-in-Publication Data

Gillespie, V. Bailey (Virgil Bailey)
    The dynamics of religious conversion / V. Bailey Gillespie.
    Includes bibliographical references and index.
    ISBN 0-89135-084-5 (alk. paper)
    1. Conversion.   I. Title.
BR110.G528 1991   91-23450
248.2'4—dc20   CIP

Religious Education Press, Inc.
5316 Meadow Brook Road
Birmingham, Alabama 35242
10 9 8 7 6 5 4 3 2

Religious Education Press publishes books exclusively in religious education and in areas closely related to religious education. It is committed to enhancing and professionalizing religious education through the publication of serious, significant, and scholarly works.

PUBLISHER TO THE PROFESSION

DEDICATION

To my students in their struggles to find God . . .

Contents

Preface

It is obvious that people change. It is equally obvious that people seek God. These two considerations provide the basis for this exploration of the process of change. The development within Christianity, particularly in the last few centuries, of emphasis on distinctive religious conversion has helped focus the study of religious experience on this particular example. Sudden conversion, however, is only one form of religious experience. Nurtured change, gradual shift, personal insight, as well as those sudden turnarounds all constitute manifestations of religion in personal life. In the secular realm, identity experience often seems paralleled to religious conversion in both its proof, presence, and impact.

This book describes both. It hopes to clarify ways in which these experiences can be efficacious in the emerging faith journey. After providing an analysis of the nature of religious conversion and the components which form some of its constituent elements—revivalism, development, ideology, emotionalism, and culture—the early chapters identify both the context of change and the factors which influence it. In a comprehensive review, the major understandings of this religious experience are probed, along with a description of that movement toward God.

Identity frames the context of the following chapters. A review of the position of Erik Erikson and others regarding identity experience clarifies the factors in this type of personal change. The relationship of religious conversion and personal identity illustrated as religious conversion is seen as a rich type of identity experience providing ideology, fit, purpose, and worldview.

No book useful to pastors, religious educators, pastoral facilitators, and counselors is particularly helpful if the implications of the theoretical construct are not explored. The practical implications for pastoral ministry, religious instruction, and counseling are suggested in the later chapters.

A word of special thanks must go to Robert Bates, a graduate assistant in the

1

department of Church and Ministry during 1988-90, who helped in the bibliographical search and collection of ten years of new material on conversion and identity. More kudos must go to Robert Dunn, Chair of the Department of English at Loma Linda University Riverside for his help in editing this new manuscript. I continue to be blessed by a wife who can somehow always add to her busy schedule some editing and insight. Judith, a court reporting agency owner, has always been encouraging. She added this manuscript to her own proofing/editing and squeezed the work between depositions and her own management tasks.

There has been such a volume of new material about religious conversion and personal identity in the past ten years that my original work in this area needed extensive reworking. This volume includes that material along with the implications of those ten years of growing research in the area of religious experience and conversion study. This book examines these issues and relationships and explores these two concepts lived out in experience—religious conversion and personal identity—with a view toward aiding those who are involved with others in the process of faith development and change. I hope that pastors, teachers, religious educators, curriculum developers, producers of materials for all age groups, parents, and all those on their own individual quest for change might find this volume worthwhile in their own growth toward God.

V. BAILEY GILLESPIE
Riverside, California

Chapter 1

Conversion: A Way to Change

"To have a conversion experience is nothing much. The real thing is to be able to keep on taking it seriously; to retain a sense of its plausibility."

Peter L. Berger

The focus of this book is religious conversion, that form of religious expression studied by psychologists of religion, preachers of righteousness, evangelists, and experienced by apostles, prophets, pastors, and men and women of God. This experience is claimed to be central to the religious change of an individual. Religious conversion is that spiritual encounter equated with the experience alluded to by Jesus of Nazareth in his evening answer to Nicodemus regarding his authority: "Verily, verily, I say unto thee, except a man be born again, he cannot see the kingdom of God."[1] The focus of this book then is how individuals change in that area of their inmost lives that touches the holy.

Conversion is most commonly understood to be a dramatic religious experience. Undoubtedly the emotionalism usually attributed to this event has caused it to be so central in most studies of religious experience. The topic is not usually analyzed in its social setting, and it is seldom understood to be multifaceted. In a sense, each conversion is unique because each occurs in a context. This context may embrace the political, social, economic, and religious centers of a person, but whatever the meaning it never takes place outside a cultural context of some kind. "Conversions, therefore, are of almost infinite variety."[2]

Because of its subjective nature conversion has had little respect from

---

1. John 3:3, King James Version.
2. John A. Gration, "Conversion in Cultural Context," *International Bulletin for Religious Research* 7 (October 1983), pp. 157-162.

3

those scholars interested in religious phenomena, since it is assumed to be supernatural by most religious groups. It therefore lies outside the realm of their investigation. The secular experience, on the other hand, such as identity, has been given considerable discussion of a more psychological nature. Since this kind of human change can be readily attributed to many sources, it has been discussed much more analytically. Questions about this topic often focus on the nature of the experience (supernatural or natural), the process itself (sudden or gradual), the causes (psychological or pathological), the sources (internal or external), or the results (personal or ideological).

Walter Houston Clark comments that conversion is "a sort of psychological slum, to be avoided by any really respected scholar"[3] while George Jackson suggests that the subject belongs in that realm in which our minds "do not easily move," an area in which we find ourselves a kind of alien. "When we hear of conversions we think immediately of revivals and the clatter of machinery which always jars upon our nerves: to us revivalism is another name for hysteria and unwholesome excitement."[4] It is also true that most of the literature about conversion, religious experience, and psychology of religion is uncritical and riddled with personal opinion. Most of the stories and personal testimonies present problems to those who would analyze them. Augustine waited some ten years to disclose his *Confessions;* Loyola finally dictated his own autobiography some thirty years after the conversional event took place; while Thomas Merton, a classic contemporary example of conversion's power, waited ten years to explain his change. Blaise Pascal was one of the few to record the experience as it happened, and but for that little piece of parchment no one would ever have known about his conversion. There are many personal accounts told to others many years later, such as the account of Henrietta Gant, an African-American slave, whose description of her conversion identifies a clearly Christian faith with Afro-American qualities. Her conversion gives hope in the midst of despair, promising "freedom despite enslavement and oppression." It was recorded in 1939, almost fifty years after the incident.[5] Even the apostle Paul may have waited until later to record the experience. This lapse between the event and its recording makes an understanding of this experience even more difficult.[6]

John Gration studied the shifts and reconstructions in the biographies of converts from a sociological perspective. He suggests that biographical

3. H. R. Bagwell, "Abrupt Religious Conversion Experience," *Journal of Religion and Health* 8 (April 1969), p. 174.

4. J. R. Scroggs and W. G. T. Douglas, "Issues in the Psychology of Religious Conversion," *Journal of Religion and Health* 6 (July 1967), p. 204.

5. Hugh T. Kerr and John M. Mulder, eds., *Conversions* (Grand Rapids, Mich.: Eerdmans, 1983), p. 155.

6. A. J. Krailsheimer, *Conversion* (London: SCM Press, 1980), p. 156.

material in testimonies should not be used as documentation for what has really happened to a person in a conversion, but rather, the story must be seen in the context of the theology or movement in which it occurs. He notes that "creating objective retrospective biographies" is difficult for converts. It is not that they are lying. They simply have a new vocabulary, and they believe a new divine power is in their lives. Consequently, "that strong postconversion understanding influences their interpretation."[7]

What can be said about conversion narratives and conversion traditions in Western Christianity? Some have argued that the pure theological (intellectual or ideological) content of the experience never lies at the moment of change. That moment exists only retrospectively when the convert—later—attempts to interpret this new insight or "light" in answering the question, "How did I get here?" And since one can only come to the past through the present understanding of the experience, it is possible that the convert constructs a narrative that renders the past and the present on one continuum of intelligible and coherent interpretive understanding. In other words, the question of "Can I trust this story?" is a real one, and the comment, "This is how I got this way" is only clearly derived through reflection. Someone has said that the retrospectoscope is the best instrument ever invented. Thus, "the seemingly historical narrative serves to reaffirm the traditions which the convert, through this event, has joined."[8] Often the conversion account is both anachronistic and apologetic. It is anachronistic because the account of the conversion experience is so much shaped and molded by the current surrounding events and context, and it may be apologetic because of the necessity for the converts to defend their newfound faith to the new, old, or opposing group. It is, as Paula Fredriksen says, "the retrospective moment through the retrospective self."[9] The subjectivity of the testimony is what gives it power. It is your own story, your eye witness account of what God has done in your life. It has an undeniable sense of authority and self-authentification. There may be a lot of questions about the Bible that you cannot answer, but on this subject you and only you are the authority.[10] And since many bizarre and unorthodox forms of religious expression exist today and are on the increase, this too adds to the problem of understanding conversion's nature. There seems to be something almost embarrassing about discussing religious experience—after all, the topic is so very personal how could it be understood by another? Nevertheless, this topic deserves probing and

---

7. Gration, "Conversion in Cultural Context," p. 28.

8. Paula A. Fredriksen, "Paul and Augustine: Conversion Narratives: Orthodox Traditions, and the Retrospective Self," *Journal of Theological Studies* 37:1 (1986), p. 33.

9. Ibid.

10. Eljee Bentley, "Making Converts: A Baptist View," *Southwestern Journal of Theology* 28 (1986), p. 54.

understanding, and a relationship with its secular counterpart—identity—should be examined.

It is not the purpose of this book to debate whether or not conversions take place, for the experience is well-documented in history. Too many cases have been cited, such as the apostle Paul on the road to Damascus, to have to debate whether or not such occurrences actually take place. William James, after courting some forceful, sudden conversion stories, says,

> I might multiply cases almost indefinitely, but these will suffice to show you how real, definite, and memorable an event a sudden conversion may be to him who has the experience. Throughout the height of it he undoubtedly seems to himself a passive spectator, or undergoer of an astounding process performed upon him from above. There is too much evidence of this for any doubt of it to be possible.[11]

John Wesley gives many examples of converts healed in soul and body in a moment.[12] St. Augustine's appraisal illustrates the definiteness of this experience where he says, "For immediately I had reached the end of this sentence it was as though my heart was filled with a light of confidence and all the shadows of my doubt were swept away."[13] Much more is known and documented regarding the mystical conversion of Pascal. He was typical in that he was a very devout type before his conversion experience. Before he was twenty-four years old, he is reported to have been enlightened by God through the reading of books of piety so that he understood perfectly what the Christian was supposed to do, yet he experienced another religious conversion at thirty years of age. He describes the experience on a piece of parchment found over his heart at his death.

> The year of grace 1654,
> On Monday, 23rd of November, Feast of St. Clement, Pope and Martyr, and others in the Martyrology,
>   Vigil of Saint Chrysogonus, Martyr, and others,
>   From about half past ten in the evening until about half past twelve,

FIRE

> God of Abraham, God of Isaac, God of Jacob, not of the philosophers

---

11. William James, *The Varieties of Religious Experience* (New York: Mentor Books, New American Library of World Literature, 1958), p. 184.

12. John Wesley, *The Journal of John Wesley,* ed. Nehemiah Curnock (London: Epworth Press, 1938), pp. 186-204.

13. Augustine, *The Confessions of St. Augustine,* trans. Rex Warner (New York: Mentor-Omega Books, New American Library of World Literature, 1963), p. 183. See also Stephen Happel and James J. Walter, *Conversion and Discipleship: A Christian Foundation for Ethics and Doctrine* (Philadelphia: Fortress, 1986), p. 15.

and scholars (Ex 3:6; Mt 22:32).
Certitude. Certitude. Feeling. Joy. Peace.
God of Jesus Christ.
Deum menum et Deum vestrum ("My God and your God," Jn 20:17).
Forgetfulness of the world and of everything except God.
   He is to be found only by the ways taught in the Gospel.
   Greatness of the human soul.
   "Righteous Father, the world hath not known Thee, but I have known Thee" (Jn 17:25).
   Joy, joy, joy, tears of joy.
   I have separated myself from Him.
Derelinquerunt me fontem aquae vivae ("They have forsaken me, the fountain of living waters," Jr 2:13).
   "My God, wilt thou leave me?" (Mt 27:46).
   Let me not be separated from Him eternally.
   "This is the eternal life, that they might know Thee, the only true God, and the one whom Thou has sent, Jesus Christ" (Jn 17:3).
   Jesus Christ
   Jesus Christ.
   I have separated myself from Him: I have fled from Him, denied Him, crucified Him.
   Let me never be separated him Him.
   We keep hold of Him only by the ways taught in the Gospel.
   Renunciation, total and sweet.
   Total submission to Jesus Christ and to my director.
   Eternally in joy for a day's training on earth.
   Non obliviscar sermones tuos ("I will not forget Thy words," Ps 118:16).
Amen.[14]

There is only fragmentary knowledge of what appears to have been a similar miraculous conversion experienced by St. Thomas Aquinas in 1273. He had led an actively religious life which culminated in his *Summa Theologica*. Then at age forty-eight he had an experience which inhibited further literary composition; he claimed: "I can write no more; for everything that I have written seems like straw, by comparison with the things I now see and which have been revealed to me."[15]

A more typical experience is that of Edward Hale's religious conversion, which was reported by Edwin Starbuck simply as growth.

---

14. Emil Cailliet and John C. Blankenagel, trans. *Great Shorter Works of Pascal* (Philadelphia: Westminster, 1948), pp. 117, 220, or see "Pensees," in Robert H. Thouless, *An Introduction to the Psychology of Religion* (Cambridge: Cambridge University Press, 1971), p. 117.
   15. Ibid., p. 116.

There had never been any dramatic, overwhelming religious crisis in his life. He had been brought up in a Christian home; since childhood he took it as a matter of course that he was to learn as much as he could about the world and was to do what he could to relieve the needs of others; all his life he had known and respected wise and intelligent men who were religious; and in spite of occasional doubts and questions, his own religious convictions had undergone a deepening and enriching through the years.[16]

There are stories of conversion outside of the specifically Western Christian context. In India, the high-caste Sadhu (holy man) Sundar Singh confessed his belief in Christianity as a result of a vision he received after he ignited a Bible and burned it with kerosene. He writes with precise detail. "At 4:30 a.m. [December 18, 1904] I saw . . . a great light, I thought the place was on fire. . . . I saw the form of the Lord Jesus Christ. It had such an appearance of glory and love."[17] As a result of this experience, history records that he became an ascetic, adopted a simple lifestyle, talked with wild beasts at night, and was last seen starting off on a pilgrimage to Tibet—a place often considered off-limits for Christians during his time. Later, Singh's books were used to inspire others to become Christian. In his words, however, he seldom again speaks of that experience.

Conversion experience has wrought considerable change in individuals' lives. Francis of Assisi may be an exemplary model. Duane Arnold and George Fry have sought to organize his life around the symbols that marked off that change. Just as Moses is a man of water, Jacob is often associated with a rock and Joseph a pit, for Francis there were symbols of dream, betrothal, pilgrimage, kiss, prayer, and trial. Each symbol was an important trigger for his change which was marked off by a significant shift in behavior and worldview. Arnold and Fry suggest that Francis saw himself first as "God's builder" in his attempts to restore God in his local environment and to upgrade the houses of worship in nearby towns. Later he is labeled "God's fool" as he tried to share God to the world. In the end, Francis could be typified as the "Light of God" whose words and deeds seemed to reflect Christ both for the church and the world. Like Christ the carpenter who died on a tree, the fool who embodied the wisdom of God, and the light which shown in darkness—so was Francis of Assisi.[18] But conversion is not always an isolated, individualistic experience, for it can have a societal ring.

The history of the world records great awakenings where conversional change took place. The great awakening in 1734-1750; Wesley's successes,

---

16. See W. S. Hill, "Psychology of Conversion," *Pastoral Psychology* 6 (November 1955), p. 44.

17. Hugh T. Kerr and John M. Mulder, eds. *Conversions: The Christian Experience* (Grand Rapids, Mich.: Eerdmans, 1983), p. xvii.

18. Duane W. H. Arnold and C. George Fry, *Francis: A Call to Conversion* (Grand Rapids, Mich.: Zondervan, 1988), pp. 32-41.

1740-1790; the reformations in Kentucky, 1796-1815; Nettelton's and Finney's revivals, 1828-1840; the revival of Millerism, 1840-1844; the American, Irish, and Welsh revivals in 1857-1859; and the revivals of Moody in the 1870-1880s—all exemplify the religious revivals of the era. Yet today, revival, with the accompanying phenomenon of conversion, still exists. The 1960s interest in the Jesus Movements, more current Neo-Pentecostalism, Born-again Christians, Moral Majority, New Age religions, and charismatic renewal groups bring this issue again to the front of experience.

To begin, we must explore religious experience and the phenomena of religious conversion.

Religious Experience

When one talks of conversion experience, one usually thinks of it as a religious experience. This necessitates an understanding of what is religious. Books have been written regarding just this. So, briefly, some comments to define "religious" are in order.

Definitions of religion and conversion are always in danger of being influenced by many of the same things—subjective standards or superficial manifestations. What some scholars label as content, others label form.[19] Some label "religious" such things as liturgy, belief, institutions, or even specific doctrines. What is here referred to as "religious" is that which Tillich asserts is of "ultimate concern."[20] It poses the aspect of a "unity of direction" that suggests how people find a unity of life and an answer to life's questions through knowledge or discovery of God's will. This God could be defined as "Being," "Other," or any of many terms used to describe the infinite. Yet religious conversion is an event that searches out unifying qualities of existence that give meaning of ultimate value to life. It is an experience with its source in God and its power of change through the Holy Spirit. In addition to this "unifying," it is a sensing of divine presence, too.[21]

The question, "What is religious," is in itself the subject of thousands of pages. One wonders if individual bias is what determines its definition. When one thinks about the feelings of knowing God, emphasis is on the personal piety and presence that transcends the mundane. For others, religion takes on a societal feel, with concerns about groups and how they learn, about responses, size, and growth in conformity with the known traditions of

---

19. Barbara Eleanor Jones, "Conversion: An Examination of the Myth of Human Change" (Ph.D. dissertation, Columbia University, 1969), p. 4.

20. Paul Tillich, *The Protestant Era* (Chicago: University of Chicago Press, 1948), pp. xv, 58, 87, 273.

21. See V. Bailey Gillespie, *The Experience of Faith* (Birmingham Ala.: Religious Education Press, 1989) for a thorough discussion of the nature of religious and faith experience.

piety. Still another definition suggests the embodiment of belief in the life of the believer. This position regarding the lives of the faithful is so vague that "faith" loses content, and clarification of the response altogether seems impossible. The general category of life as religion is too broad to examine.

John Westerhoff III suggests this: "My understanding of religion refers to those concrete communal expressions of faith which are embodied in the life of a people—a community of faith. Religion is faith given shape, form, and content."[22]

This definition is comprehensive. Religion involves the belief, the feelings, the process of becoming, and the content of faith. But religion is not limited to just the belief, feelings, and contents. It encompasses the impact of faith and belief on the world. The response of faith is part of the package of understanding what is religious. This definition is helpful and useful. It gives a fuller understanding of the inclusiveness of God in life. It is not just the feelings when one encounters the divine, yet is it not that as well? It is not just the beliefs one internalizes upon commitment, nor is it solely the response one makes when approached by the divine. It is *all* of these. It includes relationships, attitudes, friendships, meaning, and purpose. Religious experience integrates with all that we do; every experience, every attitude, and every ideological position can be influenced by it and may be generated out of it. Omitted, however, are the finer distinctions of the relationship of symbolism, superstition, or hallucination to faith and belief, nor does this definition seek to locate the cause of religious experience.

Walter Clark's definition is useful in understanding religion. He says, "Religion can be most characteristically described as the inner experience of the individual when he senses a Beyond, especially as evidenced by the effects of this experience on his behavior when he actively attempts to harmonize his life with the Beyond."[23] This definition accurately portrays an important truth, as people in their inner experience try to live their lives in tune with the experience they feel. This definition does not rule out the claims that religion is defined as being those groups organized to accomplish the task of the mission of God. When religion is used to mean this fact, the context is explicit. The insight of Max Weber—that religion claims to offer an ultimate stand toward the world by virtue of a direct grasp of the world's meaning—is equally significant.[24]

"Experience" defined is simply, according to Tillich, "the awareness of something that happens to somebody" or the "state of being grasped by the

---

22. See John H. Westerhoff III, *Generation to Generation* (Philadelphia: United Church Press, 1974).

23. Walter Houston Clark, *The Psychology of Religion* (New York: Macmillan, 1958), p. 22.

24. Ruth Ann Wallace, "Some Social Determinants of Change of Religious Affiliation" (Ph.D. dissertation, University of California at Berkeley, 1968), p. 13.

spiritual presence."[25] Some hold to the notion of a definite *kind* of experience which is itself religious and make out of that experience something very unique, marked off from every other kind of experience. This confuses the issue. Rather, every experience, be it aesthetic, scientific, moral, or political, could have religious qualities. But "religious" as a quality of experience signifies something that may belong to all these experiences.[26] Therefore, all experiences are potentially religious and contain a possible religious dimension, since religion is a perspective on life and a quality given to the experience by one who experiences it.

It is possible that a seemingly secular event such as identity experience or "crisis" could be religious in content and direction. And it is equally possible that the experience of identity might not have any specific religious connotation at all. This experience may be both religious and/or secular in content but be perceived by the experiencer as profoundly significant at the core of that person's being, and thus through interpretation it becomes religious.

The ancient Hebrew concept of personhood is helpful here. The Hebrew was viewed as being close to God and was incomplete as a person without this relationship of belonging. People were called to be saints and be sanctified. The biblical concept of "sanctification" is best understood as "to be set apart for a holy use"—to belong to God. Scripture suggests people have wandered from God. Even the first allusions in Genesis illustrate sin arising through the separation of Adam and Eve from God. The history of the Old Testament gives a picture of God and humanity attempting a reunion. Some unsuccessful attempts at finding God are thwarted by God himself because the source of reunion is from humans rather than divine. The tower of Babel story is an excellent example of this kind of attempt.

Since the ancients viewed all things in relation to God, no secular things could exist. There was religious value in all of life itself. The sacred and the secular of antiquity blurred. God was related in every way to life, and therefore to humankind. Faith, in fact, was life. Faith was seen in practice and in day-to-day activities. As humans learned to love God they felt a part of God somehow. They began to feel a deeper sense of belonging, a deeper closeness developed, until Paul could illustrate his understanding of this concept by exclaiming, "For I am sure that neither death, nor life, nor angels, nor principalities, nor things present, nor things to come, nor powers, nor height, nor depth, nor anything else in all creation, will be able to separate us from the love of God in Christ Jesus our Lord."[27] The biblical concept of sancti-

25. Paul Tillich, *Systematic Theology* (Chicago: University of Chicago Press, 1951-63), 4, p. 221.
26. John Dewey, *A Common Faith* (New Haven, Conn.: Yale University Press, 1940), p. 10.
27. Romans 8:38-39, Revised Standard Version.

fication as a sense of "belonging to God" is an appropriate symbol of humanity's relationship with the Almighty.

The popular picture of religious conversion experience, however, assumes that it is generally apart from more traditional religious expression, perhaps accompanied by various states of awareness and therefore dramatic, intense, or unique. If religious conversion is only this, then it is no wonder that many do not try to define it or at least avoid it as some sort of pathology, as Leon Salzman does when he defines all religious conversion as a pathological condition described as "cosmic feelings, states of rapture, and mystical phenomena."[28]

Conversion: Gradual or Sudden

The word conversion has been defined in many ways. Its English root has various meanings which often depend upon the context for clarity. For example, it is usually referring to a "turning" or a "change from one state to another," such as the scientific conversion of water to ice. Those with a military bent find its usage describing a change of front exposed to attack, or the change of bore in firearms. In discussion, it is thought of as a change in viewpoint or belief from ones previously held. In finance, it means a change of security, currency, or coinage. In legal circles, it is used in describing unlawful appropriation and use of another's belongings. In logic, it is the producing of a new proposition by transaction. Those involved in mathematical science find in it a change in the form of a quantity or an expression without a change in the value.[29] The word is used to describe automobile tops and hide-a-beds, and in physics it is a process of converting raw material into energy. In these domains the term conversion has a more or less clearly defined meaning. The basic connotation running throughout the technical usage is "change," "transformation," and "transposition."

Turning from the technical uses of the term, we find two other uses of the word in understanding its English usage. First, the word is used in a number of ordinary situations describing the action between people, beliefs, and attitudes; and second, in a religious sense, it is usually used in a way so vague it is barely definable. Much confusion exists as to its precise meaning. For example, it is used as a noun: "Marge is a recent convert to this viewpoint." Here the noun usage means the person herself. There are no religious overtones at all. When used as a verb, however, as in "she spoke with such conviction and argued so energetically that I know she was trying to convert me," the meaning is to exert influence over someone and the change is

28. Leon Salzman, "The Psychology of Religions and Ideological Conversion," *Psychiatry* 16 (1953), p. 117.
29. "Conversion," *Webster's New Twentieth Century Dictionary: Unabridged* (2nd ed., 1959), p. 400.

something brought about by another. A third usage is more vague, it describes an experience. For example: "You do not need to labor this point, for you see, you are already speaking to the converted." Is a state of mind or experience implied? It is not defined, and its vagueness is supposed to contain truth about experience. In the first two illustrations, the emphasis is on beliefs and viewpoints, but in the last, an experience is delineated.[30] The usage is clear, but the meaning is not.

The terminology of conversion is equally confusing. We often hear the phrase, "I got saved," or "He/she got saved." This conversional slang, so to speak, implies that this event or experience could have happened sometime in the past or at some exact moment, done in a split second, once-for-all. Religious conversion became to be understood as a complete work. It seems that nothing else need happen. John Havlik, in rebuttal of this position, notes that long after Peter first came to the Lord he was told, "When you are converted, strengthen the brothers." This implies more needs to be done in the life if full-fledged Christianity is to be evident. When Havlik was asked about the ambiguity of these phrases, a friend in full-time evangelism said, "Well, I know what it all means, and that is good enough for me." But the real question is whether or not it is good enough to communicate the truth to another person.[31]

In more recent times there has been a psychologizing of the religious conversion phenomenon, and behavioral scientists have sought other terms to describe the experience. Some have updated the jargon and ideas, but the basic ambivalence toward clarity has continued. (i.e., Tom Robbins has called the switch from one religion to another as the "invasion of the body snatchers," or "little Red Riding Hood" theory of conversion.) Instead of an omnipotent God who reaches out and blinds Paul on the Damascus road, we have techniques and processes of brainwashing, hypnotism, mind control, and coercive persuasion leading to "snapping" as means of striking down unsuspecting adults or teenagers. Conversion can even be used as a pejorative synonym for proselytizing.[32]

There are intriguing artistic and poetic allusions as to conversion's meaning. For example, John Steinbeck makes an oblique reference to significant change which might be construed as conversional in his comments about journeying and traveling. "A journey is a person in itself; no two are alike, and all our plans, safeguards, policing and coercion are fruitless. We find after years of struggle that we do not take a trip; a trip takes us."[33] Could this

30. John E. Smith, "The Concept of Conversion," *Mid-Stream* 8:3 (1966), p. 14.
31. John F. Havlik, "Trends and Issues in Evangelism Today," *Faith and Mission* 2:2 (1986), p. 11.
32. James T. Richardson, "Conversion, Brainwashing, and Deprogramming in New Religions," *Update* 6 (1982), p. 35.
33. Quoted in Joseph T. Kelley, "Some Implications of Lonergan's View of Conversion," *Journal of Pastoral Care* 40:4 (1986), p. 364.

comprehension of purpose and clarification of direction be conversion?

Artistic renderings of Paul's conversion provide equally thought-provoking scenarios. Caravaggio's painting of the conversion of the Paul seems off-centered and a bit out of focus when first viewed. The painting contains harsh diagonal lights which strike the center of the painting, and the flank of the large horse is seen first. Then, the eyes move to the large front hoof which is thrust powerfully toward the body of a strong man lying on the ground, his arms reaching upward, his eyes looking toward the light. His head is lifted and becomes the corner of what art critics refer to as the "triangle," of which the young man's arms and the ribbed back of the horse become the sides. It is obvious that Paul is blind. On the upper right in the shadows is a young lad, obviously the one who cares for the horse, who seems ignorant of the emotion before him and holds the horse's head. We have a picture of the "absolutely vulnerable Paul, frozen at the moment of his change." Here we see power turned into weakness and sight changed at once into blindness. "We do not yet know the future of his story."[34] But we do know that both Paul and the world were different because of the event on the Damascus road. While in art and poetry conversion is portrayed with emotion, the experience of religious conversion is seldom defined.

It is interesting to note that Argyle, in his work on religious conversion done in 1958, basing his study on McKeefery's review in 1949 of thirty-two studies of religious conversion experiences in the last half century, concluded that between 10 and 30 percent of Americans experienced such crisis religious conversion and that the dominant age was about fifteen years. Yet in this study he failed to define the term conversion or to explain its relationship to change in adolescence, or to explore the dynamics.[35]

Thus, the English usage varies with context. How the word is used often determines its meaning. Some conclusions seem evident.

Religious conversion can be a change from Roman Catholicism to Buddhism, a shift in beliefs without a church, or a lesser degree of change by situation, such as marriage or citizenship. This definition is the most obvious description for the experience of conversion with or without the religious element. Some in analyzing this form of conversional experience have seen five basic types in this mold: tradition transition, institution transition, affiliation, defection, and intensification. *Tradition type transitions* happen when someone leaves one major religious tradition for another, such as in conversions from Islam to Buddhism or when they occur within a framework of the tradition itself. These changes can be typified as changes in worldview rather than personal orientation and self-transcendent experiences. Transitions of this type can be painful and may yield to some form of syncretism.[36]

34. Happel and Walter, *Conversion and Discipleship,* p. 7.
35. Michael Argyle, *Religious Behavior* (London: Routledge, 1958).
36. Gration, "Conversion in Cultural Context," p. 22.

Where *institutional transitions* involve a conversion from one belief system or community to another within the same tradition, *affiliation* is understood as movement from no commitment to a nominal or strong commitment. We might illustrate this form of conversional change by looking at a Baptist university student who joins the Unification Church. This movement is often away from more conventional religion.

Intensification is the revitalization of the commitment to a religious body. Born-again conversions are usually intensifications. According to John Gration in his work on culture and conversion, Chuck Colson is a good example of someone who intensifies commitment. Gration posits conversion never occurs in a vacuum and therefore must be a social phenomenon. He claims people regularly change their allegiance, their beliefs and ideologies. This shift in loyalty and movement from *no* belief to *some* belief, community, or worldview is a valid, yet narrow, concept of conversion. There is much research using this description of conversion. Many behavioral scientific studies reflect this research. One can find studies which explore shift in commitment from most traditional religious groups to "new" religions. From this body of research comes information as to the crisis-resolution aspect of religious change and the role of stress or tension in precipitating that change.

Studies as to visibility of new converts in a religious community, their zealousness in conformity to the norms of the group which may ensure acceptance, and the concomitant behavior often associated with new membership in a new ideology or community is well-documented. Some studies have tried to associate greater commitment to greater visibility due to the excitement of the new members and their enthusiasm toward their new belief system.[37]

Understanding conversion as a shift of belief allows conversion to take on a uniquely secular character at times. David O'Rourke argues that Adolf Hitler's *Mein Kampf* is a biography of conversion of a sort—a conversion to evil. Hitler was caught and immobilized by conflicting forces and sorted them out by distinct determination to move wholeheartedly into a violent, racist, and aggressive lifestyle. He suggests that the book is an example of the noisy phase of conversional change, and his life is an example of how people can be trapped into a permanent exploitation of this phase. This however, is not religious conversion and could never be construed as such.[38]

Religious conversion may explain the crisis in which a person comes to self-realization, as did the prodigal son when "for the first time (he) faces up to the realities of his moral and spiritual situation." [39] This self-revelation may

---

37. Irwin R. Barker and Raymond F. Currie, "Do Converts Always Make the Most Committed Christians?" *Journal for the Scientific Study of Religion* 24:3 (1985), p. 312.

38. David K. O'Rourke, *A Process Called Conversion* (Garden City, N.Y.: Doubleday, 1985), p. 37.

take the form of self-disclosure or deep introspection and may be caused by any number of personal concerns and problems. Here it has close relationship to identity experience, which will be related later in this volume. More often, however, religious conversion is dramatic at some point, even if years have preceded that need to change.

It may have the emotional connotations of the revival meeting where the preacher conjures up intense emotion in the situation whereby one is "converted," or it may be simply the change that comes when one commits oneself. Religious conversion has theological overtones when it comes by means of renewal and commitment. The convert is given "new life." Often converts are given eternal assurance that their sins are gone and they can begin again. Repentance, righteousness, sanctification, and new birth are often associated with a theological understanding of the term. One's eternal destiny is determined through conversional change. Often there is a theological explanation attached to it. Conversion calls invite sinners to yield to God by an act of prayer or by public or private confession. And, as Billy Sunday insisted, "The instant you yield, God's plan of salvation is thrown into gear."[40] Obviously, some experiences are sudden and dramatic and interpreted as revolutionary. We observe lives suddenly turned around, perhaps in a moment. What usually happens when we observe such phenomena is we make such crisis-oriented experiences normative for religious life. These dramatic conversions have become historically a legitimate part of the Christian journey and, as suggested, are often associated with personal crisis. This process of coming to God has become a Protestant stereotype. Individuals focus on their moments of conscious decision in which previous lifestyles and convictions are dramatically reversed. Other traditions have a more gentle and protracted experience, but these definitions of conversion are often overlooked.[41] But we must reiterate that all momentous change takes some time. Even sudden change may be the result of years of conviction.

As you can see, the word has been used to describe change in affiliation of church membership; or it has a unique vagueness that comes from misuse and lack of clarity by meaning a religious experience one goes through. This lack of clarity is evidenced in the literature of conversion itself. Yet when religious conversion is spoken of, usually one type crops into the imagination. The sudden form of the Pauline variety has been taken as a standard by revivalists, and most people simply accept their dictum and visualize this form.

---

39. John Baillie, *Baptism and Conversion* (New York: Charles Scribner's Sons, 1963), p. 51.

40. Bernard A. Weisberger, *They Gathered at the River* (New York: Quadrangle, 1959), p. 253.

41. Peter Slater, *The Dynamics of Religion: Meaning and Change in Religious Traditions* (New York: Harper & Row, 1978), pp. 113, 114.

Few have spoken out for other understandings of this word as strongly as George Cutten, when he said in 1908, "Not only is instantaneous conversion not only the true type among several . . . it would be more true to say that no two persons ever come in the same way but each case is unique."[42]

Sudden conversional experiences are obviously the most interesting to investigate, and there are enough instances to validate its existence. Dramatic religious conversion is often preceded by a period of emotional crisis or upheaval, and the experience is marked by an altered mode of experiencing, usually brief and intense. Often the experience itself involves strong emotional arousal and in some of the cases there might be auditory or visual hallucinations. Usually, sudden experiences occur within a matrix of religious belief and result in observable, thematic changes in the subsequent behavior of the convert. They have been typified as "sudden, dramatic, spiritually awakening and emotionally transforming episode(s)."[43]

Flo Conway and Jim Siegelman in their book *Snapping: America's Epidemic of Sudden Personality Change,* investigated the phenomenon of conversion under the term "snapping," which for them designated the sudden drastic alteration of personality in all of its many forms. They concluded that conversion is a completely natural event. They suggest when you strip the experience of its supernatural components, it is simply a moment of basic human growth or some overwhelming feeling and insight where individuals push through to a higher level of consciousness.[44]

Religious conversion experience may be seen as linear or gradual in nature and therefore encompassing the whole process of change in its definition. This means that religious conversion experience itself may be the product of a long and protracted process. A gradual model may best describe its movement. When the conversion definition includes a reorientation of the personality system and involves change in the constellation of religious beliefs and practices, this extended personality reorientation may take some time.[45] Not to be taken lightly are the observations by the behavioral scientists that suggest that conversion, since it is rooted in regeneration of the personality, is a longer process than thought. What is it that these scientists are describing? Some suggest that what is happening is confusion between

42. George Barton Cutten, *The Psychological Phenomena of Christianity* (New York: Charles Scribner's Sons, 1908), p. 234.

43. Raymond J. Wooten and David F. Allen, "Dramatic Religious Conversion and Schizophrenic Decompensation," *Journal of Religion and Health* 22:3 (1983), p. 214.

44. See James Bjornstad, "Cultic and Christian Conversion: Is there a difference?" *Update* 6 (1982), pp. 50-59; or Flo Conway and Jim Siegelman, *Snapping: America's Epidemic of Sudden Personality Change* (New York: Lippincott, 1978), pp. 11-52.

45. Merrill Singer, "The Use of Folklore in Religious Conversion: The Chassidic Case," *Review of Religious Research* 22:2 (1980), p. 170.

the conversion *moment* and the conversion *incubational period*. Since a strictly biblical definition would imply that conversion is the moment when the person turns to God in faith, the period of preparation is usually not included as part of the moment of change. However, the general salvation experience usually takes more time.[46]

H. Richard Niebuhr describes aspects of God's call. First is the call to be a Christian. Next, there is a person's secret call, or the inner conviction of the Holy Spirit. Last, the call to ecclesiastical service which is the recognition of a Christian community.[47] Niebuhr's "inner" calling may be equated with conversion. Cedric Johnson and Newton Malony infer that there are three or more calls that come from God in conversion which protract the experience: 1) the preparatory call; 2) the general call; and 3) the effectual call. Each of these calls may take some length of time. Throughout all of this the Word of God is important in the process because the call of God is not a "contentless mystic experience."[48]

Dramatic changes are only one way to come to faith, and one could ask if they are as sudden as they seem to appear. More often they are the product of a long (conscious or unconscious) and protracted quest. For those individuals raised within a religious framework these shifts probably will not contain sudden decisions or even dramatic turning events but rather will be seen as a gradual reorientation in response to religious nurture.

One way to clarify the paradox in this sudden/gradual debate is to distinguish between the conversion *experience* and the conversion *event*. Bill Leonard suggests that this differentiation provides a better approach than to look at an either/or scenario. We must distinguish between experience and event because it will assist us in realizing that conversion is not a transaction we fulfill, but simply is one step in the continuum of conversion experience. Ministers must recognize the impact of this and cease forcing individuals to feel that unless they have "had conversion" or have "had the experience" they are unacceptable to God.[49] A story recounted in the Riverside, California, *Press Enterprise* illustrates the personal poignancy of this methodology.

She was in tears when she called.

Her mother, answering the phone in the middle of an art class two towns away, panicked. Her first thought was that someone had been hurt.

---

46. Cedric B. Johnson and H. Newton Malony, *Christian Conversion: Biblical and Psychological Perspectives* (Grand Rapids, Mich.: Zondervan, 1982), p. 106.

47. H. Richard Niebuhr, *The Purpose of the Church and Its Ministry: Reflections on the Aims of Theological Education* (New York: Harper & Row, 1956), p. 64.

48. Ibid.

49. Bill J. Leonard, "Getting Saved in America: Conversion Event in a Pluralistic Culture," *Review and Expositor* 82:1 (1985), p. 125.

Someone had been.
Her daughter.
But not physically.
Emotionally.
"Mama, am I saved?" the young teen asked, her voice quivering.
"What?" responded her mother.
"Am I saved?" the girl repeated.
"What are you talking about?" her mother asked.
Sobbing, the girl told of attending a church revival that evening with friends. "They asked me if I was saved and when I told them I didn't know, they told me that I'd better get saved or I'd go to hell."
The mother wasn't just mad, she was appalled.[50]

Walter Clark suggests that for an English definition, conversion best signifies a "turning about, a definite change of front, a passing from one state of being to an altogether different as a definite and specific act."[51] From the Christian perspective religious conversion is an alteration, a turning around. From the convert's perspective, conversion is not self-generated; rather, some forces beyond the control of the subject seem to effect the transformation. The change itself involves what might be called a "recentering of personal identity that marks for the convert a shift from being in some form of bondage to being in a state of liberation."[52]

Recent research on the life histories of "premies" (the followers of Guru Maharaj Ji) have found that spiritual conversion and commitment are very gradual in their development, especially upon reflection. This research was concerned with ideological shifts, as in most psychological research about religious conversion. While it does seem to be a sudden change of awareness which can transform a person's identity and perception of reality, such changes seem rare. When speaking of their conversions in 1972, the premies tended to dramatize the stories as new converts often do by simply emphasizing the significant change they had experienced. "One premie, for instance, characterized his conversion as the death of his 'old self,' so that, looking into his past, he felt as if he were examining someone else's life. Yet, after five years in the Mission, premies spoke of these conversions as having been evolutionary, not revolutionary, in their development."[53]

50. Frances Upchurch, "Teen's Painful Introduction to Ruthless Religious Bigots," Religion & Ethics, *The Press-Enterprise* (Saturday, January 7, 1989), p. H-4.
51. Elmer T. Clark, *The Psychology of Religious Awakening* (New York: Macmillan, 1929), p. 36.
52. Paula Cooey, "The Power of Transformation and the Transformation of Power," *Journal of Feminist Studies in Religion* 1 (1985), p. 26.
53. James V. Downton, "An Evolutionary Theory of Spiritual Conversion and Commitment: The Case of Divine Light Mission," *Journal for the Scientific Study of Religion* 19:4 (1980), p. 382.

To limit conversion to either sudden or gradual is to do injustice to the experience. For conversion seems to be both a crisis event and a process that takes place in the total "time-line of our life on earth. In the events leading up to the crisis of conversion we are 'becoming a Christian' and in those moments after the crisis we are 'becoming Christian.'"[54] Too often pastoral facilitators, religious educators, and personal evangelists deal only with the crisis-type modality as a means of entry into eternal life. Better stated, then, conversion for Christians is a result of the life of Christ in us. Conversion that does not deal with the whole of one's life may not be conversion in its deepest sense. "Life is living. It related to what we eat, how we think, what our attitudes are, our sex life, the stewardship of life and life's possessions. Why was God made flesh in Christ? Why the crucifixion and the resurrection?"[55] Unless a new identity is formed, unless a new sense of mission or purpose is perceived, perhaps conversion has not yet occurred. And these deep changes at the core of one's person often take long periods of time to develop and to have their impact in personal behavior.

---

54. John F. Havlik, "Trends and Issues in Evangelism Today," p. 10.
55. Ibid.

Chapter 2

Religious Conversion:
The Meaning of Change

"The clock of mercy struck in Heaven the hour and moment of my emancipation, for the time had come. Between half-past ten o'clock, when I entered that chapel, and half-past twelve o'clock, when I was back again at home, what a change had taken place in me! I had passed from darkness into marvelous light, from death to life. Simply by looking to Jesus, I had been delivered from despair, and I was brought into such a joyous state of mind that, when they saw me at home, they said to me, 'Something wonderful has happened to you'; and I was eager to tell them all about it."

Charles H. Spurgeon

Biblical descriptions of religious conversion can never be understood apart from their cultural context. The meanings are rooted in personal histories of people as they attempt to find meaning in their lives. One of the unique qualities of the Hebrew corrective in religious history is that of a personal God. In pagan cultic polytheism God was manipulated. Fate ruled most decisions. Individuals, nations, and peoples were blown by the winds of whim and fancy as the gods willed. Humankind's job was to figure out the system, find ways to enter into it and control it, when possible. Thus, cultic polytheism flourished in antiquity and people found meaning in religious ritual. They believed they could second-guess the powers of the dark.

Enter monotheism. All views of the gods change now. Suddenly there is a god that can be understood, a god that is *the* God. This God's ways become like our ways, and God's will is perceived in actions toward people. This God can give promises and keep them. Monotheism provided a theology which contained a concept of God that was personal. The terms and descriptions of

21

returning to God in conversion take on those same personal overtones. Relationship can be "broken." We need to come "home." Conversion becomes the means of return to God's personal love and care.

In a very real sense, then, every conversion story in scripture is in context, a multifaceted one which embraces political and economic domains,and religious and personal life.[1] The vocabulary of change is symbolic and God's call to lost humankind creates dynamic tension that colors our understanding of the biblical terms for religious change.

Old Testament Models

There has been a long history of the concepts of repentance and conversion in the Old Testament Hebrew Scriptures.[2] The understanding of the word conversion centers around a few words in the Old Testament. In Hebrew the word *shubh* is used to express both the transitive and intransitive moods. The word means "to return" in a general sense and is found in the following passages: Psalm 51:13, "Sinners shall be converted unto thee"; Psalm 19:7, "The law of the Lord is perfect converting the soul";[3] Isaiah 1:27, "Zion shall be redeemed with judgments and her converts with righteousness";[4] Isaiah 6:10, "Lest they see with their eyes and hear with their ears, and understand with their heart, and convert and be healed." The word is used in these passages in the active voice and in a neuter sense in all the above except Psalm 19:7, and might be as well rendered "return." It is frequently used with a second verb to give the sense of "again or back."[5] The Hebrew word *shubh* occurs in the Old Testament more than 1,100 times and means such things as 1) "to return," Genesis 18:33; 2) "to turn back," Judges 3:19; 3) "to return from a foreign land," Ruth 1:6; 4) "a turning around," 1 Kings 19:27; 5) "to turn in the course of action," 2 Kings 24:1; 6) "to turn from sin," 1 Kings 8:35; 7) "to be restored," Exodus 4:7; 8) "to return to God," Hosea 6:1.[6] An additional word is translated "conversion" in the Old Testament, too. The word *haphac* occurs once, in Isaiah 60:5: "The abundance of the sea shall be converted unto thee." Here the word simply means "turn."

---

1. See John A. Gration, "Conversion in Cultural Context," *International Bulletin for Religious Research* 7 (October 1983), pp. 157-162.

2. See *metanoia,* in *Theological Dictionary of the New Testament,* ed. Gerhard Kittel, trans. Geoffrey W. Bromiley, 4 (Grands Rapids, Mich.: Eerdmans, 1967), pp. 975-1008; and David F. Wells' discussion in *Turning to God: Biblical Conversion in the Modern World* (Grand Rapids: Mich.: Baker Book House, 1989), p. 31.

3. The Revised Standard Version's rendition of this passage translates *shub* as "reviving the soul."

4. The New English Version here translates *shub* "repentant."

5. Robert Baker Girdlestone, *Synonyms of the Old Testament* (Grand Rapids, Mich.: Eerdmans, 1948), p. 92.

6. William Barclay, *Turning to God* (London: Epworth Press, 1963), p. 24.

The Hebrew preserves much of the real nature of conversion as an actual turning around in one's way especially in the social and political spheres.[7] Tillich points out that conversion for the Hebrew person pointed to a turning around, a reversal *from* to a turning *to* something. The turning might be from injustice to justice, or from inhumanity to humanity, or from idols to gods. This twofold stress in the Hebrew is important in understanding its usage.[8] For the Hebrew, conversion was never just the experience of changing, but included a goal of action on the part of the believer where the conception of God's will was being fulfilled in turning around. It was movement back to knowing God. This movement had religious implications and was considered true religious conversion.

There are many examples of the experience of conversion in scripture—individual stories of people experiencing it. Abraham, Moses, Jacob, the Widow of Zaraphath, Samuel, Miriam, and the prophets were summoned by an insistent God in such a way that the experience could only be called a right-about-face, direct turn-around, or redirection to a calling. An exception to this might be Ruth which shows the blessing that comes to a foreigner who turns to Israel's God and so becomes part of God's faithful people. The basic elements of conversional change seem to be repeated in almost every Old Testament conversion experience. First, there is a flashing vision of truth. Then some kind of conviction of one's worthlessness. Next, the joy of being forgiven with the purging of absolution. And finally, some kind of consciousness of new vision, personal mission, or life of service.[9] One can multiply this "sudden" model throughout Old Testament scripture.

The story of David is an example of this schema. 2 Samuel 11-12 records the story of David, the plot to have Uriah the Hittite killed, and the subsequent confrontation by God through the prophet Nathan. David's turning point is captured in the line, "I have sinned against the Lord." Only after forgiveness could David again begin to work for God.

The story of Job, who comes to know the mystery of God, underscores the truth that even the just person is called to turn around in conversion. The key biblical words for conversion suggest a radical turning or a redirection of one's life. Some have argued that the biblical words for "conversion" and "return" imply a turning *from* sin and turning *toward* God.[10] Both directions are implicit in the vocabulary of conversional change in the Old Testament.

In some instances there were certain rituals that could be performed which

---

7. Bernhard Citron, *New Birth: A Study of the Evangelical Doctrine of Conversion in the Protestant Fathers* (Edinburgh: University Press, 1951), p. 14.

8. Paul Tillich, *Systematic Theology* (3 vols.; Chicago: University of Chicago Press, 1951-63), III, p. 218.

9. Hugh T. Kerr and John M. Mulder, eds., *Conversions: The Christian Experience* (Grand Rapids, Mich.: Eerdmans, 1983), p. x.

10. Walter Conn, *Christian Conversion* (New York: Paulist, 1986), p. 5.

would precipitate conversion. Penitential observances were expected of everyone who wanted to change (1 Kgs 8:33). For example, fasting and prayer were requirements used to avert divine anger as in the case of Ahab, who had Naboth murdered to steal his vineyard.[11] Prayer and fasting, temple rituals and penitence were means to secure divine favor and were precursors and/or the means for the change to begin.

The psalms contain some of the richest insights into the spiritual lives of the Old Testament saints and the nature of religious conversion. There is a clear distinction made between righteous and wicked. But even those following God's will must at times repent and be changed. Even believers must return to God and be restored in order to receive God's rich blessings. Psalm 32 speaks of just such an experience. Here is seen forgiveness followed by absolution of sin and iniquity. Some religious groups argue that regeneration through conversional change was not possible until the coming of the Holy Spirit at Pentecost. This belief is not founded in the Bible. Change brought through God is in evidence in the Hebrew scriptures. For example, the stories of change are myriad in the Old Testament and this change occurs in all levels of society and among people of all ages. Conviction and conversion are linked together in the Old and New Testaments.

Arthur Lewis refutes five arguments that imply the Old Testament knew nothing about return and conversion to God. He claims that the Old Testament does speak of the new birth, however infrequently, with terms and phrases that are clearly the language of regeneration. He believes that the Holy Spirit acted then as now as the omnipresent power of God in their hearts. God worked conversion in their lives through conviction and sanctification. He also suspects that the New Testament writers regarded the saints in the Old Testament as another part in the long continuum of history. He believes that all share the same life from above and notes that the gift of the Spirit in the New Testament only signaled the mission to the Gentiles and provided new power for an old task rather than offer a new way of entry into God's kingdom.[12] For Lewis, regeneration is a human requirement for salvation and has always been important to God's people.

New Testament Models

Terms in the New Testament serve to reinforce the concept of return and regeneration. They include such phrases as "born again," "born from above," "newness of life," "made alive in Christ," "a new creation," "as new-born babes," and "being raised from the dead." The New Testament records

11. Stephen Happel and James J. Walter, *Conversion and Discipleship* (Philadelphia: Fortress, 1986), p. 10.

12. Arthur H. Lewis, "The New Birth Under the Old Covenant," *Evangelical Quarterly* 56, p. 43.

instances of change from one way of life to another. The disciples were called to follow Jesus; those who met Jesus of Nazareth were healed in spirit and called to follow a new way of life. The three thousand at Pentecost, the Greeks at Antioch, the Ethiopian eunuch, the jailer, Lydia, Paul, Barnabas, Martha, and Mary—all were called to follow and were changed. In these stories a change from Judaism to Christianity is implied and a movement toward God in a personal sense is illustrated.

Religious conversion in the New Testament is from the Hebrew *shubh* and is translated in Greek by *epistrephein,* a word used more than thirty-five times with the sense of 1) "turning around," Luke 1:16, 17; James speaks of the duty and privilege of bringing back, or turning back to someone who has strayed away from God, James 5:19, 20; in the "physical sense of turning or returning," Matthew 12:44, Luke 2:30, Matthew 24:18, Mark 13:16, Matthew 10:3, Luke 8:55, Luke 17:31, 2 Peter 2:22, and others. 2) It is used as a person turning around (Mk 5:30, Mk 8:33), but most frequently it is used to denote a mental or a spiritual turn such as in Acts :19, "Repent ye therefore, and be converted, that your sins may be blotted out, when the times of refreshing shall come from the presence of the Lord."[13]

Epistrephein in classical and secular Greek reflects no experiential religious sense at all. It means to turn one's back upon someone. It is found as a Hebraism in the sense of returning to do something again or to turn the mind or the attention to someone or something. William Barclay suggests that in secular Greek more meanings for conversion are asserted: "To turn the attention of a person to someone or to something can be to warn him, to correct him to cause him to repent, and hence to convert him; and to have the attention so turned is to heed to repent, to take warning, and so to be converted."[14]

A closely related word used in the New Testament is *strephein* meaning 1) "to return something to someone," Matthew 5:39; 2) "to change something into something," to bring back, return *ti* (something), Matthew 27:3; 3) "turn away" as God turning away from them, Acts 7:42; or 4) "to turn, or change inwardly, or be converted," emphasizing the turning to something positive, while its opposite, "to turn evil" would be to be "perverted."

One of the most controversial passages in scripture regarding conversion, Matthew 18:3, "I tell you this: unless you be converted and become as little children you will not enter the kingdom of heaven" is translated in the New English Bible in its true sense as "I tell you this: unless you turn around and become like children, you will never enter the kingdom of heaven," indicating the relationship of change, deep change, going to the core of the

13. The New English Bible has this text translated, "Repent then and turn to God, so that your sins may be wiped out." This implied a turning *from* something again and a return *to* God.

14. Barclay, *Turning to God,* pp. 18, 19.

person. It is a turning around or a coming home.[15]

There are instances in New Testament translations where other Greek words have been called "conversion." These instances include three other Greek words whose meaning is clear. These words are 1) *proselutos*, a "proselyte," or a "convert" to a type of belief, Matthew 23:15, Acts 2:10, 6:5, 13:43; 2) *aparche*, translated "first fruits" in the K.J.V., but modern translators update this term to "converts," Romans 15:5, 1 Corinthians 16:15; and 3) *neophutos* translated as "neophite." Modern translators update this word found in 1 Timothy 3:6 to "recent converts." The meanings of these related words are clear—a person newly changed in beliefs, attitudes, or lifestyle.

Another closely related term sometimes translated by more modern biblical scholars is the Greek term *metanoia*, "a change of mind."[16] *Metanoia* seems to have several connotations of conversion including a change of mind after reflection; a going beyond the present attitude, status, or outlook; or repentance, which is also its translation. Karl Barth made a distinction between *shubh* as a once-and-for-all or repeated individual movement, and *metanoia* as an inclusive movement in which "man moves forward steadily to continually new things."[17] It can perhaps be implied that the Hebrew and Greek understanding of this movement are denoting a far more profound reorganization to reality than is usually meant in the popular usage of the term conversion. Erick Routley in his book *Religious Conversion* states that the word does not inevitably imply a turning for the first time, still less "a turning for the first and only time. It means simply stopping, turning, attending and pursuing the new course."[18] Other words in the Latin, for example, are reflections of these basic comments, meaning again

---

15. William Barclay (*Turning to God,* p. 22) suggests for the text in Matthew 18:3 the following and interesting comment in explanation: "In this passage the word which is translated converted is exactly the same word and the same tense of the word which is used of Jesus turning around. In the passages in which it is used of Jesus, it is the aorist particle *strapheis* which is used. Here it is the aorist tense *straphete*. When *strephein* is so used for turning it is middle; that is to say, the verb is passive in form, but active in meaning, as with deponent verbs in Latin, it is therefore quite clear that in the Matthew passage the translation should be active and not passive. It ought to be, not 'except ye be converted,' but unless you turn, unless you change. Both the word convert and passive use of the word introduce wrong overtones into the translation. It is not technical conversion which is being spoken of; it is a turning of the mind so that man's outlook on, and attitude to, life are altered from pride to humility."

16. William Arndt and F. Wilbur Gingrich, *A Greek-English Lexicon of the New Testament and Other Early Christian Literature* (Chicago: University of Chicago Press, 1957), p. 778.

17. Karl Barth, *Church Dogmatics,* trans. G. W. Bromiley et al., 4 (4 vols., Edinburgh: T. and T. Clark, 1936-1962), p. 567.

18. Erick Routley, *Religious Conversion,* trans. Helen Augur (New York: Harcourt, Brace, 1927), p. 31.

to "turn around."[19]

The word "conversion" as you can see, does not appear often in the Bible. Certain synonyms translated in the English such as "repentance," "regeneration," and "being born again," occur with greater frequency throughout the Bible. The notion of a "turning" is most often used. To be converted is like making a "U-turn," it is like "starting at square one again" or going "back to the drawing board."[20] Conversion, no matter how it may be described, implies a change from one lifestyle to another by abandoning an aimless and unsatisfying perspective in exchange for a new and more promising incentive to live a more meaningful life. It may mean that call to holiness and discipleship which draws a person to the ethical demands of Christian life.

One cannot simply equate renewal and regeneration with mere activity and enthusiasm nor with primarily secular change. These terms are too vital to be depleted by equating them with evangelistic activity. "For in biblical thoughts and experience, renewal is linked with divine visitation, purging judgment and restoration through repentance, and no amount of hustle and bustle qualifies as renewal where these notes are absent."[21] Renewal becomes the inward exercise of the heart. While this term is filled with affective associations rather than cognitive understandings, *metanoia* implies that if change is real, it will be God's work alone. Scripture indicates that it is a pneumatological activity in which the community and individual believers are infused with power from the Holy Spirit (Eph 1:17-23; 3:14-19; Rom 6:4; 8:2-11). This activity of the Spirit leads the community to understand its cosmic identity and mission. Joseph Allen has expertly identified various personal qualities of renewal which the biblical record supports. They include an acceptance

---

19. Theologian Seward Hiltner ("Toward a Theology of Conversion in the Light of Psychology," *Pastoral Psychology* 17 (1966), pp. 35-42 suggests this interesting discussion with himself as he discovered the Latin usage of this term. "Recently I got out my Latin dictionary and looked up *converto*. I was not surprised to find 'turn around,' even though I got a slight jar from the synonym, "whirl around.' In Cicero, I found, it meant 'to turn in the opposite direction,' which is not so surprising if you get a proper definition of what 'opposite' means. But I was truly startled to find that *conversio* meant, in Cicero, 'a periodical return.' No once and for allness here! And I was even more astonished to think of the relationship between *conversio* and *conversatio,* the root of our modern 'conversation,' which routinely meant 'frequent use,' but which in Seneca, meant 'dealings with person'. . . . Conversion it seems, is a real turning around, even in the opposite direction (if you can figure out just what opposite means). Like a weather vane, it may be periodic; and like the related conversation, it may have a truly social reference. . . . An alcoholic who turns around and now kissed his wife and pays the bills is equally converted."

20. Kerr and Mulder, eds., *Conversions,* p. ix.

21. See James I. Packer, *Summons to Faith and Renewal* (Ann Arbor, Mich.: Servant Books, 1983), p. 110; and Joseph Allen, "Renewal of the Christian Community: A Challenge for Pastoral Ministry," *St. Vladimir's Theological Quarterly* 29 (1985), pp. 305-323.

of the integrity of God's Word, sensitivity to sin, fruitfulness in community life, and a sense of God's nearness.[22]

The New Testament concept of religious conversion has Jesus or the Holy Spirit as the instigator of conversion. The experiences are often referred to as "the stunning acts of God."[23] The resurrection of Jesus is the historic instance that changes things for everyone in the Christian church. Jesus was dead and is now alive. What is normally experienced as absence due to that death is now sensed as the "presence" of the Holy Spirit. Guilt and despair are given way to joy and comfort. Whenever these shifts in perspective appear in the New Testament, Jesus is present in Spirit to nudge and inspire. Christ is the source of change in the New Testament.

It seems that the primary biblical viewpoint regarding a definition of religious conversion is that it means change, a turning around from and to a viewpoint, or a return to God's principles. Conversion is a thorough-going turn-around, with a reorientation to the meaning of life. Since the early church spoke in symbols to portray the realities of God, conversion was the symbol used for the transformation. It takes on no special mystical or emotional tone in biblical usage but becomes the phrase used to describe the shift of attention and to point toward new direction. The New Testament is full of other symbols of this type to describe the shift of attention, direction, and change people of God are to experience. Followers are called out of the darkness into light; they are to be born anew; are told to take off the old nature and put on the new. They are told to believe and be saved. They are challenged to cultivate faith like children and to enter into the kingdom of God. When they enter the relationship with God they are new creations and experience freedom.

Conversion experience thrives in biblical figures of speech. For example, it is talked of as restoration from impurity (Tim 2:14); a translation from death to life (Jn 5:24); getting rid of the old and acquiring a new type of humanity (Col 3:9); and a dying of self and rising again to newness in Christ (Rom 6:2-8).[24]

Conversion is used to emphasize an entering into a new way, in contrast to the old; a turning around in a mental sense or the more literally used physical way. It is interesting to note that religious conversion in the Bible does not include an analysis of the experience. Where the word is used there is no connotation of an emotional upheaval or pathological break from reality which many psychologists have suggested.

The process in the Bible is considered to be supernatural and, therefore,

---

22. Joseph Allen, "Renewal of the Christian Community: A Challenge for Pastoral Ministry," *St. Vladimir's Theological Quarterly* 29 (1985), pp. 305-323.

23. Robert C. Fuller, *Religion and the Life Cycle* (Philadelphia: Fortress, 1988), p. 103.

24. Ibid., p. xi.

God-sent, yet person-centered. Any person who participates in the event of Jesus Christ will have a new existence, enabling in all those areas that constitute personhood. It is obviously a mystical kind of union—one that skirts definition, but one that the Bible suggests has no specific emotional overtones. This perhaps is why it can often be spoken of as gradual as well as instantaneous. The results are the evidence. A person has been changed, and is changed, and stands changed before God. The status of condemnation is no longer valid. Life is different from that point, rejoicing in Jesus Christ with victory over sin.

Historical Models

In antiquity we have intriguing examples of the effects of change on daily life. We note that at certain times people's names were changed when they had undergone a shift in allegiance or affiliation. What are we to make of these name changes? Modern analogies will readily come to mind, for name changes are often a statement about the individual self-perception, or the perception which others may have. For example, we often use nicknames to describe individuality. We all remember classmates doomed to low self-image because of nicknames like "bird-legs," "skinny," "buzzy," or "nerd." For the Egyptians, the nearest equivalent was perhaps the "beautiful" name attached to one's own, which was often an abbreviation of the person's name.[25] Nicknames provide a new statement about individuality. The term "Christian" given to early believers identified them with Christ, for example.

Early in America much of what we think of conversion was associated with the Puritans who provided a theological vocabulary for describing the conversional process. They introduced into the language of piety terms like "regeneration," "election," and "predestination" which have remained a part of the language of theology to this day. Such inventions as the "anxious seat"—the place for repentant sinners to think about their relationship with God—were an integral part of getting saved in America. It created what some have called, "the sacrament of walking the aisle, an outward and visible sign of an inward and evangelical grace." Converts began to describe salvation's event in terms appropriate to the invitation: "when I 'walked the aisle,' when I shook the preacher's hand,' 'when I went forward.' Walking the aisle seemed to replace baptism a public profession of faith. Indeed, many testified that salvation seemed to come to the very act of moving from pew to aisle."[26]

25. G. H. R. Horsley, "Name Change as an Indication of Religious Conversion in Antiquity," *Numen* 34 (1987), p. 2.
26. Bill J. Leonard, "Getting Saved in America: Conversion Event in a Pluralistic Culture," *Review and Expositor* 82:1 (1985), pp. 120, 121. The quotation is from Charles G. Finney, "Sinners Hoping to Change Their Own Hearts," *Sermons On*

In the nineteenth century new propositions began to be introduced. Calvinistic morphology of salvation was often modified in more Arminian directions giving a larger role to free will and human response in salvation. What was before a lengthy process (conversion) became shortened to a more immediate action. The growth of American religious pluralism contributed to the great diversity of conversional morphologies.[27] Some denominations stressed cognitive shift while others emphasized emotional response.

Popular understandings of conversion were emerging in contrast to the serious work soon to be done by psychologists and theologians. Perhaps no single person influenced the way nineteenth-century America understood conversion than the famous evangelist Charles Grandison Finney. Finney's interest in free will, immediate salvation, and the proper use of "means" continue to provide significant insight. He felt that conversion did not need a long and lengthy protracted conviction and advocated that sinners should rely on their own free will to change their minds and turn to God by their "own voluntary act."[28] Bill Leonard observes that the masses seeking salvation were often unable to tell the difference between the gradual and sudden conversion in the light of Finney's preaching. But as revivals came, instructions for conducting them followed with appropriate case studies as illustrations of the suddenness of the experience. Most case studies showed the importance of sudden, immediate change—still a process but radically shortened. As Calvin Colton wrote in 1932, "The more sudden the conversion then the better."[29]

Looking at the academic research and opinion about conversion can be confusing. We shall review from a historical perspective various psychological definitions of religious conversion with the hope of finding common themes in our understanding of this experience. There is no attempt to examine the dynamics of conversion yet; this aspect will be discussed in the following chapter. This analysis of definitions will serve as a summary of some of the literature available on conversion.

Early studies of religious conversion had their beginnings with G. Stanley Hall. As early as 1881 he shocked a Boston audience by suggesting that adolescence was the typical age for conversion.[30] His basic definition of conversion suggested a fundamental redirection of life, a process necessary to maturity, and a movement out of the earlier stages of development. That redirection involved basic changes from egotism to

Important Subjects (New York: John S. Taylor, 1836), pp. 37, 38.

27. Ibid., p. 118.

28. Quoted in Leonard, "Getting Saved in America," p. 119.

29. Ibid., p. 120.

30. Walter Houston Clark, "Intense Religious Experience," *Research on Religious Development: A Comprehensive Handbook,* ed. M. Strommen (New York: Hawthorne Books, 1971), p. 532.

altruism and from pantheism to transcendence. In these changes each person recapitulates the history of the race in its advance from animism to ethical practice. This definition draws heavily upon Hall's basic concepts of genetic psychology. "In its most fundamental sense, conversion is a natural, normal, universal, and necessary process at the stage when life pivots over the autocentric to a heterocentric basis."[31]

Along with Hall was Edwin Starbuck, whose studies published in his *Psychology of Religion* proved to be monumental in establishing interest in psychology of religious phenomena.[32] Some told of an overwhelming experience at revival meetings, in fields, jails, or bars, leaving each person changed. Starbuck defined conversion by its *cause* rather than specifically delineating the experience. Conversion is "a process of struggling away from sin rather than of striving toward righteousness."[33] It is primarily an "un-selfing."[34] He stressed the suddenness of the experience in his definitions by characterizing it as more or less sudden changes of character from evil to goodness, from sinfulness to righteousness, and from indifference to spiritual insight and activity.[35] Thus for Starbuck religious conversion was a process of growth, and he wished to study all psychological manifestations which preceded, accompanied, and followed this experience. His definition of conversion, however, reflected a new typology that was to form a basis for other studies on conversion. He found conversion to be of two types: 1) volitional, which he described as a spontaneous awakening and sense of the divine, and also 2) an intermediate form described as self-surrender. This insight was new and focused many scholars on the conversion phenomena.[36] He opened the way for psychological definitions of this interesting experience.

A major contributor to an understanding of conversion experience was William James. It has been suggested that James could theorize and systematize with the best of researchers, but on the whole his

---

31. Robert N. Beck, "Hall's Genetic Psychology and Religious Conversion," *Pastoral Psychology* 16 (September 1965), p. 47.

32. Starbuck was early in the modern American movement in the study of religion and when one reads his volume, one is impressed with the tremendous time given to his conversion experience. Clark (*Psychology of Religion*, p. 7) suggests that this was the fashion of the day in most Protestant evangelical circles and that the book only reflects the times. Yet his book received wide acclaim and was later translated into German.

33. E. D. Starbuck, *The Psychology of Religion* (New York: Charles Scribner's Sons, 1915), p. 64.

34. Ibid., p. 145.

35. Ibid., p. 21.

36. William Paterson, *Conversion* (New York: Charles Scribner's Sons, 1940), p. 161.

temperament led him to be more of an expander than an innovator. His interests led him to consort with mediums and to sniff nitrous oxide.[37] James has been criticized for the lack of statistics in his study on the *Varieties of Religious Experience,* originally given as the substance of the "Gifford Lectures" at the University of Edinburgh at the turn of the century. His work is based upon case studies and he allows, as much as possible, individuals to tell their own story. In *Varieties* James selected for study extreme and highly individualized forms of religious life. This represented his feeling that religion is basically an individual rather than a social phenomenon and his conviction that religion shows itself more clearly in extremes.[38] The pragmatism of William James shows through his work, for he is not as concerned in the origin of a religious experience (which may be rank superstition or pure madness for all he cares), but rather his concern is in its results. Therefore, though he is interested in the process of religious conversion, it is the usefulness and value of conversion to the person that is essential[39] W. H. Clark's comments about James are relevant here: He insists that it is neither the origins nor the processes of the religious life that justify it so much as the results. No matter how disreputable the genesis of a religious impulse or how psychopathic the founders of a religious movement, if the consequent religious activities are beneficial to the individual or to society, the religion is thereby justified.[40]

James' contributions to this discussion lie in four areas: 1) an emphasis on the role of experience and its results; 2) a unique concern for the individual in religion; 3) the use in mass of individual cases for the study of experiences; and 4) a respect for the role of the unconscious.[41] With these emphases James defines conversion through numerous case examples and declares:

> To be converted, to be regenerated, to receive grace, to experience religion, to gain assurance, are so many phrases hitherto divided, and consciously right, superior, and happy in consequence of its firmer hold upon religious realities. This is at least what conversion signifies in general terms, whether or not we believe that a direct divine operation is needed to bring such a moral change about.[42]

---

37. See Walter Houston Clark, "William James: Contributions to the Psychology of Religious Conversion," *Pastoral Psychology* 16 (September 1965), p. 30.

38. William James, *The Varieties of Religious Experience* (New York: Mentor Books, New American Library of World Literature, 1958), pp. 21-37; pp. 168-174; lecture 20.

39. Walter Houston Clark, "William James: Contributions to the Psychology of Religious Conversion," *Christianity Today* (May 12, 1967), pp. 5-20.

40. Walter Houston Clark, *The Psychology of Religion* (New York: Macmillan, 1958), p. 8.

41. James, *Religious Experience,* see pp. 367-390.

42. Ibid., p. 157.

He places stress in the suddenness and crisis effect of religious conversion.

> Now there may be great oscillation in the emotional interest, and the hot places may shift before one almost as rapidly as the sparks that run through burnt-up paper. Then we have the wavering and divided self we heard so much of in the previous lecture. Or focus of excitement and heat, the point of view from which the aim is taken, may come to lie permanently within a certain system; and then, if the change be a religious one, we call it a *conversion,* especially if it be by crisis, or sudden.[43]

It is interesting to note that James considers change to be just change, but when given a religious context it becomes religious conversion.

James further defines conversion: "To say that a man is 'converted' means, in these terms, that religious ideas, previously peripheral in his consciousness, now take a central place, and that religious aims form the habitual center of his energy."[44] In James' definition, religious conversion becomes a unifying experience, and his definition centers in on an understanding of the nature of it and a dichotomy between sudden and gradual concerns, between conscious or voluntary types and involuntary or unconscious types.[45] In defining conversion using this type of description, he advocated that the sudden and gradual changes are not basically different experiences. They are both conversion. Yet as he goes on to work within this framework of experience, his own analysis does not conform to his own definition. It is well said by Earl Furgeson:

> By describing the gradual process as common and "less interesting" he implies that psychodynamically there is a difference. . . . If James had affirmed only two ways by which changes in personality come about, one by gradual process of growth and the other by the sudden more agonizing process of conversion, he would have been on sage psychological ground, but when he identified the two as not being radically different he introduced a fault into the definition which his own analysis will not support and which the subsequent confusion will not sustain.[46]

James speculated that those who had dramatic conversion experiences might have been born with a certain disposition toward them. He identified the "melancholy disposition" or the chronically "divided" mind as characters with possibilities toward religious change. Within the context of his radically empirical methodology, James broadens his original psychology of consciousness in an effort to not only describe the

---

43. Ibid., p. 162.
44. Ibid.
45. Ibid., p. 202.
46. Earl H. Furgeson, "The Definition of Religious Conversion," *Pastoral Psychology* 16 (September 1965), p. 9.

phenomenon of conversion, but also to grasp its meaning as a "lived experience" and he does this by expanding an awareness of the relationship between consciousness and experience.[47] James' definition therefore stresses unification of the self and is defined by the *nature* of the experience as well as the *causes*.[48]

George Albert Coe, religious educator and theorist, made a unique contribution in the 1900s by adding an additional insight. Coe reacted somewhat against the contemporary emphasis of conversion—that it was sudden and crisis-oriented. His stress was on the religious nurture of youth, and he added that if individuals who worked with youth especially would play down the conflict nature, the storm and stress of religious decision, and concentrate on the normal nurture of youth, they would have a more gradual and fruitful type of religious development.[49] Religious change would be more normal, and religious growth would be seen in a more natural light. Coe's stress on the gradual nature of spiritual change was a necessary corrective for a psychology rooted in evangelistic and revival nomenclature.

George Coe saw six senses in religious conversion that aid in its definition: 1) Conversion is a voluntary turning about or change of attitude. This reflects the biblical understanding of conversion. 2) It is the renunciation of one religion and the start of another kind. Here is a change of one branch of religious belief to another. 3) It is the means of individual salvation according to an evangelical "plan of salvation." 4) It is the growing consciousness of the religious mores of the family. 5) It is a quality of life of the Christian ("he [she] is converted"). 6) It is any abrupt transfer, particularly a rapid transfer, from one standpoint to another. This transformation is usually from one form of living to a higher one in an ethical sense.[50] However, he identifies "unreligious conversions," too. Coe suggested that conversion was not coextensive with religion, and James recognized that various interpersonal processes paralleled conversion, even the experience of falling in love.[51] His definition is fairly complete in that it provides various definitions to cover the many aspects of change and reflects the complexity of the experience in its sociological and psychological aspects.

In those early years there seem to be at least three major concerns

---

47. Gary T. Alexander, "Psychological Foundations of William James's Theory of Religious Experience," *Journal of Religion* 59 (October 1979), pp. 426, 428.

48. James, *Religious Experience,* p. 169.

49. George Albert Coe, *The Spiritual Life* (New York: Eaton and Mains, 1900), pp. 35-52.

50. George Albert Coe, *Psychology of Religion* (Chicago: University of Chicago Press, 1916), p. 152.

51. Ibid., p. 54.

which most typically appear to have been central in studies of conversion. They are 1) the role of time in identifying types of conversions; 2) the age at which conversion occurs; 3) explanations of the processes which account for conversion.[52] In understanding the role of time, consensus suggested the sudden/gradual typologies be accepted and that the change noted in the experience of conversion was one of complete shift of one's life with a new "centering of concern, interest, and action."[53] The age issue was settled by looking at adolescence as the opportune time for conversion. More recent studies tend to refute that conclusion. Such things as emotionalism, revivalism, adolescence, deprivations, and personal crisis resolutions were often included in the causes of sudden change.[54]

With concern for growth and the vocabulary of nurture becoming important it is no wonder that the discussions of conversion began to stress nurture and emphasis on family as the source of change. Mary Boys traces this movement in her book, *Educating in Faith,* where she points out that conversion became the subject of empirical study as those who studied it "had often themselves undergone a sort of a conversion to the methods of science." Somewhat of an anti-empirical mentality herself, Boys suggests that they embraced empiricism which devalued supernaturalism.[55]

George Jackson in the "Cole Lectures" for 1908, given before Vanderbilt University in the area of the psychology of conversion and later published in his book *The Fact of Conversion,* vaguely defines religious conversion and emphasizes the mystique surrounding the experience. He says, "For one man conversion means the slaying of the beast within him; in another it brings the calm of conviction to an inquiet mind; for a third it is the entrance into a larger liberty and a more abundant life; and yet again it is the gathering into one the forces of the soul at war within itself."[56] A contemporary of Jackson, Harold Begbie defines conversion as a "revolution in character." He stresses "turn around" rather than suddenness and the traumatic nature of change.[57] The definitions of conversion were beginning to reflect a concern for the experience rather than to stress only its sudden or gradual nature. There

---

52. Bernard Spilka, Ralph W. Hood Jr., and Richard L. Gorsuch, *The Psychology of Religion: An Empirical Approach* (Englewood Cliffs, N. J.: Prentice-Hall, 1985), p. 201.

53. Ibid., p. 203.

54. Ibid., pp. 205, 206.

55. Mary C. Boys, *Educating in Faith* (San Francisco: Harper & Row, 1989), p. 57.

56. George Jackson, *The Fact of Conversion: The Cole Lectures for 1908* (New York: Revell, 1908), p. 97.

57. Harold Begbie, *Twice-Born Man* (New York: Revell 1909), p. 18.

was hope for understanding what was going on in this change process now.

All in all, the early work on religious conversion, relying heavily upon questionnaire and case study information, established conversion as a fact of the Christian life. This fact reflected the times as well, for conversion was an actual form of entry into the Christian life stemming from revivals in the eighteenth and nineteenth centuries. William James, quoting the New England Puritan Joseph Alleine, points to the symbolic nature of conversion by saying it is "not the putting in a patch of holiness; but with the true convert holiness is woven into all his powers, principles, and practice. The sincere Christian is quite a new fabric, from the foundation to the topstone. He is a new man, a new creature."[58] Conversion was considered a depth change, characterized by typologies that included those defined by *nature* (sudden or gradual) and those defined by *cause* (volitional or self-surrender), and a new concern about the *type* of change was beginning to be important.

In 1910, *Psychology of Religious Experience* was published by E. S. Ames. His viewpoint was that religion has its origin in the attempt to conserve social value. Ames agrees with Begbie in his definition in seeing conversion only as sudden, intense, and extreme emotional experience.[59] James Leuba began to publish during this same time. Leuba differed in his approach to psychology of religion and tended toward naturalistic explanations of religious phenomena, pointing out, for example, the similarity of the reports of mystics to those of people who have been under the influence of drugs.[60] Yet he defined religious conversion by its *causes* rather than specifically defining it. He understood conversion to be the result of the conflict within people and believed it to be a method of seeking "wholeness" within a person. He is one of the first to assume the integrating force within conversion for personality.[61]

Later in the century, Robert Thouless defined religious conversion on the basis of *content* rather than nature or cause. He defines conversion as a process with contents primarily intellectual, moral, or social. He stated:

> Religious conversion is the name commonly given to the process which leads to the adoption of a religious attitude; the process may be gradual or sudden. It is likely to include a change in belief on religious topics, but this will be accompanied by changes in the motivation to behavior and in reactions to the social environment. One or another of these directions of change may seem to play the pre-

---

58. James, *Religious Experience,* p. 185.

59. Ed S. Ames, *The Psychology of Religious Experience* (Boston: Houghton-Mifflin, 1910), p. 251.

60. Clark, *The Psychology of Religion*, p. 9.

61. Carl W. Christensen, "Religious Conversion in Adolescence," *Pastoral Psychology* 16 (September 1965), p. 19.

dominant role in the conversion change. One may then speak of intellectual, or moral, or social conversions. The distinctions between them are not, however, clear-cut; every intellectual change has its implications for behavior and for social allegiances, and no one is likely to change his social allegiance in religion or his behavior motivation without some corresponding change in what he believes.[62]

In illustrating these types of change he suggests that of the three kinds of conversion, Paul's would be of the social variety. Paul's change seems to have been from one system of loyalties to another, and he claims that there is no evidence that the conflict was one between opposing opinions, nor was the change from a wrong to a right system. Rather, Paul's change was from two systems equally right at the time.[63] This question could be debated, however, for Paul's conversion was to a new way of life, one that condemned the previous way as being wrong. Therefore, there would have to be moral tones within the conversion, especially if one is to define conversion according to content.

An illustration of moral conversion is that of one "swearing Tom," whose conflict was primarily a moral one and the change to be adopted was from an old way of life, one of swearing, to a new way where the old lifestyle was ruled out.[64]

Finding examples of religious conversion defined by its intellectual elements is much more difficult, according to Thouless. A choice between two systems of thought where the decision is between true and false claims is rare indeed. Thouless states that they may only be found in literature. He quotes two examples of this type, Ward's novel, *Robert Ellsmere,* and Masefield's *The Everlasting Mercy.* These are illustrations of change—one from Christianity to agnosticism and the other from agnosticism to Christianity.[65] An interesting historical commentary on evangelistic technique is given by Thouless as a reason for so few documented intellectual conversions.

> A purely intellectual conversion, uncomplicated by elements of moral or social conflict, is perhaps not to be found in real life. Certainly one will not find them in the records of evangelists since these do not commonly argue with individual members of their audiences and generally doubt the value of an intellectual appeal. Yet there are cases of individuals whose main problem has been that of accepting as true the propositions of religion and whose central change has been the acceptance of a system of beliefs that was previously held to be false. No doubt, other factors come into such a person's conversion; he must change his behavior motivation and loyalties too, but the belief may seem to him to be the primary thing from which these others follow.[66]

---

62. Robert Thouless, *Introduction to the Psychology of Religion* (Cambridge: Cambridge University Press, 1971), p. 104.

63. Ibid., p. 105.

64. Ibid., p. 106.

65. Ibid., pp. 106-107.

66. Ibid., p. 107.

In the 1920s a book appeared in the field of psychology of religion which is second only to James' *Varieties of Religious Experience*. This was James Pratt's *The Religious Consciousness*. Pratt had done some work in this field while a graduate student at Harvard and had published earlier in 1907 in this area. He was a member of the gradualist school of thought regarding religious conversion and claims that religious conversion is "a gradual and almost imperceptible process." Little consideration is given for the "sudden" typology of James or Ames, but he spends some time defending the idea that all change is gradual, even Paul's, perhaps.[67] Pratt's typology provided a balance to the discussion.

John Oman at the same time suggests that conversion is not a subconscious change of nature, but is itself a "conscious discernment of our true relation to God and man."[68] His emphasis on the centrality of personal awareness in the conversion process reflects James's concern for individuality in these kinds of experiences. Integral to the sense of awareness of the process is a conscious decision in which the reality of "ultimate Being is acknowledged, confessed, apprehended, returned to."[69]

By the 1920s there was also a more generalized acceptance of the concepts of psychoanalysis. Sigmund Freud himself dealt with religious conversion only briefly in a short paper in 1927. A young physician had written to Freud about a religious experience of his that had happened shortly after he had seen an old woman on a dissecting table. Because of this the young man was temporarily thrown into religious disbelief, conflict, then strong belief. He was analyzed as undergoing a stimulated Oedipal jealously and anger which had been directed at the father for the sadistic, sexualized degradation of the mother, represented by the old woman. Freud theorized that because the man's understanding of God and father was basically interrelated, the anger and rebellion that were experienced were expressed in atheistic form. But for fear of the omnipotence of God he was forced to a sudden return to faith, which was experienced at a moment called conversion.[70] Religious conversion was defined as a reaction process and differentiated by its cause again. Omitted were the essential imperatives of gender differences and cultural impact on the experience.

During the 1920s Oskar Pfister wrote about the apostle Paul's conversion. Through a detailed reconstruction of Paul's life, most notably his childhood, he arrived at some interesting conclusions. He labeled Paul a "hysteric"

---

67. James Bissett Pratt, *The Religious Consciousness: A Psychological Study* (New York: Macmillan, 1926), p. 153.

68. John Oman, *Grace and Personality* (Cambridge: Cambridge University Press, 1925).

69. Ibid.

70. Sigmund Freud, "A Religious Experience," *Sigmund Freud: Collected Papers,* ed. James Strachey, Vol. 5 (New York: Basic Books, 1959), p. 243.

dealing with unconscious sexual guilt. And thus, religious conversion was again defined by *cause*.[71] Those of this school of thought, like Pfister, tend to classify conversion experience as a phenomenon of psychopathology. Surely some religious conversion experiences find their source in pathology, yet this definition alone does not seem to be broad enough to fit what is generally considered conversion, nor validate the broad scope of research.[72]

Henry Nelson Wieman used the word "unification" to define religious conversion and stressed a sort of fusion that makes people whole; "it means that he is made whole . . . fused into a single total system in which each element sustains every other."[73] This reflects later concerns of Gordon Allport and Leslie Weatherhead as they discuss conversion as an integration or reintegration process.[74] This aspect of wholeness and unification is an essential element in defining religious conversion, I believe, for its role in identity formation may encourage this sense of wholeness and unification of reality.

In 1927 a volume that dealt with the typical experiences of those converted to Catholicism was released by Sancte de Sanctis. He saw conversion only as a gradual process, the end result of a lifelong development.[75] Being a gradualist it allowed him to define conversion by *nature* rather than by *cause*, yet his rather one-sided definition allowed the developmental process of growth to be emphasized. Since religious beliefs and ideas typically begin in childhood, equating conversion with growth was natural. Since religious conversion is gradual and is often preceded by precipating experiences or conditions, then it is like growth in its occurrence; they therefore must be alike. This is the logical outcome of illogical reasoning, for it empties conversion of its dynamics and tends to make the experience so vague as to generalize a specific experience away. His definition reads: "The crisis conversion . . . need, therefore, be nothing but an episode in a slow psychic

---

71. Oskar Pfister, "Die Entwinkling des Apostels Paulus," *Imago* 4 (1920), p. 243.

72. Carl Christensen, a physician, in "Religious Conversion in Adolescence," p. 17, suggests "since psychiatry is concerned with mental disorders, much of the psychiatric contributions to the understanding of religious belief have emphasized psychopathology. Sometimes, psychiatrists tend to forget that religion is a normal part of man's individual and cultural life." Scroggs and Douglas in "Issues in the Psychology of Religious Conversion," *Journal of Religion and Health* 6 (July 1967), pp. 213-215, conclude that those psychologists whose commitment is to the Christian faith tend to view conversion as healthy, normal, and leading to maturity, while those who do not share this concern are most likely to see religious conversion as regressive and pathological. James avoids the issue altogether and focuses instead on fruits rather than roots.

73. Henry Nelson Wieman, *Religious Experience and Scientific Method* (New York: Macmillan, 1926), p. 219.

74. See Gordon Allport, *The Individual and His Religion: A Psychological Interpretation* (New York: Macmillan, 1950), pp. 92-95; or Leslie D. Weatherhead, *Psychology, Religion and Healing* (London: Hodder and Stoughton, 1952), p. 467.

75. H. R. Bagwell, "Abrupt Religious Conversion Experience," *Journal of*

process."[76] The fact that his studies were on change of experience within the Catholic community may have tempered his decision, since crisis, sudden experiences, or experiences that, though gradual, had a decisive act of decision involved in them, were seldom experienced in his audience.

Elmer Clark proposed during this same time that religious conversion be defined solely as a radical or emotional change for irreligion to religion. He adds the term "religious awakening" to describe the entry into a religious experience.[77] His study was one of the largest ever done as he examined a sample which included 985 Methodists, 366 Presbyterians, 252 Baptists, and 133 members of the confirmation group of churches. He is criticized because his study portrayed a cross section during a religious period when conversion had gone out of style as a way of entry into faith. Perhaps he could be expected to report only in the terms he did.[78] He is also criticized that his subjects were practically all middle-class college students—mostly male—and therefore not typical of the population of the day. Of his group only a small proportion reported sudden religious conversions.[79]

By the 1930s, understanding behavior in terms of adaptation was a common viewpoint and the definitions of religious conversions reflect this. Up to now most defining conversion made use of descriptions which incorporated either a sudden or gradual dichotomy, or looked to its contents to classify it; most did not signify conversion by its *cause*. W. Lawson Jones, a British psychologist, formulated religious conversion as part of a general adaptational process dealing with the whole of an individual's life situation. He included both intrapsychic and environmental conflict resolution as its cause.[80] In the 1930s, a most intriguing definition of conversion, almost secular, was also presented by L. W. Grensted. He stated that religious conversion is the building up of a sense of wholeness. This stress on the *function* of conversion became a new trend. His conviction that the central issue in conversion was wholeness allowed him to see persons as total units and to see conversion as a positive aid in unifying humankind. His definition was very broad. He would call conversion any change in any sphere that tended toward wholeness, but classified those changes with a religious sound as holiness or sanctity, "the outcome of the process of sanctification."[81]

Religion and Health 8 (April 1969), p. 167.

76. Sante de Sanctis, *Religious Conversion: A Bio-Psychological Study* (London: Kegan Paul, Trench, Trubner & Co., 1927), p. 84.

77. Elmer T. Clark, *The Psychology of Religious Awakening* (New York: Macmillan, 1929), p. 96.

78. William Paterson, *Conversion* (New York: Charles Scribner's Sons, 1940), pp. 154-155.

79. Clark, "Intense Religious Experience," p. 532.

80. H. R. Bagwell, "Abrupt Religious Conversion Experience," p. 169.

81. L. W. Grensted, *Psychology and God: A Study of the Implications of Recent Psychology for Religious Belief and Practice* (London: Longmans, Green, 1930), p. 86.

Another definition at this period of history was Mary Ewer's three understandings of this process: 1) the gradual transmutation of the nature itself; 2) a conscious, usually catastrophic, "new birth" into a filial relationship with God; and 3) a turning point or change of direction.[82] This simplistic concept brings all concerns about religious conversion to the front.

From a context of mental illness, both personal and theoretical, Anton Boisen formulated in 1936 a theory of conversion as an alternative to schizophrenia or schizoid states in the resolution of personal problems. When he added his author's note to the 1952 edition of his book, *The Exploration of the Inner World,* he resubstantiated his earlier viewpoint that religious conversion is the more or less sudden change of character from sinfulness to righteousness or from indifference to spiritual awakening arising out of the problem-solving of mental tasks. He stated:

> Both may arise out of a common situation—that of inner conflict and disharmony, accompanied by a keen awareness of ultimate loyalties and unattained possibilities. Religious experience as well as mental disorder may involve severe emotional upheaval and mental disorder as well as religious experience may represent the operation of the healing forces of nature. The conclusion follows that certain types of mental disorder and certain types of religious experience are alike attempts at reorganization. The difference lies in the outcome. Where the attempt is successful and some degree of victory is won, it is commonly recognized as religious experience. Where it is unsuccessful or indeterminate, it is commonly spoken of as "insanity."[83]

With this viewpoint, some types of honest, desperate mental illness are literally the same as this sudden, eruptive kind of conversion. For Boisen, abrupt and disruptive religious conversion is caused by distress or from evasion and concealment of one's feelings. "Such disturbances often serve as a sort of judgment day, the patient blurting out what before, for the life of him, he would not have dared to say."[84] Religious conversion is defined as an attempt at repair or elimination. It is experienced as a reorganization of one's entire mental structure with a reevaluation of values. Boisen refers to Starbuck's concepts on conversion as he describes his own understanding. It is important to bear in mind that such acute disturbances are closely related to the religious conversion experience. According to Starbuck's findings such conversion experiences are likewise an eruptive breaking up of evil habits and abnormal tastes and turning vital forces to new channels. In mental disorders of this type we have a manifestation of power that makes for health just as surely as in the religious conversion.[85]

82. Mary Anita Ewer, *A Survey of Mystical Symbolism* (New York: Macmillan, 1933), p. 197.

83. Anton T. Boisen, *The Exploration of the Inner World* (New York: Harper & Bros., 1936), p. viii.

84. Ibid., p. 196.

85. Ibid., p. 159.

Leon Salzman makes one of the best contributions to conversion in terms of its *dynamics*. Linking religious conversion with any change accomplished at a given time, he stresses its suddenness and defines it in terms of its *psychodynamics,* or, as he says, "It is any change of religion or of moral, political, ethical, or esthetic views which occur in the life of a person either with or without a mystical experience, and which is motivated by strong pressures."[86] In every case of conversion, religious or nonreligious, he recognizes an incubation period and a precipitating event and therefore labels two types of conversion according to result: 1) the progressive or maturational kind, and 2) the regressive or psychopathological kind.[87]

> Religious conversion is a specific instance of the general principle of change in the process of human adaptation. Conversion is a generic term for change and generally implies a drastic alteration of a former state . . . in theological terms it has been used in a special sense to imply a marked alteration of one's spiritual state through a superior power, generally meaning a Godhead.[88]

His insight that conversion may be caused by natural factors proves helpful. His addendum regarding changes caused by pressing personal and interpersonal difficulties which have no spiritual significance, yet may be dressed in religious language or symbolism, gives a broader understanding to the process of change.[89] This does not deny that God is in some way active in these natural changes; it only opens the person to find some actual cause for the change. If that change is beneficial, then it serves its purpose in integrating life. In my own opinion, if a knowledge of Deity and our relationship to others is enhanced, the experience will be actualizing in the believer's life, growth will occur, and religious identity will be established.

Two others in this period have proposed definitions—Owen Brandon and Pitirim Sorokin. Brandon seems unsatisfied to rely upon defining conversion as gradual or sudden change, but amplifies these two types of religious conversion to include some four or five other kinds, each gradations of the two basic, usual types.[90] Sorokin isolates factors in any conversion experience itself rather than to define it, seeing identification with a supreme value as the cause of the possible rearrangement of values and new group affiliation.[91]

---

86. Leon Salzman, "The Psychology of Regressive Religious Conversion," *Journal of Pastoral Care* 8:2 (1954), p. 63.

87. Christensen, "Religious Conversion in Adolescence," p. 20.

88. Leon Salzman, "Types of Religious Conversion," *Pastoral Psychology* 17 (1966), p. 10.

89. Ibid.

90 Owen Brandon, *The Battle for the Soul* (Philadelphia: Westminster, 1959), p. 27.

91. Pitirim A. Sorokin, *The Ways of Power and Love: Types, Factors, and Techniques of Moral Transformation* (Boston: Beacon, 1954), pp. 119-120, 148-154.

Functional Models

One of the most interesting contributions to the study of religious conversion experience has been William Sargent's additions. His *Battle for the Mind* correlated conversion with Chinese brain-washing and thought-reform techniques. He defined religious conversion by *function*. Conversion for Sargent becomes a process akin to self-abnegation and brain-washing. He traced the long history of the many uses of psychological conditioning through the generation of intense anxiety or strong emotion, such as fear, hate, guilt, anger, which are used to wipe the cortical slate clean and thus disorganize the individual so new patterns of belief and action can be established. These new ways are usually induced by suggestion and hinted at by the one who suggests them.[92] His definition of conversion points to the relationship of suggestion to conversion process and gives an important insight into the way the mind functions in causing changes. Yet he attributed conversion to a normal brain process and stresses the *cause* (suggestion) and *function* (reorganization) in his definition.

Orlo Strunk, writing about psychology of religion, included a unique emphasis regarding religious conversion. His position reflects modern psychology. He suggested that the process active in conversion is a "binding" which is conversion's fundamental dynamic and leads to an organization and completion of human life. Strunk equated religious conversion experience with that of "actualization," the process which helps to stabilize, interiorize, and motivate people. Conversion is defined by its *effect*, and is the process by which individuals realize themselves.[93]

In the 1960s Carl Christensen, a psychiatrist, made perhaps one of the most complete contributions to the long list of those who concerned themselves with religious conversion. His 1963 paper, "Religious Conversion," reported on twenty-two patients who had experienced conversions during adolescence. In each of the reported cases, these people suffered unusual conflict in their early childhood and, according to Christensen, significant ego impairment too.[94] The people he studied had rigid church backgrounds, which he theorized originally served as a haven for acceptance but later became their source for anxiety and guilt. It was during these times of stress that extreme hallucinatory conversion most often occurred.[95] Christensen is unique among

---

92. See William Sargent, *Battle for the Mind* (New York: Harper & Row, 1957) as an example.

93. Orlo Strunk, *Religion: A Psychological Interpretation* (New York: Abingdon, 1962), p. 74.

94. As reported by Carl W. Christensen, "Religious Conversion," *Archives of General Psychiatry* 9 (September, 1963), pp. 207-216. The patients studied were two with schizophrenia, one schizoid, and nineteen others with various tendencies.

95. Ibid.

writers on conversion in that he is quick to inform us that he narrowly defines conversion. Conversion for Christensen is an "acute hallucinatory episode occurring within the framework of religious belief and characterized by its subjective intensity, apparent suddenness of onset, brief duration, auditory, and sometimes visual hallucinations, and an observable change in the subsequent behavior of the convert."[96] His emphasis on *suddenness* limits his usefulness in understanding the whole range of conversion experience.

Beit-Hallahmi, Argyle, as well as Gallemore, Wilson, and Rhoads suggested that religious conversions are more common to those who suffer from some sort of affective disorders, like Christensen's "acute confusional state." The conditions that mark the early stages of psychosis are variously represented as typical conversional concerns such as: unsolved problems, cumulative stress, nervousness, anxiety conditions, and a sense of being overwhelmed, overstimulated, and even depressed. This close resemblance to the kinds of pressures and situations that contribute to deep change of direction in the psychological realm makes mental disorder and religious conversion common allies and shows what have come to be called "triggers" for experience.

Since Christensen is mostly concerned with conversion as an adolescent experience, he stresses the suddenness of it and suggests that conversion does not include other forms of religious experience which, while they may eventually have a similar result, lack the acute reactions.[97]

Another contributor to the literature of conversion is William Barclay, who sees religious conversion in the biblical sense as a "change" and considers "the most serious mistake . . . is to standardize the experience of conversion, and to (invite) the inevitable result . . . that the normal conversion experience must be sudden, shattering, and complete . . . there will be no one standardized conversion experience; but the experience of conversion will be as infinitely varied as human experience itself."[98]

Other contemporary writers discuss conversional change as well. W. S. Hill sees religious conversion defined by its *depth*, not its *speed*,[99] while John Smith suggests that conversion can be categorized as a total transformation, or an alteration in some identifiable feature of a person's life and experience, or "it may be thought of as a more radical transformation involving a change of total personality."[100]

Seward Hiltner, a theologian, presents a variation to the usual definition of religious conversion when he suggests that it is to be defined as a "move-

96. Ibid., p. 207.

97. Christensen, "Religious Conversion in Adolescence, " p. 18.

98. Barclay, *Turning to God,* pp. 92-93.

99. W. S. Hill, "Psychology of Conversion," *Pastoral Psychology* 6 (November 1955), p. 46.

100. John E. Smith, "The Concept of Conversion," *Mid-Stream* 8:3 (1966), p. 16.

ment" rather than a "once-for-all completed fact." Second, it should be considered a common compelling growth experience to those in their thirties rather than as just an adolescent experience; it is as well a function of the church through education and pastoral care and is truly to be defined as the decisive joining of a fellowship to those who "though sinners, yet saved, reach out in evangelism, in missions, and in social service and reform to share the treasure that God's grace in Jesus Christ had brought to them."[101] His definition is obviously limited to a function of mission of the church; even though this type of conversion experience may be considered a valid function of the church, it negates the vast amount of evidence that it is more. Hiltner's "conversion" is only one kind and his definition is too narrow to provide a good, meaningful description to those who seek to understand the experience.

Those who do not provide a definition of their concepts of religious conversion include Joel Allison, who suggests that its cause is "a regression in the service of the ego" and very well may be a positive activity.[102] Some writers, such as Charles Stewart, define religious conversion very specifically as "the change from egocentricity to concern for other persons, from separation from persons to reconciliation with them, or from isolation to community may occur in the adolescent by a sudden overturn of his emotions and by emergence of a new and different orientation."[103] William Silverberg calls it the "schizoid maneuver," yet Stewart deals with a concern for adolescence and his definition reflects this. Stewart's definition is based on social distinctions, thus adding another dimension to the definition.

W. H. Clark, psychologist of religion, more recently had suggested that conversion should be defined as a sharp and sudden break with a person's "past ideas, attitudes, values, or behavior, more generally all four of these, accompanied by intense feeling. . . . It is always recognized by the participants as religious."[104] Clark reflects earlier concerns with the nature of the experience and deals with conversion as gradual, which contradicts his earlier definition. He concludes that most sudden conversions have their gradual elements.[105] James Dittes defines it like the broad concept—religion. Conversion may represent primarily a change of institutional allegiance, may take place within highly emotional frameworks, or may occur when it is the generally prescribed form which is normative within the group. Or "conversion may

---

101. Seward Hiltner, "Toward a Theology of Conversion in the Light of Psychology," *Pastoral Psychology* 17 (September 1966), p. 35.

102. Joel Allison, "Recent Empirical Studies of Religious Conversion Experiences," *Pastoral Psychology* 17 (September 1966), p. 22.

103. Charles William Stewart, *Adolescent Religion: A Developmental Study of the Religion of Youth* (Nashville: Abingdon, 1967), p. 266.

104. Clark, "Intense Religious Experience," p. 531.

105. Ibid.

simply refer to a much more subjective and private change of orientation and values."[106]

André Godin had noted that the sudden nature of a transformation "is obviously not religious in itself. Furthermore, it is also apparent in abrupt changes of values, beliefs, and attitudes leading to 'diversion' (abandonment of religious faith or membership of religious groups)."[107] He indicates that the character of a change in beliefs, faith, abandonment of or return to religious faith in conversion is not to be directly associated with any type of divine intervention. He even goes so far as to suggest that "'sudden conversion' should be ascribed rather to character traits in the personality of the converts."[108] He attributes the notion of meeting God in conversion to the realm of psychological reflection. He even suggests that meeting God is usually through "words, messages, in dialogue, or possibly in orders that are difficult to execute."[109] Godin suggests that in the reconstructions of the past (conversion stories) we are caught up by the possibility of meeting God. In reality, we are seeing God in absence, not in presence. It is here that there is power for change.

Quoting André Frossard's story of change, Godin argues that religious certainty was the result. "God exists and it is all true." In most stories of conversion, says Godin, the transformations are largely anticipated and are often the results of previous wishes of the convert. He claims:

> The more the author focuses attention on his own life without presenting anything that might renew and enrich the image each one has of God, the more religiously insignificant his story is. In an extreme case, it would no longer be a question of God at all; it would flatter the reader's wish without drawing him toward the reality it claims to talk about. As for suddenness, real or pretended, it has *no* valid claim to be a criterion in discerning an experience of God. Sudden or not, this experience is only said to be "of God" by an interpretation that must seek justification elsewhere.[110]

Godin defines religious experience using rational understandings rather than spiritual or religious categories. He sees Christian experience as both a transforming experience and as an active synthesis between "inner attitudes and an action that can transform the world; it is also a synthesis between the wishes originating in man, even religious man, and those derived from the

---

106. James E. Dittes, "Two Issues in Measuring Religion," in *Research on Religious Development: A Comprehensive Handbook*, ed. Merton P. Strommen (New York: Hawthorn Books, 1971), p. 81.
107. André Godin, *The Psychological Dynamics of Religious Experience* (Birmingham, Ala.: Religious Education Press, 1985), p. 73.
108. Ibid., p. 75.
109. Ibid., p. 77.
110. Ibid., p. 82.

God revealed in the gospels."[111] Religious experience also functions at the level of resistance which may or may not be repressed and as an experience of identification (identity).[112] For Godin religious experience functions best at the level of identification. For example, children identify and transfer their loyalties to religious personages, are formed by the modeling of significant religious figures, and understand themselves in light of these others. Their idealized wishes and perceptions are fulfilled in their identification with religious people (both historical and biblical), and their religious wishes are realized. While Godin's approach seems a bit self-directed without lending credence to the transcendent in life, his insight is useful. He stresses the importance of identity in religious experience. While conversion may or may not be externally triggered by any transcendent God, the results are perceived as religious and therefore useful in interpreting one's world and the religious symbolism therein.

While Godin argues that the experience of God is never immediate, usually has intensity, contains fusional joy, and excitement is found in the resolution of conflict, his major point is that the experience of God is never a *first* experience.[113] Long before any illustration of God's presence the experiencer has his or her story. These preconditions always determine the understanding of the experience of God. When critiquing Godin's assumptions one is reminded of Kirke Farnsworth's comments on psychology of religion. He says,

> If a psychologist were conducting long-term research on the personality development of a person who suddenly experiences new meaning and direction in life, how would the psychologist explain it? Probably as some combination of socio-cultural formative influences, physiological concomitants of the emotional side of the experience, and behavorial changes that can be associated with the person's stage of life and predisposing personality characteristics. But if the psychologist failed to entertain the possibility of the occurrence of a religious conversion, would it mean that he or she was not thorough enough, that the psychological analysis should have included something more? Not at all. Any tacked-on spiritual language would add nothing to the psychological account of the event.[114]

Some would argue that theological categories are more helpful than are psychological ones. That may be the reason it is often hard to understand the transcendent. And to have a religious experience such as a conversion might

---

111. Ibid., p. 209.
112. Ibid., p. 195.
113. Ibid., pp. 3-6.
114. Kirke E. Farnsworth, *Whole-Hearted Integration: Harmonizing Psychology and Christianity Through Word and Deed* (Grand Rapids, Mich.: Baker Book House, 1985), p. 106.
115. David G. Myers and Malcolm A. Jeeves, *Psychology Through the Eyes of Faith* (New York: Harper & Row, 1987), p. 58.

suggest is thus to assign to "sensory experience spiritual significance."[115] Religious people regularly interpret phenomena with a sensitivity to the presence of God. As Myers and Jeeves suggest, when one holds such a schema of faith, a whole new set of perceptions rule one's consciousness. Jesus now is seen "not as a psychotic but as an incarnation of God. The universe is seen not as a meaningless material reality, but as God's creative handiwork—the ultimate miracle that makes little sense without a Creator."[116]

A recent renaissance of research on religious change has provided better analysis of the conversional event and a clarity of definition. Allen Moore notes that conversion has usually been emphasized as the goal of education especially during the evangelical movement; however he defines conversion as "a radical change in one's life orientation, or a turning point leading to a new state of being and a new posture in the world."[117] The changes are both personal and social.

John Kildahl's research on sudden converts explored the relationship of personality structures of the once-born and twice-born person. Basing his work on that of Starbuck, Coe, Clark, and Freud he hypothesized that sudden converts would be less intelligent, perceive authority figures as more threatening, and more authoritarian themselves, more hysteric, depressed, less humanitarian, and more religiously conservative.[118] While his research was tentative he did conclude that sudden converts were less intelligent and more hysteric than those of the gradual change variety. He also notes that the conversion experience is immensely complex and it is well to "keep in mind that conversions are rather widespread psychological phenomena, occurring within the Christian church, but also in non-Christian situations as well."[119] This being the case, Kildahl suggests that one should remember that conversions may or may not be conducive to better emotional integration because of the conflict relationship of most occurrences. Due to this fact, a conversion experience of the sudden type often falls short of optimally promoting mental or emotional growth and maturity.

A major contribution was made by J. R. Scroggs and W. G. T. Douglas in the late 1970s. They explored the definitional, pathology, personality type, age readiness, voluntaristic, and conceptual scheme issues in conversion. Their conclusions are particularly helpful.

Regarding the definition of conversion and the range of behaviors that are

---

116. Ibid.

117. Allen J. Moore, "A Social Theory of Religious Education," in *Religious Education As Social Transformation,* ed. Allen J. Moore (Birmingham Ala.: Religious Education Press, 1989), p. 29.

118. John P. Kildahl, "The Personalties of Sudden Religious Converts," in *Current Perspectives in the Psychology of Religion,* ed. Newton Malony (Grand Rapids, Mich.: Eerdmans, 1977), p. 241.

119. Ibid., p. 245.

often labeled conversion they suggest that both sudden and gradual typologies are needed. They conclude that "those who choose to write on this issue are generally interested in advancing the thesis that religious conversion, brainwashing, and/or psychotherapy are fundamentally identical or very similar processes."[120] Their review of the literature suggests the same conclusions as Windemiller: that conversions are crisis experiences and problem-solving processes which aid in stability of the personality; that they usually involve emotional upheavals which result in changed thinking and rely on group pressures as their active methodology. Conversion often results from involvement in confession and discussion and utilization of highly structured organizational approaches where new vocabularies, exhaustion, surrender and suggestion may be factors. The results include self-criticism, doubt, fear, and guilt. But both Scroggs and Douglas realize that conversion may also be the product of a pastoral counseling session with just as focused results with less dramatic personal experience.[121]

In a bibliography on conversion studies finished in 1982 only twenty-five psychological studies are identified since 1970. In looking at the bibliography one notices that many are clinical studies. During the same time period over a hundred are sociologically oriented. This shift in focus in recent years has continued to make a clear definition of conversion problematic.[122]

In a more recent study Paloutzian approaches the topic from a "cognitive need" theory which suggests that individuals often tend to sort out and bring meaning into their lives. Paloutzian hypothesized that religious conversion would fulfill just such a need.[123] He noted that those who professed to conversion seemed to respond to a higher purpose in life. He also identified a type of "forgetting curve" in which the initial enthusiasm wears off after a few weeks evidenced by a drop in understanding one's purpose. His research did not support the classic assumption that more gradual conversions enhance one's understanding of the meaning and purpose in life.

John Lofland and Norman Skonovd have provided a significant contribution in their work on "Conversion Motifs."[124] This research identified five major underlying variations within six major motifs of religious change (see chart 1). These motifs include: intellectual, mystical, experimental, affectional, revivalist, and coercive ones. They suspect that conversion motifs differ

120. Ibid., p. 257.

121. Ibid.

122. See L. R. Rambo, "Current Research in Religious Conversion," *Religious Studies Review* 1982, 8, p. 146.

123. R. F. Paloutzian, "Purpose in Life and Value Changes Following Conversion," *Journal of Personality and Social Psychology* 41 (1981), pp. 1153-60.

124. John Lofland and Norman Skonovd, "Conversion Motifs," *Journal for the Scientific Study of Religion* 18 (1979), pp. 419-423.

significantly from one historical epoch to another and even change across varied societal boundaries and subcultures within a single society. They also postulated that certain religious ideologies and organizations may have an affinity with some unique conversion motifs and in fact predispose the converts to such experiences if the convert is accepted into that cultural matrix which expounds them. This analysis of the motifs in conversion aid in organizing a more systematic approach to a definition of religious conversion and is most helpful in understanding the process itself.

Chart 1: Conversion Motifs

CONVERSION MOTIFS					
	1. Intellectual	**2. Mystical**	**3. Experimental**	**4. Affectional**	**5. Revivalist**	**6. Coercive**
1. Degree of Social Pressure	low or none	none or little	low	medium	high	high
2. Temporal Duration	medium	short	long	long	short	long
3. Level of Affective Arousal	medium	high	low	medium	high	high
4. Affective Content	illumination	awe love fear	curiosity	affection	love & fear	fear & love
5. Belief-Participation Sequence	belief-participation	belief-participation	participation-belief	participation-belief	participation-belief	participation-belief

* From John Lofland and Norman Skonovd, "Conversion Motifs," *Journal for the Scientific Study of Religion* 18 (1979), pp. 419-423.

Intellectual motifs in conversion are relatively uncommon according to Lofland and Skonovd. They begin within the person through private investigation of possible new approaches to "being" and with study into alternate theodicies. The means of self-discovery in this motif can be as simple as reading books, watching television, or attending lectures. The mode of transmission is impersonal or "disembodied." During the course of this research it was suggested that some people convert themselves in isolation from actual interaction with devotees of the respective religion. This motif defines religious conversion as shift in *allegiance*.[125]

---

125. Ibid., p. 377.

Mystical motifs in religious conversion experience are the best known. This motif suggests that the experience itself cannot be expressed in logical or coherent terms. While the apostle Paul has functioned as the ideal of what conversion should be in the Western world, this experience is reminiscent of James (1911), Starbuck (1911), and E. T. Clark (1929), who focused on mystical conversion which was further characterized by the experience coming onto an individual rather than being brought on by the subjects themselves. The convert senses a brief encounter. It is usually brought on in isolation and with little or no social pressure even though a period of stress often comes before the critical event and may stretch back for some days or even weeks. This motif is characterized by the brevity of the encounter with what the convert knows to be God. Lofland and Skonovd argue that the level of emotional arousal is extremely high, "sometimes involving theophanic ecstasies, awe, love, or even fear."[126] A definition of conversion using this motif is difficult to universalize since this experience is self-authenticating in its presence and force.

Experimental motifs have curiosity as their motivation. This type of change was identified by Howard Becker as "situational adjustment—commitment being the end result of increasing adaptation and the making of side-bets."[127] This shift is often tentative in nature but can result in a radical reorganization of identity and meaning in life. Social pressure and affective arousal is relatively low while the temporal duration of the experience may be quite long. The *affective* content of the experience is that of curiosity.

Affectional motifs in religious conversion experience are often difficult to understand for they deal with the feeling world which may or may not seem real. Here the cognitive element is obviously deemphasized and social pressure is medium, while the feelings of God's approval and the present reality of "something-out-there" are high.[128] Religious conversion is understood by its "sense" or feeling tones.

Revivalist motifs find their sources in the evangelical emphasis of the early century. While this motif seems out of vogue today, occasionally this theme is reintroduced through evangelism, traumatic messages, or enthusiasm. One such example today might be the Unification Church's approach to conversion with its rapid growth in the United States in the past decade.[129]

Coercive motifs in understanding conversion are even more rare and occur only under unusual circumstances. Lofland and Skonovd suggest that this type of change may be rampant among the new religions of the Western world where brainwashing, programing, mind control, and coercive persuasion

126. Ibid.
127. Howard S. Becker, "Personal Change in Adult Life," *Sociometry* 27 (1964), p. 40-53.
128. Lofland and Skonovd, "Conversion Motifs," p. 378.
129. Ibid., p. 379.

are the modes of entrance. Two key features of this motif of conversional change are evident: First, there is compulsion; second, sincerity and will-ingness to confess guilt or embrace an ideological system. One flaw in the conversional mechanism is that individuals changing through the use of coercive means tend to return to open social ideology when brought back into the mainstream of life. In this model it often takes a large staff in order to pro-cess a single person or even a small group of new believers. Belief often follows participation with this motif.[130] Conversion is defined by the *mode* of change rather than by any insight into the change itself.

Feminist Perspectives

One perspective which is often overlooked in discussions about change is that of personal differences which may trigger conversion or provide a dif-ferent perspective on the discussion. More recently a number of scholars have provided a balance in academic discussions which before had been only male dominated. They have been successful in bringing to the fore-front of the academic community the need for a thorough understanding of the paradigms which have modeled ways of knowing over the past decades. What often appears in this body of literature is the need to listen to "a different voice"—this is used often as a metaphor for new approaches to intellectual, ethical, and spiritual development.[131] While there is really no "one voice" of women in research of this kind, a cognizance of the uniqueness of the feminine approach provides a balance to any discussion. For example, we often generalize about the stages of growth and later in this book as we look at Erikson's model of identity theory we will use his work as a model. But we cannot forget that women's studies have provided a new agenda for scholars in this decade. This perspective initiates consideration for more informa-tion and makes most past research somewhat tentative in the areas of moral, intellectual, and faith development. What is often correctly argued is that most research has been male dominated. Mary Boys asks, "Do the cate-gories formulated by men take women's perspectives into account?"[132] Carol

130. Ibid., p. 380.
131. There is a developing body of literature in this area. See for example, Mary Field Belenky, Blythe McVicker Clinchy, Nancy Rule Goldberger, and Jill Mattuck Tarule, *Women's Ways of Knowing: The Development of Self, Voice, and Mind* (New York: Basic Books, 1986); Carol Gilligan, *In a Different Voice: Psychological Theory and Women's Development* (Cambridge, Mass.: Harvard University Press, 1977); Nicola Slee, "Parables and Women's Experiences," *Religious Education* 80:2 (Spring 1985), pp. 232-245; Jo Durden-Smith, "Male and Female—Why? *Quest/80* (October 1980); Robert W. Goy and Bruce S. McEwen, *Sexual Differentiation of the Brain* (Cambridge, Mass.: MIT Press, 1980), Elisabeth Schüssler Fiorenza, *In Memory of Her: A Feminist Theological Reconstruction of Christian Origins* (New York: Seabury, 1983).
132. Mary C. Boys, *Educating in Faith* (San Francisco: Harper & Row, 1989), p. 159.

Gilligan argues that most psychological theories depreciate the role of women. She especially targets Lawrence Kohlberg's research regarding moral reasoning as discriminating. She points out that an ethic of *care* and *intimacy* rather than one of *justice* as Kohlberg suggested needs to be understood.[133]

Another significant work is that of Mary Belenky and others who describe women's experiences and the impact they have on how women build an epistemology. She suggests that women learn to know differently than men. For example, women focus on received knowledge more than on creating it. Women move toward subjective knowledge—a kind which is personal and almost intuited. Another form of knowing for women is that of constructed knowledge which views all knowledge in its context as it interplays with intuition and the knowledge of others.[134] How women construct reality is significant when religious change deals with the reality of life. Women, it seems, have been influenced by the cultural mores of society and have in the past responded in kind. Conversion, which is a personal shift in loyalties, would be understood by women in a unique way if the research is consistent. Both the experience of God and the processes which trigger it may be uniquely feminine.

In the area of conversion studies there is little which reflects this balanced nonbiased research approach. We believe that girls learn of a "personal" God earlier than boys. Girls in their early teens often have deeper, more personal religious experiences than do boys of the same age. This is often attributed to maturity differences and girls' ability to picture abstractions earlier than boys. Almost every study that includes measures of religiousness reports the same type of findings: "a decline for boys (some say sharp, others say slight), especially of frequent worship attendance or prayer, but little, if any, decline for girls of the same age."[135] Arguments exist as to the reasons for this decline. For boys it is often explained by the lingering cultural pressure for boys to project a "macho, self-sufficient image."[136] One Search Institute study of approximately 8,000 young adolescents conducted in the 1980s focusing on the nature of religious experience noted that boys, more than girls, tended toward a religious concept "that is a means to some other end" while girls showed a greater tendency toward a religious concept that sees belief as an end in itself—intrinsic religion as contrasted with extrinsic religious belief for boys. Girls felt a greater "sense of connection with God and with other people through their faith.[137] If this is so, then the texture

---

133. See Gilligan, *In a Different Voice.*

134. Belenky et al., *Women's Ways of Knowing,* pp. 113-114.

135. "Religion in Adolescence: Dying, Dormant, or Developing?" *Source: A Quarterly Information Resource on Issues Facing Children, Adolescents, and Families* 5:4 (December 1989), p. 2.

136. Ibid.

of the experience may as well be different. Since much of the vocabulary used to define God is symbolic in nature, the ability to deal with abstractions enhances articulation of religious concepts. Preliminary research which identifies differences in the sexes as to their understanding of God, their values, and faith often pictures the mothering figure in the home as the earliest significant introduction to God-like-ness and the most powerful influence for good.[138]

Feminist definitions of spirituality which emerge relate to conversion experience in the same way. Mary Boys quotes Anne Carr, Joann Wolski Conn, and Carol Ochs who suggest a spirituality for women which is at the deepest self-transcending core of life. What is needed is understanding into an experience with God that takes "experience seriously" and one that allows new insights into relationships with regard to what is real and forces our concept of spirituality to deal with *this* world rather than to be concerned with the mysteries of heaven. Ochs uses the mother figure as a core image of mature spirituality. Some women have a way of relating to others while many men strive for individuality and independence and this perspective impacts spirituality. This attitude makes women's experience more nurturing and possibly gradual. There is a rich wealth of material which indirectly relates to understanding conversion in this research, but what is needed is a clear focus on conversion or identity per se in order for it to directly impact our conclusions. Feminist studies have emphasized the need to provide a balanced look at spirituality and to recognize the differences between men and women in the areas of religious experience.[139] One however does not want to generalize here again. There is great texture in men and women's religious experience, and in their conversional change.

What women's studies have brought to religious education is a deep and valid concern for the *process* of instruction. If, for example, women experience God differently or the triggers in their religious change are somewhat dissimilar to men, then there must be an attempt to understand these differences and construct religious educational activities which minister to this end.

Nicola Slee suggests that we need to attempt to re-read and reclaim scripture in light of women's experience, and the attempt to hear what the Bible

---

137. Ibid. See P. Benson, D. Williams, and A. Johnson. *The Quicksilver Years: The Hopes and Fears of Early Adolescence* (San Francisco: Harper & Row, 1987).

138. Preliminary research in a massive study called *Valuegenesis,* funded by the General Conference of Seventh-Day Adventists and coordinated by Peter Benson and Michael Donohue of Search Institute, Minneapolis, Minnesota has suggested this concept in early data analysis. Complete work with the massive data of grades 6-12 in North America needs more time for reliable and definitive conclusions regarding sexual differences regarding faith, values, and commitment.

139. Boys, *Educating in Faith,* p. 167.

says to women's lives is an important consideration for anyone trying to make sense out of how people change.[140] The beauty of the biblical lessons may be enhanced when this balanced approach is tried. Dwayne Huebner illustrates the texture by including women in a description of faith by citing an inclusive story in Matthew's gospel.

> Jesus acknowledges the "little faith" of the disciples, and the faith of the centurions, the hemorrhaging woman, the friends of the paralytic, and the Syrophoenician woman. Recognizing their faith in them, he grants that it need be no more than the grain of a mustard seed. It is, however, a faith that must be acted upon—used. Or as our Story proclaims, "Ask (as the Syrophoenician woman did) and it will be given to you; seek (as the hemorrhaging woman did) and you will find; knock (as the paralytic's friends did with boldness) and it will be opened to you.[141]

Developmentalist Models of Conversion

A discussion about conversion would not be complete without including the more contemporary writers who occasionally refer to conversion. While not specifically concerned about the phenomenon per se, the developmentalist school of research has obliquely provided information helpful in understanding the nature of the experience. Jean Piaget outlined the course of cognitive growth from the early infant years through the development of language, the various symbolic functions that emerge in early childhood, the growth of concrete operational thinking in later childhood, and the final emergence of formal operations in adolescence. Each new stage develops as a consequence of a former stage and the transitions which one goes through introduce new elements into that process.[142] His concepts suggest that there are some structural dynamics in persons that strive for renewal and growth which seem to be governed by laws that are internal to the person involved.[143] The necessity for renewal and change seems deeply seated in the person. Conversion in the developmentalist view is to be expected and perhaps even predicted at certain stages or situations in the faith-emergence process. While this "change" may be different between the sexes, the movement to be different seems real.

Scholars such as James Fowler, Lawrence Kohlberg, and James Loder provide additional insights into conversion experience but shed little light on its definition specifically. Conversion for them is viewed from the perspective of *structure* rather than *content* or *dynamics* and in the vocabulary of the

---

140. Slee, "Parables and Women's Experiences," p. 233.

141. Dwayne Huebner, "Christian Growth in Faith," *Religious Education* 81:4 (Fall 1986), pp. 514-515.

142. Conn, *Christian Conversion,* p. 29.

143. Ibid., p. 22.

developmentalists is called a movement that is "vertical" in nature rather than "horizontal" where radically new questions creatively restructure old and new content into a totally new horizon.[144]

James Fowler's analysis of faith development suggests that somewhere between Stage 3 (Conventional-Synthetic) and Stage 4 (Intuitive-Projective) the individual begins to make a cognitive shift to a more critical, personal view of one's own authority in religious decisions. Fowler even moves beyond this to suggest an almost mystical falling in love with the uncomprehended God as the person is grasped by an other-worldly love and is transformed. While Fowler indicates that such deep devotion is rare, it does typify a model of conversional change. More will be said about the developmental schema in later discussions about the impact of conversion on growth and youth. In a critique of James Loder and James Fowler, Andrew Grannel suggests that their two approaches stand in a "paradoxical tension." "Fowler's study tends to emphasize the first part of the equation [i.e., 'without the long process of formation, there could be no transformation'] while Loder's study tends to emphasize the second part [i.e., 'no amount of careful formation can transform']."[145] Each uses a differing view of transformation. Fowler looks at the social-psychological implications of a lifelong search for ultimate meaning while Loder suggests the importance be placed in the life-transforming process of being "grasped" by God.[146]

Kohlberg, on the other hand, claims that individuals move to autonomous, postconventional morality as they grow. But the basic question of "why should I be moral?" cannot be answered by any explanation other than by an orientation to a cosmic perspective rooted in "nondualistic contemplative experience."[147] While these definitions and suggestions regarding change seem esoteric, others have spoken of this radical movement to such an orientation in terms of surrender or conversion.[148] The product of this change for Kohlberg would include new concern for ethical behavior since religious conversion involves a demand for "total, permanent self-surrender, without conditions, qualifications, or reservations.[149] Meeting God at this level requires responsible action because Kohlberg's third, postconventional level of moral reasoning which is rooted in self-chosen, personal ethical principles requires a cognitive conversion in areas of morality. He implies that only at a more

144. Ibid., p. 183.

145. Andrew Grannel, "The Paradox of Formation and Transformation," *Religious Education* 80 (Spring 1985), p. 387.

146. Ibid.

147. Walter E. Conn, "Merton's True Self: Moral Autonomy and Religious Conversion," *Journal of Religion* 65 (1985), p. 514.

148. See Lawrence Kohlberg, *The Philosophy of Moral Development* (San Francisco: Harper & Row, 1981), pp. 344-372.

149. James P. Hanigan, "Conversion and Christian Ethics," *Theology Today* 40 (April 1983), p. 30.

adult age—at a time of postconventional morality—would conversion be significant, and therefore conversion may be expected only at an older, more adult age.

Critics often question Kohlberg's assumptions when he suggests that thinking and morality are more closely related than are actions. They strongly question his humanistic individualism, his sexual bias, and his conclusions that the "highest" or most "mature" moral stage is exhibited by those who make moral decisions consistent with their self-chosen convictions and perspective.[150] Carol Gilligan again argues that Kohlberg's ideas are those of a typical Western male. She believes that Kohlberg ignores that moral maturity for women is not a matter of abstract ethical principles but derives from responsible, committed relationships. This might imply that an understanding of conversion in a woman's context might be more related to role modeling and relationships than to purely intellectual or abstract commitment. More research needs to be completed in this area to do more than infer conclusions in this area.

Against the biblical understanding of religious conversion's impact on the first century Christians—that of a people gathered to celebrate the process of conversion—Bernard Lonergan posits conversion as *the* fundamental quality of being a religious person. In his essay focusing on "Theology in its New Context," he actually equates religion with conversion. His book, *Methods in Theology,* develops the sources and ramifications of religious shifts in "horizons" through a model of religious change that includes at least four types of change: *intellectual, affective, moral,* and *religious* conversions.[151]

For Lonergan, "conversion is not a set of propositions that a theologian utters, but a fundamental and momentous change in the human reality that a theologian is."[152] Yet, while the concept of conversion is the linchpin of Lonergan's theological thought, a clear understanding of what he means by conversion is often lost. Some have argued that this is due to his rather broad and general treatment of the subject. A most unique analysis of Lonergan's thought is presented by James Price as he attempts to apply Lonergan's theory to the life of John Climacus, a monk whose work, "The Ladder of Divine Ascent," outlines steps to spiritual awareness and change in conversion.[153] In this work Price concludes that Lonergan's structure is basically sound and that

---

150. Myers and Jeeves, *Psychology Through the Eyes of Faith*, p. 14.

151. See Bernard Lonergan, "Theology in Its New Context" in his *A Second Collection,* ed. W. F. J. Ryan and B. J. Tyrrell (London: Darton, Longman & Todd, 1974), pp. 55-67; and *Method In Theology* (New York: Herder and Herder, 1972).

152. Lonergan, *Method,* p. 276.

153. James Robertson Price, "Conversion and the Doctrine of Grace in Bernard Lonergan and John Climacus," *Anglican Theological Journal* 62 (October 1980), pp. 338-362.

Climacus' story of religious change illustrates the movement to be gradual over a long period of time and seems to reflect Lonergan's views as "otherworldly falling in love."[154] Since Lonergan treats the subject of conversion structurally rather than illustratively his language on the topic is necessarily general and vague rather than concrete.

Lonergan argues that a real conversion is necessary if one is to shift the "horizons" of one's life. This shift will permit us to differentiate and interrelate the worlds of common sense and of theory and poetics.

Intellectual conversion for Lonergan, interpreted accurately by Mary Boys, is a turning from the idolatry of easy answers and certitude. It is deep commitment to knowing—experiencing, understanding, integrating, differentiating, and believing. Intellectual conversion helps one live with the uncertainty of ambiguity and not be frozen and stopped by it. It is a clarification in the way one thinks. Former intellectual or ideological concepts weaken under the pressure of an ever-expanding experience of God and eventually old views are discarded, according to Lonergan. As Boys aptly says, "Intellectual conversion asks that we believe in a God who is not threatened by our doubts and questions. It enables us to pray, as does Elie Wiesel: 'I no longer ask you to resolve my questions, only to receive them and make them part of you.'"[155]

Moral conversion on the other hand implies a shift in the basis for moral and ethical choice. It draws out the person to be what he should be.[156] This moral shift of horizon provides a substantial change in the criterion of choices. There is movement from satisfaction to values in decision making. This model reflects the most basic biblical concepts of return and change. Kohlberg has, of course, developed this moral reasoning to a fine edge when he suggests that our ethical values later in life determine our moral choices, but Lonergan's view implies much the same thing, with somewhat less clarity.[157]

Religious conversion is the most difficult to understand in Lonergan's trilogy. This complete change involves a total and permanent self-surrender without any reservations. [158] In a sense it is the feeling of being grasped by God. From it we recognize the joy of returning home to God where we should be. In religious conversion the radical change is initiated not by ourselves, but is in response to the experience of being approached, somewhat

154. Stephen Happel and James J. Walter, *Conversion and Discipleship* (Philadelphia: Fortress, 1986), p. 20; or see Lonergan, *Methods*, pp. 240-244.

155. Quoted in Mary C. Boys, "Conversion as a Foundation of Christian Education," *Religious Education* 77 (March-April 1982), p. 220; from Elie Wiesel, *One Generation After* (New York: Avon Books, 1972), p. 241.

156. Conn, *Christian Conversion*, p. 28.

157. Joseph T. Kelley, "Some Implications of Lonergan's View of Conversion," *Journal of Pastoral Care* 40:4 (1986), p. 363.

158. Happel and Walter, *Conversion and Discipleship*, p. 22.

like the messianic presence for the apostle Paul on the Damascus road.

Affective conversion is equally difficult to understand. This change involves at least three aspects of "attachment and detachment," according to Happel and Walter. It requires 1) a "recentering in the patterns of the subject from detached scrutiny or irony to attachment; 2) a shift in the object toward which the subject's affections are drawn (from self-interest to concern for others—family, society, nation, world); and 3) the location of the appropriate aesthetic symbol to express one's affective meanings.[159] Like all conversion, it can occur gradually or rapidly in a single place or piecemeal in many situations.

Walter Conn builds on Lonergan's views in his seminal volume, *Christian Conversion: A Developmental Interpretation of Autonomy and Surrender,* and uses the same categories to understand conversional change. His discussion of the religious dimension of conversion is especially helpful as we come to understand Christian conversion as essentially an *"invitation to a life not only dedicated to the love of neighbor but focused and empowered by the mysterious presence of God at its vital center."*[160] What is especially helpful here is his clarification of the relationship of conversion to religious and personal development. These insights are especially useful later in this volume when factors that contribute to religious conversion are explored.

Other individuals could be cited, for almost everyone who has written about religious experience attempts some type of definition of religious conversion. And these definitions and descriptions cover the time-line completely. Writers as diverse as Søren Kierkegaard and T. S. Eliot have hinted at an understanding of conversion, one as the father of existentialism and the other by new ways and moods of poetry. The Dane sought all of his life to understand what being a Christian truly meant. And he concluded that a person could not have anything upon his conscience if God did not exist, for the conscience is the God-relationship. Therefore, the terrible weight of having even the slightest guilt on one's conscience because one is immediately conscious of the judgment of God and the need to move close to God in order to find forgiveness; thus, the need for conversion.[161] There is only one curious note in Kierkegaard's *Journals.* It was entered with the exact time and date. *"May 19, [1838]. Half-past ten in the morning.* There is an indescribable joy . . ."[162] And Eliot, in his later, more mature years, quietly and without any showboating, joined the Church of England as a symbol of his Christian commitment. Conversion had worked its way in his heart.

---

159. Ibid.

160. Conn, *Christian Conversion*, p. 212.

161. See Søren Kierkegaard, *Works of Love,* trans. David F. Swenson and Lillian Marvin Swenson (Princeton: Princeton University Press, 1946); or a discussion about Kierkegaard in ARCS: *"Metanois," Parabola* 8 (Winter 1983), pp. 27-33.

162. Quoted in Kerr and Mulder, eds. *Conversions,* p. xvii

There is little uniform agreement in contemporary literature regarding the definitions of conversion. Some identify the process, others focus on the time it occurs. Still others deal with parallel experiences of both religious and secular nature in determining its understanding. Some investigators have tried to identify conversion types or motifs. Those with a more sociological bent have confused religious socialization with the conversion experience itself. Other scholars have suggested that conversions must be identified by their impact on one's life.[163] Those effects range from simple personality changes to alterations in lifestyle and ideology. Given this interest, most modern research has focused on the processes which impact religious change.

Whether a gradual change, a sudden emotional experience, a changing of allegiance, or a turning from self to others or God, conversion is a vital force in the life. The Bible suggests that it is part of the scheme of salvation. Individuals should come home—to God. This return transforms. This renewal makes life different for the saint and sinner. Religious conversion has many definitions and throughout history the meanings have shifted as the need to explore yet another dimension of the process of change is felt. It plays a significant role in the construction of personal identity, pointing a life in a particular direction, giving it an aim, giving it new meaning and purpose. To determine the way conversion provides these functions, it is necessary to examine the constituent elements of the phenomena.

---

163. See Spilka, Hood, and Gorsuch, *The Psychology of Religion: An Empirical Approach,* pp. 199-222 for a complete discussion of the research regarding conversion. His treatment of the classical history of conversion is especially helpful in understanding the shifting emphasis in this research.

Chapter 3

Wholeness: The Constructs of Change

"In the evening I went very unwillingly to a society in Aldersgate Street where one was reading Luther's preface to the Epistle to the Romans. About a quarter of nine, while he was describing the change which God works in the heart through faith in Christ, I felt my heart strangely warmed. I felt I did trust in Christ alone for my salvation; and an assurance was given me that He had taken away my sins, even mine, and saved me from the law of sin and death."

John Wesley

There are many definitions and foci of concern regarding religious conversion experience. Contemporary research has moved from a typically biblical definition to an attempt to define the experience as it integrates with the development of personality. Some early definitions of conversion stress *causality* when describing such things as motives, intuition, or volition. When attempting to analyze conversion itself as sudden or gradual, acute, confusional, dramatic, pathological, or positive, the definitions reflect an attempt to define its *essence* or *nature*. Those who wish to look at the *content* stress the intellectual, emotional, social, moral, philosophical, or religious elements or beliefs involved. Definitions that are especially *theological* tend to be biased by religious tradition and ethereal hopes, while those which stress the *function* in the life of the believer see the binding, integrating, and bonding function of the experience. Those definitions of conversion that are simply *symbolic* tend to be too vague and therefore are not very helpful; an example is Lonergan's "otherworldly-faithing-in-love" or de Sanctis's definition of conversion as a "displacement of psychic energy or a new economy of love."[1]

---

1. Sante de Sanctis, *Religious Conversion: A Bio-Psychological Study* (London: Kegan Paul, Trench Trubner, 1927), pp. 92, 115, 127, 142.

61

There has been a gradual shift throughout the history of studies about religious conversion in this century. Early studies of conversion simply described the process. Then as people began studying the issue afresh, elaboration of the hypothesis that the process of religious conversion be related to general theories of personality and behavioral change emerged. This is only logical because the new insights of psychoanalysis and psychology since Freud have centered on the changing aspects of humankind as lived, which would necessarily include religious expression.

Psychology is especially good at observing different kinds of conversion experience. In particular the psychological school observes that Christianity continues to produce examples of a radical transformation of character, but that there is much greater variety than theology had recognized in the attainment, the forms, and the content of the experience.[2] There is no consensus as to religious conversion's moment—whether prolonged by some crisis, or sudden in its event. Both seem to be the categories of conversion. One is tempted to agree with George Jackson when he criticized attempts to define conversion in a limited sense by saying, "It matters . . . little what principle of classification we adopt, or whether we adopt any at all—the best is imperfect—what does matter is that we steadfastly resist all attempts to 'standardize' conversion. There are types of conversion to which many do not conform. There is none to which any must conform."[3]

It is important then to insist that there are many varieties of religious conversion and any definition that does not allow for the individual variations due to genetics, environment, gender, tradition, or personality variables has negated an important fundamental point. Conversion is primarily a personal, private affair, and any attempt to model a generic type is fruitless. It is a personal experience because religious expression and belief is usually a personal affair. It is an attitude, since faith is an attitude of our whole person toward God and life in general. It is an integrative experience because it seems to involve all those factors in our personality which constitute us as whole—for example, change impacts behavior, ideology, outlook, worldview, and lifestyle. It has historical or cultural relationships; when we speak of religious conversion we usually think of it in a Christian context, however, and our faith-perspective gives shape and definition to our understanding of the experience. As David Hoffman says:

> To speak of conversion from a Christian perspective is to speak of a turning from all other gods to the God of Jesus Christ. . . [it is a movement toward] a reorientation of our personal lives; that not only [impacts] structures and institutions

2. William Paterson, *Conversion* (New York: Charles Scribner's Sons, 1940), pp. 155-156.

3. George Jackson, *The Fact of Conversion: The Cole Lecturers for 1908* (New York: Revell, 1908), p. 97.

but we as individuals are in fundamental need of transformation . . . a change in what we as persons stake our lives on . . . a change of faith which involves a change of those stories that make sense of our lives . . . a reinterpretation of our past . . a change of our value-center from ourselves, our groups and our causes to the God of creation.[4]

We have seen that religious conversion hints at 1) a change in denominational affiliation or status; 2) a movement *back* or to God through personal introspection or outward encounter; 3) a sense in which a person solves or resolves a religious identity crisis which integrates the personality and informs one's purpose. Each description points to an important aspect of religion in the life. Finding an adequate center of beliefs and values is a significant aspect of religion's function in the life, and religious conversion assists in that process. Individuality, uniqueness, and separateness must be allowed in the experience. Since it is not the purpose to decide whether conversion experiences are religiously true or not, a definition that stresses *function* and *process* is perhaps the most decisive for use in this book and the most useful in understanding the experience. Therefore, I suggest that religious conversion be defined by constituent elements, those processes that operate in the religious experience. This process would then be considered religious conversion.

It is obvious that the most consistent theme that runs throughout the research on conversion is that the experience typifies "change." The original words signify that change of a deep nature, a return to earlier allegiances, or a shifting around of attitude and belief constitute the best understanding of the word. If conversion means "change," the converted person is one who has changed his or her way of life. That change can be in cognition, affection, or praxis. But, if conversion only means change, then obviously all types of change, good or bad, toward helpful or harmful things would constitute religious conversion, or as Earl Furgeson suggests, "A person who gets married has changed his way of life, but he is not usually thought of as having been converted."[5] There are with religious conversion various connotations that equally influence the definition. Most of these are the connotations of the wild emotionalist, revivalist, Bible-beating circuit preacher who scared hell-fire and damnation into those who watched. Or we think of the dramatic tongue-speaker who shouts or shakes.[6] Or we think about persons changing their styles of living. Heroin addicts who have shot up for twelve years suddenly

---

4. David Hoffman, "Conversion and Evangelism," *Touchstone* 3 (1983), pp. 28, 29.

5. Earl Furgeson, "The Definition of Religious Conversion," *Pastoral Psychology* 16 (September 1956), p. 9.

6. See Barbara Eleanor Jones, "Conversion: An Examination of the Myth of Human Change" (Ph.D. dissertation, Columbia University, 1969), for a detailed accounting of how terms for religious change have been altered.

come to themselves, or the Teen Challenge graduate who has found in Jesus a way out of his or her compulsive behavior all are preconceived notions of conversion in religious thought and tradition.

When religious conversion is totally equated with change, the psychological essence of the experience itself is dissipated. This was the motivation for E. T. Clark in 1929 to eliminate the use and confusion of the term conversion by simply avoiding the use of the word. Attention must also be called to the fact that, as illustrated by the previous discussion of definitions, conversion is only a part of a total process, of which the final product is religious experience.

Therefore I suggest that for an experience of change to be religious conversion constituent elements must be present. These elements make up the essence of religious conversion, and without them the experience should not be classified as religious, but perhaps simply psychological or societal change. Chart 2 (following) shows the elements joining to define religious conversion. This will be used as a basis for reflecting upon the identity experience later. A brief discussion of each element in the definition will follow.

Chart 2: CONSTITUENT ELEMENTS OF CONVERSION
Conversion is a word used to describe "change,"
but a kind of change that includes the following constituent elements

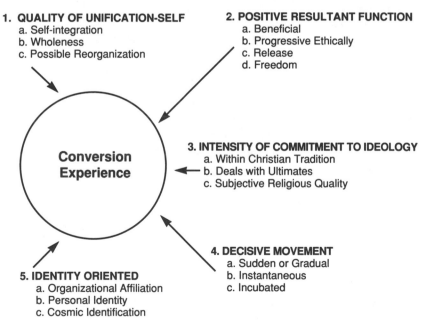

1. QUALITY OF UNIFICATION-SELF
   a. Self-integration
   b. Wholeness
   c. Possible Reorganization

2. POSITIVE RESULTANT FUNCTION
   a. Beneficial
   b. Progressive Ethically
   c. Release
   d. Freedom

Conversion Experience

3. INTENSITY OF COMMITMENT TO IDEOLOGY
   a. Within Christian Tradition
   b. Deals with Ultimates
   c. Subjective Religious Quality

4. DECISIVE MOVEMENT
   a. Sudden or Gradual
   b. Instantaneous
   c. Incubated

5. IDENTITY ORIENTED
   a. Organizational Affiliation
   b. Personal Identity
   c. Cosmic Identification

Religious conversion then is a word used to describe "change" but, more specifically, a kind of change that has the following elements: 1) a unifying quality for self, which includes self-integration, wholeness, and possible reorganization and integration; 2) a positive behavior; 3) an intensity of commitment to an ideology, usually thought of as occurring within the Christian tradition as a confrontation with ultimates but may include change with any subjective religious quality; 4) includes a decisive "change or returning to" brought on suddenly or gradually, seen as either instantaneous or incubational; 5) a sense of belonging or understanding of personal identity itself. The "triggers of change" may be influenced by personality, gender differences, environment, mystical experience, or practical (pedagogical) influences.

One reason that there is so much diversity of definition regarding religious conversion is that each person views conversion definitions from a personal vantage point. If that view is theological, then the definition might speak of it as a divine act that engages and changes one. Those who select a naturalistic viewpoint simply eliminate the religious connotations. So it is not simply a matter of selecting the twenty-two major definitions and getting at their substance. The result of this type of definition would probably not be too comprehensive. But looking at the constituent elements in the process may provide an observable base for understanding that allows one to explore the various causes and contexts wherein religious conversion is manifest. Therefore, conversion is evident when these elements are in operation. This does not take into account those whose religious conversions are pathological in nature, wherein the experience may not culminate in positive results; such changes can be examined according to their causes and explained by them. Nevertheless, if the elements listed are present, it is safe to define the conversion as religious. God is active in this change, in this return, but it is not explained totally by "a feeling" about God.

Unifying Quality

This element in religious conversion stresses the *function* of the change itself, taking into consideration earlier definitions that reflect this aspect of conversion. Religious conversion is seen as providing for the emerging self both integrity and completeness. This process of becoming whole then includes all aspects of "unselfing," disintegration, reflection, reorientation, recommitment, and self-transcendence. In a sense, conversion, since it involves a new set of images, symbols, issues, goals, and values, helps in providing a transformation in the "concrete shape and texture of one's life, in one's character."[7] Barbara Jones suggests that the process of conversion would perhaps better be described as a reintegration, a return to one's self, for in this psychological sense reintegration implies a return to a former state of

---

7. Walter Conn, *Christian Conversion* (New York: Paulist, 1986), p. 208.

completeness. This position is a difficult one to maintain psychologically. She suggests however that "in a religious sense, 'return' is a helpful concept if we are clear as to precisely what is meant. That in a wider sense all religious conversion is a return to, a reorganization and appropriation of the source of that which is."[8] In a more restricted sense, some have suggested that conversion is a return to the original teachings from childhood later rejected in adolescence.[9] This concept of conversion as a return would not fit many of the conversion examples throughout history or recorded in the Bible. Although Pascal and Augustine might fit this definition, the apostle Paul certainly would not. Yet, the concept of return is biblical, and reflects this theological understanding of the Old Testament view of humankind alluded to earlier. Since we are to be with God, since reconciliation through Jesus Christ in the New Testament sense reflects this reunion with God, it is a good concept to use in understanding this change. One does in a sense return to God, back to the place of origin, back to the home of God.

When one confronts what someone considers to be infinite and makes a positive move in lining up with that perception, integration often happens. This change, intense, deep, and profound, this reorganization and reorientation, involves the whole person and is, though it may or may not be permanent. James in his *Religious Experience* suggests that permanence not be the requirement of effectiveness.

> One word, before I close this lecture, on the question of the transiency or permanence of these abrupt conversions. Some of you, I feel sure, knowing that numerous backslidings and relapses take place, make of these their apperceiving mass for interpreting the whole subject and dismiss it with a pitying smile as so much "hysterics." Psychologically, as well as religiously, however, this is shallow. It misses the point of serious interest, which is not so much the duration as the nature and quality of these shiftings of character to higher levels. Men lapse from every level—we need no statistics to tell us that. Love is, for instance, well known not to be irrevocable, yet, constant or inconstant, it reveals new flights and reaches of ideality while it lasts. . . . So with the conversion experience; that it should for even a short time show a human being what the high-water mark of his spiritual capacity is, this is what constitutes its importance—an importance which backsliding cannot diminish, although persistence might increase it.[10]

It is interesting to note that James himself in his study found *no* instances of backsliding among those he studied. He gives an example of a M. Ratisbonne, whose whole future was shaped by the few minutes of his conversion decision; he subsequently gave up his project of marriage, became a priest, went to Jerusalem, and founded a mission to work for the Jews.

---

8. Jones, "The Myth of Human Change," p. 76.
9. William James, *The Varieties of Religious Experience* (New York: Mentor Books New American Library, 1958), p. 205.
10. Ibid.

The experience was a finding of identity—for him, a holistic, integrating, new selfhood through the process of religious conversion. And Starbuck suggests that the effect of conversion is to "bring with it a changed attitude toward life, which is fairly constant and permanent, although the feelings fluctuate."[11]

Some of the most interesting research comes from women's issues. While the experience of change seems to have no sexual limitations, its personal impact may be different between the sexes. Paula Cooey points out a significant variant among women whose sensitivities toward transformation may result in a new sense of power. She uses conversion to describe the consciousness-raising experience that comes through enlightenment. She suggests that conversion may in essence refer to a large range of consciousness-transforming experiences which differ not only in the cognitive beliefs incorporating ideological change but involve a new sense of power, not an alien experience to women in their struggle and new-found freedom.[12]

One unique aspect of this unifying movement in the conversion process is that for conversion to be religious even this unifying quality is seen to be wrought by God. The result, a sense of self-understanding, comes often only in the light of a new understanding of God's purposing in one's life.[13]

Results and the Life

Any deep change, brought on by any of hundreds of causes, results in various effects. In a religious conversion, the effects are always for the better even if only so defined by the one experiencing it. Some psychologists, however, would be quick to point out that converts have a reactive, regressive, and degenerative experience because of religious change.[14] These may be the overall effects as observed by those analyzing the experience, or when viewing a pathological experience, but for the one experiencing conversion the results appear positive. Conversion seems to promise positive change in most of the areas that constitute wholeness. All of life seems impacted in this experience. Behavior may change, ideas may refocus, pur-

11. E.D. Starbuck, *The Psychology of Religion* (New York: Charles Scribner"s Sons, 1915), pp. 357-360. In addition to this, Starbuck found that as he collected facts on the duration of conversion experienced from some one hundred subjects, more than half Methodists, 93 percent of the women and 77 percent of the men had been backsliders before their conversion. Starbuck concluded that people experiencing conversion once having taken their stand and identified with a church do not leave it even if their previous enthusiasm declines.

12. Paula Cooey, "The Power of Transformation and the Transformation of Power," *Journal of Feminist Studies in Religion* 1 (1985), pp. 32, 33.

13. Leroy T Howe, "A Developmental Perspective on Conversion," *Perkins Journal* 33 (1979), p. 20.

14. Furgeson, "Religious Conversion," p. 8.

pose and mission may become clear on a very personal level. The lifestyle choices that seem mandated by such an encounter with God may not be seen as necessarily positive by those with whom the convert meets, but, personally, they are considered a movement toward God and wholeness. The postcrisis process is notable for the clarity of feeling and attentiveness to purpose that accompany it. For example, those who have experienced religious conversion note the characteristics of the new life: the newness, the revival of cheer and fullness, the developments of positive virtues such as courage and hope. These postcrisis feelings do, however, relate to the temperament of the individual, yet generally do typify conversion experience.[15]

Ethel Waters' dramatic conversion is illustrative of the resultant sense of peace, joy, and positive attitude.

> On the last of the three extra nights of the meeting I got down on the mourners' bench, down on my knees once more. And I told myself, "If nothing happens tonight, I'll not come back again."
>
> Nobody had come that night to the meeting, nobody but the very old people who were always there. I was praying hard and hopefully, asking God, "What am I seeking here? What do I want of You? Help me! If nothing happens, I can't come back here any more!"
>
> And then it happened! The peace of heart and of mind, the peace I had been seeking all my life.
>
> I know that never again, so long as I live, can I experience that wonderful reaction I had that night in the little church. Love flooded my heart and I knew I had found God and that now and for always I would have an ally, a friend close by to strengthen me and cheer me on.
>
> I don't know exactly what happened or when I got up. I don't even know whether I talked. But the people who were there that night were astounded. Afterward they told me that I was radiant and like one transfixed. . . . And I did feel full of light and warmth. . . . I knew it was not just wintertime religion with me and that my feeling of being watched over and protected would never leave me.[16]

Others suggest that the post state can *only* be seen by its positive results. While James Pratt speaks of it as the loss of evil habits, David Roberts describes the experience as trust in God and inward harmony. While Benjamin Weininger delineates a period free of anxiety with a new, clearer perception that includes concerns of brotherly love, William James hints that the results of the converted life are total, final, complete, and in some way irreversible.[17] These reflect the biblical concept that "it is a fearful thing to fall into the hands of the living God,"[18] for those who experienced the divine

---

15. George Barton Cutten, *The Psychological Phenomena of Christianity* (New York: Charles Scribner's Sons, 1908), p. 250.

16. Ethel Waters and Charles Samuels, *His Eye Is on the Sparrow* (Garden City, N.Y.: Doubleday, 1951), pp. 50-52. Quoted in Hugh T. Kerr and John M. Mulder, eds. *Conversions* (Grand Rapids, Mich.: Eerdmans, 1983), pp. 220-222.

17. Starbuck, *The Psychology of Religion*, pp. 123-124; James Bisset Pratt, *The*

presence historically have been changed dramatically.

Encounter with the Almighty cannot be taken lightly. Meeting God and being changed through conversion, both gradual or sudden, creates new ethical and social demands. The story in the New Testament about selling all that you have to purchase the kingdom of God, the language of real estate, shows the claim of God on a person and what that new identity demands. One is continually confronted with the ethical and moral implications of making a commitment to God and allowing divine power to motivate. The change is often deep and noteworthy.

Of the group that Salzman studied, those with neurotic tendencies, the results of religious conversion, do not come away sounding quite so positive for the observer. He suggests that in his group the convert has

> 1) an exaggerated, irrational intensity of belief in the new doctrine; 2) the convert is more concerned with the form and doctrine than with the greater principle of his new belief; 3) the convert's attitude toward previous belief is one of contempt, hatred, and denial, and he/she rejects the possibility that there might be any truth to it; 4) the convert is intolerant toward all deviates, with frequent acting-out by denouncing and endangering previous friends and associates; 5) the convert shows a crusading zeal and a need to involve others by seeking new conversions; and, 6) the convert engages in masochistic and sadistic activities, displaying a need for martyrdom and self-punishment.[19]

Nevertheless, for the participant in religious conversion even these observed negative results, because of the emotional involvement and intense conviction, are viewed and assumed as beneficial. The inevitable difference may solely arise from the viewpoint of the observer. Robert Thouless describes just such a concept, "The convert may be impressed by her new feeling of love for everybody; her neighbors may observe only the behavior reaction of walking on the curbstone to avoid contact with ungodly people."[20] George Albert Coe, on the other hand, clarified this experience and is quoted by William James as saying, "What is attained is often an altogether new level of spiritual vitality, a relatively heroic level, in which impossible things have become possible, and new energies and endurances are

---

Religious Consciousness: A Psychological Study (New York: Macmillan, 1926), pp. 162-163; David F. Roberts, *Psychotherapy and a Christian View of Man* (New York: Charles Scribner's Sons, 1950); Benjamin Weininger, "The Interpersonal Factor in the Religious Experience," *Psychoanalysis* (March 1955), p. 31; James, *Religious Experience*, pp. 195-207.

18. Hebrews 10:31.

19. Leon Slazman, "Types of Religious Conversion," *Pastoral Psychology* 17 (1966), p. 18.

20. Robert H. Thouless, *An Introduction to the Psychology of Religion* (Cambridge: Cambridge University Press, 1971), p. 113.

shown."[21]

Thus positive results is an element for conversion. These may be simply new directions, and therefore they are interpreted as "good" by the believer because of the intensity of commitment and definiteness of experience decisions to eliminate past problems are incorporated into the individuals, who see themselves as better. Or the believer may actually be ethically a better person according to the mores of the society due to the new organization of values. Or the commitments and values which have been internalized direct the convert to new heights of attainment.

Commitment and Growth

Not only new ideologies result through religious conversion but the intensity of commitment to them is emphasized. This intense commitment is usually thought of as reflecting in some way the Christian tradition but may as well incorporate subjective qualities of religion as well. This would allow an individual who perceives that the experience has religious qualities or essence to define it as religious conversion. There is in conversion a perceived "confrontation" and a resultant intense commitment to an ethical, creedal, or ideological framework even if the process which assisted that commitment was long and protracted. This is especially true in conversion's outward allegiance—joining a church or religious community. Growth is usually the result. This growth can be understood in a number of ways.

Lewis Sherrill points out, "God confronts man" in this crisis.[22] And in the decision to advance toward growth or shrink back from its perils, religious conversion may take place. Conversion thus would include a growth toward loyalty to a new way of life, to the ideological framework of a group, church, or organization. It would be a commitment to *not* go back. Only the future has potential in Sherrill's view. But remember it must include a religious quality if it is to be considered religious conversion. This quality may only be perceived by those who are involved, but it must be present.

The intensity of belief is an important factor as well. Intensity may take the form of emotionalism, deep concern, insight, or calm understanding, each with clarity and definiteness. The process of conversion may follow many significant points of crisis. When a person shows active involvement symbolically significant outward actions are often encouraged. Baptism takes place in many religious communities as a symbol and significant step in validating that inward commitment. The convert accepts membership in a community and ideally the values of that group. Hopefully, those values center around the will of God and show a growth toward maturity for the person

---

21. James, *Religious Experience,* p. 194.
22. Lewis Joseph Sherrill, *The Struggle of the Soul* (New York: Macmillan, 1951), p. 27.

who joins that group.[23]

Decisive Movement

True religious conversion demands movement, whether a movement toward a total life reorganization or a return to a former belief and lifestyle. The decision is crucial; it points to a way that is different and, since it also includes a call toward integration, a decisive element is suggested. This change can, I believe, be expressed as either gradual or sudden. Since most discussions about religious conversion stress the suddenness of the experience, conversion is usually thought of as a fast, sudden crisis. We must always, however, include change that is either gradual or sudden as a movement in religious conversion. Long protracted changes we have seen are all a part of the conversion process. The event may be particularly momentous, but the decisive movement may have occurred, nudged by many months, or even years, of careful, thoughtful concern about religion in the life. Finally as the change comes, months may have passed with more time in which to sort out the implications of that change.

If this deep change that causes reorganization of the self is *always* and *only* sudden, and by sudden is meant a spur of the moment thing, a wrong impression has been given. Those who differentiate between sudden and gradual conversions, each being called religious conversion, do perhaps the best job at defining. It seems a shame that even James in his great work identified gradual conversion as a type, then illustrated only sudden varieties. It is important to note, as does Earl Furgeson, "James was indeed correct in affirming that there are two ways in which mental results may be accomplished, the way of gradual growth and the way of more sudden conversion, but he was probably not correct in affirming that these are psychologically the same process."[24] The typologies of sudden and gradual are in themselves misleading for they do not take into account the possible period of incubation which leads up to the crisis of change. Even sudden experiences of conversion have their gradual elements. And the most gradual experiences have their decisive moments. Yet if one studies just the actual change that comes after conversion, that sudden turn-around in behavior or belief, then the temptation is to list the experience as sudden, even though the causes may have been extended far into the prehistory of the event itself. One perhaps would be true to the term of religious conversion if the exact change cannot be totally understood unless the preceding conflicts, wishes, desires, or circumstances are truly taken into consideration. Or as Leon Salzman suggests, "Most change—possibly all—is gradual in its development, but since it culminates

---

23. Cedric B. Johnson and H. Newton Malony, *Christian Conversion: Biblical and Psychological Perspectives* (Grand Rapids, Mich.: Zondervan, 1982), p. 110.
24. Furgeson, "Religious Conversion," p. 10.

in a specific moment of alteration or conversion, it may seem to . . . be an instantaneous, or unexplained, mysterious event. However in every case there has been an incubation or preparation."[25]

The insight of Tillich is also significant to this idea.

> The image of turning around in one's way produces the impression of something momentary and sudden, and, in spite of all pietistic misuse of it, the element of suddenness should not be excluded from a prescription of conversion. It is a decision, and the very word decision points to the momentary act of cutting off other possibilities.[26]

It is evident that the debate as to whether sudden or gradual is the proper word will remain one of the larger questions of any study of religious change. Few have been willing to let go of the gradual Bushnellian connotations of change of this type, and it is important to stress that within religious conversion, there is a decisive, or crucial, moment of change, and this seems to be closer to a proper understanding of the word. This decisive moment is crucial for conversion to be truly in operation within experience. However, if we are to be saved from definitional bedlam we must reassert that the experience of religious conversion has a decisiveness about it often interpreted as sudden and is not the same as gradual growth, yet has many of its aspects, even if only the moment of decision is what is sudden. Since one objective of this book is to look at the decisive moment of change, we will spend time looking at its dynamics and process rather than try to determine which is proper, gradual or sudden. In either case, change occurs, and it is this change that we want to understand.

The event of conversion is decisive for it is a personal event, at the core of being in that it changes individuals drastically. Many may be confronted with ultimate decisions over again, yet perhaps may not acknowledge it or be decisive about the encounter. Jones suggests that conversion therefore may be the first encounter with "sacred" that humans respond to, accept, digest, absorb, and actualize.[27] It is not however the first interest or the normal meeting, but rightly suggests that the meeting is significant in that it is within this experience that we appropriate the power of ultimate Being. This meeting then is the first real mature realization of the fact that things of ultimate value affect our lives. This decisiveness or cruciality of decision is significant, and it is this movement that makes it important in the change process.

---

25. Leon Salzman, "The Psychology of Regressive Religion Conversions," *Journal of Pastoral Care* 8:2 (1954), p. 63.

26. Paul Tillich, *Systematic Theology* (3 Vols; Chicago: University of Chicago Press, 1951-63), 3, p. 220.

27. Jones, "Human Change," p. 69.

Identity Oriented

Since this much-debated issue of religious conversion, as it has classically been described, contains a psychology of individual transformation and often results in a formation of an intense commitment to some sort of ideology with a subjective religious quality, it is logical to note that this commitment often forms a sociological bonding in community. This raises in a general way the topic of the relationship with identity experience. This multi-faceted aspect of the conversional change has captured the interest of psychologists and sociologists, as well as historians and theologians. For the psychologist conversional change is of special interest since it aids in understanding the development of the human personality.[28] And since there is often some resolution of crisis in the formation of religious commitment, logic would demand that there be identity issues resolved in the movement too. Three aspects of the identity issue come to mind in dealing with the experience of religious conversion in a general way.

First, the obvious organizational affiliation of the conversional change provides a new sense of belonging and acceptance. Those churches which provide rich community life and a biblical sense of *koinonia* (fellowship) often are the fastest growing and most active in a community. For the new believer who is developing new ideological concepts, this sense of fitting and belonging which the community provides can only strengthen his or her desire for change.

Second, religious conversion may provide a sense of personal identity. Particularly important has been Erik Erikson's work on the development of personal identity through the resolution of various crises. Personal identity calls us to be new. Religious conversion does the same and "challenges the person to reorganize himself or herself on a deep level of consciousness; it very often involves a heightened awareness of one's finitude."[29] A person who sees himself or herself with new purpose, a sense of mission, and a personal identity founded in the love of God often is capable of doing much more than ever thought. Conversion as the experience of personal identity creates personal change in a unique way. A thorough look at the factors in personal identity and the experience of finding oneself will be explored later.

Third, religious conversion, broadly understood, provides a sense of cosmic identity. After all, religion at its best uplifts humans to new potential in this world. At its worst it abuses individuality, but in either case religious conversion provides a touchstone to the other world of power. One of the most basic theological insights of the religious message to this world is that indi-

---

28. James V. Howe, "A Developmental Perspective on Conversion," *Perkins Journal* 33 (1979), p. 25.

29. Mary C. Boys, "Conversion as a Foundation of Christian Education," *Religious Education* 77 (March-April 1982), p. 216.

viduals must learn the proper use of power. For Christians, Jesus was the perfect example. He used his power only for others and not for himself. Any institution, government, or individual that places himself or herself above others is not to find a place in the kingdom. The first shall be last, the last first, and the kingdom message for the masses were concepts proposed by Jesus while he ministered on earth. Recognizing the proper use of power can be Christianity's greatest gift to the world. Individuals who find God in religious conversion sense a bit of the power that is theirs for the benefit of others and humankind. Identification with this cosmic purpose, this universal message, this apocalyptical promise provides hope and motivation to be different and to make a difference. One can only remember the impact on the world of Schweitzer, Ghandi, Martin Luther King Jr., or Mother Teresa and understand that they are motivated by more universal issues than petty one-up-manship or self-aggrandizement.

Now in conversional change the purpose and meaning of life is appropriated to the mind and takes on major importance to the convert; the decision to change forms the fabric in which all of life is now viewed. The mission is clarified, and one's place in the grand scheme of things is identified.

We shift now the focus of this study from the actual understanding of conversion, to the dynamics of the experience itself. In order for a relationship of any kind to be properly drawn, significant dynamics, causes, results must be examined. Especially if we see identity in some way paralleling this experience as we have hinted in the previous chapter. What follows is an attempt to arrive at the actualities that are the underlining dynamics, and centering in on the identity aspects of religious conversion before actual discussion of identity formation takes place.

Chapter 4

Life: The Context of Change

"Religion is not so much theology as life. It is to be lived rather than reasoned about."

James Pratt

"A Presbyterian middle-class teenager raised in a conservative church in a southern city will probably be more like a Scots middle-class teenager raised in a conservative church in Scotland than the American Presbyterian teenager will be like a liberal Jewish teenager raised in the same southern town. In this case, the southern town presents us with the same society for the Jewish and the Presbyterian teenager. However, the primary society (conservative Presbyterian church) interprets a religious tradition (Calvinism) in such a way that another teenager raised in a similar religious environment, though it be four thousand miles away, will be more like the American Presbyterian than the latter will be like his liberal Jewish fellow citizen."

C. Ellis Nelson

We have seen that the form of religious conversion experience most easily observed is the sudden variety—with rather abrupt and immediate behavioral change. The reason little is said about the dynamics operant in the more gradual variety is due to the unavailability of observation over long periods of time. Longitudinal studies of religious change are seldom funded or examined and simply do not exist.[1] Life changes people slowly at times, as

---

1. Longitudinal studies of religious change take a great deal of time. Studies of this nature are being attempted however. Roger Dudley a professor of Church and Ministry at Andrews University, an expert researcher, is beginning a ten-year study of Seventh-Day Adventist students. Another study, *Valuegenesis* funded by the Seventh-Day Adventist Church and coordinated through Search Institute with Peter

Pratt suggests, but still the intensity of change seems deep, the commitment to ideology equally intense, yet because of its nature, little is said as to the dynamics functioning in this situation. Sudden experience, however, has been more thoroughly studied, and that research has probably biased the conclusions about conversion experience. We are interested in the dynamics of change in this chapter—both protracted and instantaneous. What is going on when people change in a religious context? Both dramatic conversion and gradual conversion experience will be explored with a view to understand the situations or environments that both assist in and provide the context for religious conversion.

As we have seen, contributions to the knowledge of religious conversion appeared early in the century with Hall, James, and Starbuck. With the beginning of the study of behaviorism, little of scientific value was accomplished until the resurgence of psychodynamic methods and insight. Writers concerned with the psychology of religious conversion see that the experience does not just happen; it seems caused. Persons are not struck outside their own situation, and, therefore, it would seem that understanding the psychological and sociological dynamics involved with religious conversion would aid immensely in understanding the relationship with identity. This provides another focus for study. Various contexts exist which seem to enhance the possibility of conversion and may be significant in its occurrence.

Most writers see several factors operating in religious conversion—the individual's environment, past and present situations, the very psyche of the person is involved.[2] Others, such as James or Salzman, explore the issue of distinguishing the validity of the experience by examining it according to its *results*.[3] Hiltner suggests that the turning around may be a political, eco-

---

Benson as chief researcher may begin to provide some answers as to those factors that influence religious commitment, values, and faith in those from grades six through twelve. Data for this study have been collected and the results will be available in the future.

2. Carl W. Christensen, "Religious Conversion in Adolescence," *Pastoral Psychology* 16 (September 1965), p. 21.

3. William James, *The Varieties of Religious Experience* (New York: Mentor Books, New American Library, 1958), p. 192, suggests that the believers in the nonnatural character of sudden religious conversion admit that class plays little part in conversion. "The supernormal incidents, such as voices and visions and overpowering impressions of the meaning of suddenly presented scripture texts, the melting of emotions and tumultuous affections connected with the crisis of change, may all come by way of nature, or worse still, be counterfeited by Satan. The real witness of the Spirit to the second birth is to be found only in the disposition of the genuine child of God, the permanently patient heart, the love of self-eradicated." Thus, the experience or the natural causes or even effects are not a test of conversion's validity.

Ellen G. White adds, *The Great Controversy* (Mountain View, Calif.: Pacific Press, 1888), p. 473, "Popular revivals are too often carried by appeals to the imag-

nomic, as well as a religious kind of event and yet still be a conversion experience. Here Hiltner's focus is on the reality of change determining the experience. And according to our definition, if conversion is perceived as "religious," that event could be classified as religious conversion.

No real turning point is without antecedents, such as dissatisfaction with the status quo or a lure away from an ideal. Often in discussions about religious experience these antecedents are called "triggers" of experience. With the modern insights of psychodynamics and social psychology, the actual internal process may very well be that of resolution, in one sphere or many. Thus secular forms of change or conversion may have their roots in observable social forms. In looking at religious conversion, others may see an effective cause in developmental sources, and yet another group may see psychological factors and developmental readiness operating in the change.

One may be converted to communism, the John Birch Society, Alcoholics Anonymous, jazz, Mahler, or many other things other than the Christian faith. The commitments in this kind of conversion may be strong and behavior may be redirected because of it, however, this should not be confused with religious conversion and perhaps could better be called just simply change, but the intensity of that redirection demands consideration of the term "conversion" and the new direction which results from the experience must be taken seriously. For in no instance does the actual event of turning around itself attest to the soundness of the new ideology espoused. For a decision of that kind, other criteria than personal experience are needed. Likewise, the occurrence of the experience in no way validates religious conversion itself. Others interested in validation and truth must decide this. The authority on which "truth" is validated is personal and, for some, revealed. Understanding how one makes something or someone an authority cannot be discussed here, although it would provide an interesting research topic for another book. But first a discussion of the experience itself is needed.

---

ination, by exciting the emotions, by gratifying the love for what is new and startling. Converts thus gained have little desire to listen to Bible truth, little interest in the testimony of prophets and apostles. Unless a religious service has something of a sensational character, it has no attraction for them. A message which appeals to unimpassioned reason awakens no response. The plain warnings of God's words, relating directly to their eternal interests, are unheeded. . . . In the truly converted . . . the relation to God and to eternal things will be the great topic of life." Leon Salzman in "Types of Religious Conversion," *Pastoral Psychology* 17 (1966), p. 12, lists two kinds of conversion—the progressive type: "Only in the sense that the movement is forward in terms of personality development, permitting greater maturity. . . . This conversion could be called a conjunctive one, brought about by a lessening of anxiety; it is the integrating maturing development in the life of the person . . . equivalent to the 'Aha' experience . . . insight . . . the experience of *satori* arrived at in Eastern religions." Another type of conversion he calls regressive where pathology operates in the experience.

Experiential Knowing

There are many accounts of religious conversion, most recorded in history or religion. The apostle Paul is cited as a chief example; Augustine of Hippo and Pascal are others. Little current research has recorded the experiential factors of the happening. John Lilly does an excellent job of describing drug-induced experiences in his volume, *The Center of the Cyclone: An Autobiography of Inner Space,* but the changes induced here in personality were from external sources, drugs, and finally in his book, meditation.[4] These experiences, although related to experiences labeled conversion, do not fit the definition, due to their chemical source.

Often converts identify the concept of conversion by using their imagination. The use of metaphor is common in describing the religious conversion experience. C.S. Lewis uses the metaphor of being "surprised by joy." While this had double meaning for Lewis, it suggested conversion was an unexpected bounty or something unasked for. Thomas Merton in his book, *The Seven Storey Mountain,* borrows a figure from Dante which hinted at both a cleansing and purifying ascent to God.[5] Bede Griffiths chose a metaphor of the golden string in his conversion allusion derived from a poem by William Blake:

> I will give you the end of a golden string
> Only wind it into a ball
> It will lead you in at heaven's gate
> Built in Jerusalem's wall.[6]

Religious conversion is often precipitated by a longing or desire, "a heart's ache for something we have never quite experienced and cannot fully describe."[7] This sense of longing is not something especially new to individuals. Everyone has sensed it since childhood, and it may even be part of everyone's personality constructs. Gordon Allport, in his book *The Individual and His Religion,* identifies this need as "the appetite for meaning" and claims that this appetite may differ from individual to individual yet is there

---

4. John C. Lilley, *The Center of the Cyclone: An Autobiography of Inner Space* (New York: Julian Press, 1972), pp. 6-23.

5. See C. S. Lewis, *Surprised by Joy: The Shape of My Early Life* (New York: Harcourt Brace, 1955); and Thomas Merton, *The Seven Storey Mountain* (New York: Image Books, 1970), or a discussion of the metaphor of conversion experience in Emilie Griffin, *Turning: Reflections on the Experience of Conversion* (New York: Doubleday, 1980), pp. 18-20.

6. Lines attributed to William Blake, Bede Griffiths, *The Golden String* (New York: Kenedy, 1954), p. 9, in Griffin, *Turning,* p. 19.

7. Griffin, *Turning,* p. 31.

to a greater or lesser degree in everyone.[8]

It seems that the conversion brings knowledge through experience.There is a sense in which the convert "knows" in a way that only those that have had "that kind" of experience can know. Obviously, scientific research cannot touch understanding of this type. For example, after the conversion of John Delorean to Christianity some accused him of being a smooth-talking opportunist rather than a committed Christian. Some saw the personal change evident in his life as due to the crisis he and his family had experienced due to the loss of his automobile franchise. In talking about his change Delorean said, "I know what's in my heart, and he (God) knows what's in my heart. Nothing else really counts, does it?"[9]

Stages of Change

Individuals seem to go through change with some order. It has been argued that this process has developmental stages or steps which predispose the convert to change. The first step, as Emilie Griffin suggests, moves one to God. The statements of Jesus in the Sermon on the Mount in Matthew 5 reflect this same concern. Jesus said, "Blessed are those who are poor in spirit, for theirs is the kingdom of heaven."[10] What is often understood here is that the first step in finding God is knowing that you have a need. Getting in touch with the distance you are from God is the essence of the religious conversional motivation—a personal sense of spiritual poverty is needed. Griffin also describes the religious conversion process as having a dialectic— the argumentative or reasoning stage of conversion, struggle—the tension that exists in sensing one's distance from God, and surrender—that aspect of giving in, all are described as aspects of the process of religious change itself. After the process of conversion has happened, one finds a new sense of thankfulness, even a kind of euphoria, "a spontaneous charity for everyone and everything. I wanted to shout from the rooftops!"[11] Griffin quotes Charles Dickens in writing of the conversion of Ebenezer Scrooge to understand the after effects of change:

> The chuckle with which he (spoke) and the chuckle with which he paid for the turkey, and the chuckle with which he paid for the cab, and the chuckle with which he recompensed the boy, were only to be exceeded by the chuckle with which he sat down breathless in his chair again, and chuckled till he cried.[12]

---

8. See Gordon Allport, *The Individual and His Religion* (New York: Macmillan, 1950), pp. 15-20.

9. John F. Havlik, "Trends and Issues in Evangelism Today," *Faith and Mission* 2:2 (1986), p. 64.

10. Matthew 5:3 (RSV).

11. Griffin, *Turning,* p. 151.

12. Quoted in Griffin, *Turning,* p. 151. From Charles Dickens, *A Christmas Carol* (London: Chapman and Hall, 1843), pp. 157-60.

Analyzing religious conversion experience has provided some clear categories. Religious conversion has traditionally been divided into three phases: 1) preconversion experience, 2) crisis, and 3) postconversion. Each has distinctive parts. First, in the preconversion stage, such feelings as intense intrapsychic conflict (causes of this state will be discussed under social context), a distinctive sense of unrest, dissatisfaction with self, a vague lack in the life of some kind, a general feelings of discontent or a feeling of wanting something or wanting to be something that is not yet clear to oneself, is evident.[13]

We have already seen Christensen's model of conversion which is based upon the conflicts typical of what is often referred to as an "acute confusional state." When converts are compared to patients who are undergoing decompensation to psychosis some of the same conditions mark the initiation of both experiences. Such things as unsolved problems, cumulative stress, nervousness, anxiety conditions, a sense of being overwhelmed, overstimulation, and even depression are feelings that both converts and mentally ill patients share.[14]

The process of religious conversion eventually brings a person to that point in which he/she is willing to surrender to God. As a result of the sense of needing to change, the process of conversion seems to include a crisis of faith which is often described as being evidenced by one or more stages. 1) A period of growing awareness in which persons find themselves in divided allegiance and dissatisfaction with life. In light of this tension they often assume something is missing in their lives and move into a problem-solving mode motivated by the tension. This is due to many things. Both personal developmental crises and unconscious experience may play in this tension, but regardless of the immediate cause, at the end of the incubation period a point of realization seems to occur when commitment to God appears to be the only way out. 2) A period of consideration of an alternate focus or commitment becomes possible. This may arise out of association with advocates from other faiths, preachers, or significant others who espouse that belief structure or experience, and there is a distinct movement toward a religious center. We argue, however, that the type of crisis may be very personal and, as we have seen, some may come with intellectual content or emotional baggage which may be gradual or sudden. 3) Finally there is a period of incorporation where the convert actually changes lifestyle practice and allegiance. Often in this final stage, we find new orientation in life rather than change of personality. We hear of a state of subjective peace and well-

---

13. George Albert Coe, *The Spiritual Life* (New York: Eaton & Mains, 1900), p. 51.

14. See Raymond Wooten and David F. Allen, "Dramatic Religious Conversion and Schizophrenic Decompensation," *Journal of Religion and Health* 22:3 (1983), pp. 212-220.

being which may be short-lived, although this feeling is certainly not a requirement for conversion.[15]

Early on in the history of research on religious conversion, Starbuck recognized that the preconvert suffered from a sense of dividedness, "the contrast between what is, and what might be"[16] Leuba and Starbuck during the same time in history described the religious conversion experience in great detail showing the initial period as one of anxiety, doubt, depression, or guilt. There is as well a state of tension that exists, perhaps brought on by the dissonance between certain feelings that the preconvert is unable to reconcile with his traditional, culturally determined world view. There is an acute intensification of the discomfort that occurs, then frequently a feeling of the "awesome," the "uncanny," which is interpreted as a religious communication.[17]

Thouless suggests that it is worthy to note in Paul's preconversion experience an exhibition of an intensified hostility shown in his persecution of Christians.[18] In Starbuck's early studies of 1899 he found the most prominent experiences in the preconversion state to be in descending order: depression, pensive sadness, calling on God, restless anxiety and uncertainty, sense of sin, loss of sleep or appetite, feelings of estrangement from God, desire for a better life, doubt and question, earnest seriousness, weeping, and nervousness.[19] The sense of sin seemed predominant in adolescent religious conversion experiences as well, and sin was very vivid. The conflict that arises from wishing one was something else, and the knowledge of what one really is, is significant here, for part of the emotional experience of conversion is that one's previous life appears so bad. This may even be one reason that conversion stories are told with such vividness in revivals. Their potency for change may very well rely upon the dramatic abandonment of sin, for sin is more easily eliminated when the audience sees its depth and the greater distance the listeners are from the goal proposed by the evangelist. Even though this agonizing period precedes the experience and may be evident gradually over long periods of time or come rather suddenly, the period seems necessary for change, if only for reflection. Deep change may not be forthcoming through this one instance of agony, but conflict tends to break old patterns and thus leads the way for deep change. It would seem log-

---

15. Cedric B. Johnson and H. Newton Malony, *Christian Conversion: Biblical and Psychological Perspectives* (Grand Rapids, Mich.: Zondervan, 1982), pp. 71, 82.

16. E. D. Starbuck, *The Psychology of Religion* (New York: Charles Scribner's Sons, 1915), p. 155.

17. H. R. Bagwell, "Abrupt Religious Conversion Experience," *Journal of Religion and Health* 8 (April 1969), pp. 164-165.

18. Robert H. Thouless, *An Introduction to the Psychology of Religion* (Cambridge: Cambridge University Press, 1971), p. 104.

19. Paul E. Johnson, *Psychology of Religion* (Nashville: Abingdon, 1959), p. 127.

ical to assert that this may be the reason for the conflict in conversional change. What must, however, be pointed out is that unity exists with much unique variety, as in all realms of living. There are many marked differences in each experience, and the above prestate can only be taken as outlining general areas of early emotional stress which may lead to this returning to God. This matter becomes even more complex when we try to define conversion in psychophysiological terms. Trying to understand the changes that the brain goes through during these crisis times is difficult to explain. Perhaps William Sargent (1957) has done more than most researchers in seeking the relationship between religious conversion and the mechanisms of the brain itself.[20]

There are marked differences in the time taken to effect changes in individuals. For example, impressions differed widely among those experiencing religious conversion regarding the most dominant feelings in the preconversion state, which was also evident in the nature of the blessings converts believed they had received, as well as in attributing the source for the conversion. In reply to the question, "In what did the change consist?" Starbuck's group found "forgiveness" in first place by 16 percent and "oneness with friends," 14 percent.[21] Salzman points out that of those in his regressive category, or those with pathological basis for change in religious conversion, most had feelings of hatred, resentment, and hostility. Destructive attitudes were in each case he examined, and he stresses that the role of hatred in conversion is as true for the mentally imbalanced as conflict or lack of identity is for the more normal person.[22] Even through his negative assessment of the sources of religious conversion, he correctly sees the close identity-forming function of the change.

Moving from the preconversion state into the crisis phase itself, James recorded the feelings which immediately filled the hour of the religious conversion experience as being primarily a sense of a higher control; he called this the "subliminal other."[23] This concept was validated by the more recent studies of Carl Christensen, who suggests that Edoardo Weiss's concept of the "psychic" presence is applicable here and forms a useful hypothesis for this subjective feeling. (Briefly, the psychic presence is thought to be the non-egotized mental image of another person which affects the individual's emotions and behavior.) The religious convert would never accept such a statement. The presence is supernatural for the convert. This presence was not always strong, however, in Christensen's studies: "A part of the conversion experience included a sense of presence. The intensity of this subjective feeling varied from person to person, some vague, others a definite

---

20. From Johnson and Malony, *Christian Conversion*, p. 13.
21. Starbuck, *Psychology of Religion*, p. 94, table 11.
22. Salzman, "Types of Religious Conversion," p. 17.
23. James, *Religious Experience*, p. 195.

sense of someone being close by . . . it is a part of the convert's concept of God."[24]

Sometimes among various Pentecostal groups the believer senses something that is different and extraordinary. For this group, *glossolalia* has sometimes been present along with religious conversion and becomes the validifying mark of the experience. The believer feels God must be present because of the miracle of linguistics.[25] Starbuck found the central factors in the experience itself to be spontaneous awakening, forgiveness, public confession, a sense of oneness and sameness, determination and direction, and self-surrender.[26] This last factor of self-surrender is an important experiential factor.

"Giving up" and final choice is the event that resolves the crisis. The decision to change is significant, then, to the release of the crisis and to complete conversion. James quotes Starbuck and suggests the following dialogue by a convert regarding this self-surrender.

> I had said I would not give up; but when my will was broken, it was all over."
> . . . Another says: "I simply said: 'Lord, I have done all I can; I leave the whole matter with thee'; and immediately there came to me a great peace."—Another: "All at once it occurred to me that I might be saved, too, if I would stop trying to do it all myself, and follow Jesus: somehow I lost my load."—Another: "I finally ceased to resist, and gave myself up, though it was a hard struggle. Gradually the feeling came over me that I had done my part, and God was willing to do his."—"Lord, Thy will be done; damn or save!" cries John Nelson, exhausted with anxious struggle to escape damnation; and at the moment his soul was filled with peace.[27]

The sense of giving up has been equated with submitting to authority, interpreted by the convert as God centered. Christensen even suggests it is a form of giving up to the mother image.[28] This self-surrender is brought on by the conviction of sin. Up to this point the person may be aware of the feelings exhibited in the preconversion state, those of incompleteness, doubt, alienation, restlessness, and anxiety. The convert suffers. This suffering is conviction of sin, and the release is brought about by self-surrender.

> To begin with, there are two things in the mind of the candidate for conversion: The present incompleteness or wrongness, the "sin" which he is eager to escape from; and second, the positive ideal which he longs to find. Now with most of us the sense of present wrongness is a far more distinct piece of our consciousness than is the imagination of any positive ideal we can aim at. In a majority of cases,

24. Christensen, "Religious Conversion in Adolescence," p. 26.
25. William J. Samarin, "Glossolalia," *Psychology Today* (August 1972), p. 79.
26. Johnson, *Psychology of Religion*, p. 127.
27. James, *Religious Experience*, p. 171.
28. Christensen, "Religious Conversion in Adolescence," p. 26.

indeed, the "sin" almost exclusively engrosses the attention, so that conversion is a process of struggling away from sin rather than a striving towards righteousness.[29]

There are other experiences accompanying religious conversion. Such things as hallucinations, visions, even photisms are seen, but always conviction, self-surrender, and crisis seem to be commonalties with the experience itself. After the crisis comes a moment of turning. And it is here that the experience and the word for conversion itself come together. Crisis here is essential to the turning for humankind. It seems that times of accounting are inherent within the structure of living, and growth seems to be associated with turning points.[30] And since life is growth itself, crises are inevitable. The points of turning may not be acute or especially dramatic, but they are real and are seen as actual events. "The crisis is understood to be capitulated by similar factors as the preconversion period; . . . The crisis is seen as the source from which the rest flows, rather than merely the point from which the results are marked."[31] The resolution of the crisis, or the solution of the struggle between the higher and lower parts of human nature, using theological language, is the endeavor on the part of the convert to make the new ideology, or concepts, or way of life personal. This may be contrary to habit patterns and lifestyle, and this precipitates the struggle and crisis. George Cutten suggests that in some, rather than a sense of sin before surrender, the term *conviction* should be used to describe this feeling. This feeling may last for weeks, hours, or days, and may appear with varying degrees of intensity, yet it is always determined and definite.[32]

For Starbuck, the conversion phenomenon in the conviction of sin lasts about one-fifth as long as the periods of adolescent storm and stress, for which he had statistics. This stress period in religious conversion is not so

29. James, *Religious Experience,* p. 171.

30. See Lewis Sherrill, *The Struggle for the Soul* (New York: Macmillan, 1955), pp. 25-40, for a significant contribution to the relationship of crisis to growth within the Christian life.

31. Barbara Eleanor Jones, "Conversion: An Examination of the Myth of Human Change" (Ph.D. dissertation, Columbia University, 1969), p. 249.

32. George Barton Cutten, *The Psychological Phenomena of Christianity* (New York: Charles Scribner's Sons, 1908), p. 241. It is also interesting that theologian Seward Hiltner, "Toward a Theology of Conversion in the Light of Psychology," *Pastoral Psychology* 17 (1966), p. 38, suggests a cognitive element in any type of conviction. Using the Alcoholics Anonymous experience of conversion, equally dramatic or gradual, he lists the following cognitive factors in their change: "1) accurate understanding of the immediate enemy from which deliverance has been won; 2) social support that transcends one's natural psychological defenses; 3) a discipline which is not prevented by pride from looking ever and again at the source of deliverance and which is aware that it has been saved in 'principle' rather than all over. This is, in truth, a spelling out of what Martin Luther meant by saying that the redeemed man in Christ is *simuli ustus et peccator.*"

long, yet much more intense. Bodily manifestations, such as loss of sleep and appetite, accompanied the experience. Starbuck found that these signs of stress and unrest were more prominent in adolescence.[33]

The act of giving in (decision, resolution, of crisis sublimination), or any other term, results in the final state of conversion, the postexperience briefly stated in chapter 3. James calls the result resolution of stress, a "state of assurance rather than a 'faith-state.' Central to the experience was the loss of all worry, a sense of ultimate well-being, peace, harmony, the willingness to be, even though outer conditions should remain the same. A new certainty of God's grace ensued and a passion of willingness of acquiescence, of admiration followed."[34] A typical description of this experience is recorded by Tillich.

> This process of conversion has not turned my world upside down, although at times it has seemed to do so. It has, instead, set me on my feet again, whereas for nearly half a century I was trying to think things out while standing on my head; there is this pervasive quality to the appropriative encounter: all of man is transformed in a total reconstruction.[35]

This experience is call a "postdisaster Utopia" or postcrisis feeling, and is noted for its clarity, liberating sense, and healing potential.[36] Starbuck cites such feelings as joy, peace, acceptance and oneness with God or Christ, a new happiness, bodily lightness, weeping or shouting, partial relief, a sense of responsibility or a sense of redirection and subdued calm. Of the 151 men studied, 43 mentioned as a result being closer to God, 4 suggested a closer feeling of knowing Christ, 34 suggested a closer relation with nature, and 42 found a closer love for others or a desire to help others. Of women surveyed the results were substantially the same.[37] One would assume that the language used by women in describing conversion may be different, at least if the research of Carol Gilligan is as important as it seems when she relates information about faith emergence and the vocabulary of change to women's studies.[38]

When one undergoes a serious crisis and its subsequent resolution, a natural sense of relief is found and with it comes the desire to share it with oth-

---

33. James, *Religious Experience,* p. 164.

34. Ibid., p. 198.

35. Paul Tillich, *The New Being* (New York: Charles Scribner's Sons, 1955), p. 116.

36. See Robert Jay Lifton, *Thought Reform and the Psychology of Totalism: A Study of "Brainwashing" in China* (New York: Norton, 1956), p. 49; Barbara E. Jones, "The Myth of Human Change," p. 254; or J. D. Frank, *Persuasion and Healing* (Baltimore: Johns Hopkins Press, 1961), for a discussion of healing power.

37. Starbuck, *Psychology of Religion,* p. 128, table 16.

38. Carol Gilligan, *In a Different Voice* (Cambridge, Mass.: Harvard University Press, 1963), p. 12.

ers. This too is an aspect of religious conversion experience. An experience of this nature is not valid until it is shared, for one function of commitment is witness to that conviction.

The postcrisis feelings are related to the surrender act as its cause. In answer to why the positive phase follows religious conversion, H. M. Tiebout suggests this answer based on his dealings with alcoholics:

> I know the positive phase comes, but not just why. Surrender means cessation of fight and cessation of fight seems logically to be followed by internal peace and quiet. That point seems fairly obvious, but why the whole feeling tone switches from negative to positive with all the concomitant changes is not so clear. Nevertheless, despite my inability to explain the phenomenon, there is no question that the change does take place and that it may be initiated by an act of surrender.[39]

The surrender, then, triggers reactions with the person and his or her perception of life changes. For him/her the world is different; its difference may simply be the new look of things through eyes of faith, but the newness brings meaning that the observer never before experienced. James refers to a "shifting of man's [women's] centers of personal energy" in this same vein.[40] But under any terminology, the result is problem solving and identity forming. It seems tragic that the realm of religious experience for many psychologists has fallen into the area of the abnormal and psychologically unhealthy. The evidence of religion is not in fact real evidence of any pathology. For the religious conversion experience in its problem-solving function and identity-forming aspect serves as a framework for maturity in coping with the problems of living and eternity. Religious beliefs fulfill many of the basic needs of humankind in that they motivate human behavior. Because of this they are therefore subject to investigation and psychiatric scrutiny. Again Christensen's claim comes to mind: "Since psychiatry is concerned with mental disorders, many of the psychiatric contributions to the understanding of religious beliefs have emphasized psychopathology. Sometimes, psychiatrists tend to forget that religion is a normal part of man's [women's] individual and cultural life."[41]

Another factor in looking at the experience is the notion that the convert feels religious conversion to be something that was not brought on by will or reason. In Starbuck's study, 23 percent felt that the awakening into new life was a spontaneous happening like a bursting forth without any apparent cause. While only a surprising 10 percent gave credit to God, 11 percent

---

39. H. M. Tiebout, "Conversion as a Psychological Phenomenon in the Treatment of the Alcoholic: Therapeutic Mechanisms of Alcoholics," *The American Journal of Psychiatry* (January 1944), p. 469.

40. James, *Religious Experience,* p. 186.

41. Christensen, "Religious Conversion in Adolescence," p. 17.

recalled the experience as a self-surrender in which they themselves actually participated.[42] Those who found a more gradual conversional change to their personality construct saw the volitional powers dominate the judgment in the change.[43] James gave credit to unconscious factors, in psychoanalytic tradition, as prefactors for religious conversion.[44] It is evident, in many cases, that change is brought about through factors unseen to the rational mind. Those with newer existential viewpoints such as Allport, Maslow, and Rogers, however, stress the role of conscious, present decision for behavior change; but as important as the willing-of behavior is, early life situations, genetics, intelligence, culture, and environment are factors in any kind of change that cannot be negated and therefore play a role in the effective results.

The process of religious conversion has some elements in common with other change behaviors. First there is a fascination which attracts attention and begins the process of destruction of self-confidence, and then a construction of a new identity. In the case of religious conversion this identity comes through a new sense of center or a personal feeling of acceptance in a group, or can be more mystically understood as acceptance by God. Secular change, without any religious overtones, proceeds the same way. First there is an interest in changing (need), there is a reorientation to new values, concepts, or ideology (content), and there is the euphoria of decision making (feelings). Lewis Rambo would use the term "transformation" to define the whole process of conversional change, and from his observations of change he identifies various interacting elements such as: death and rebirth, self and others, and ritual changes where the convert learns new activities. One contribution I find particularly helpful is his identification of various "triggers" or stimuli which encourage change.[45] Rambo identifies a series of states which precede transformation. His stages include: "ordinary life" or the routine activities that might encourage turmoil; "breakdown," the awareness of the inability to cope with that turmoil or dissatisfaction; "quest," which involves looking for new options; "commitment," the decision to make some move from the old and internalize the new; "postconversion depression," which comes naturally when the new is perceived in reality; and "pilgrimage," the growth and maturity that come from a longer affiliation with the new.[46]

In summary, then, the experience of religious conversion is outlined in

42. Starbuck, *The Psychology of Religion,* p. 94, table 11.
43. Clarence Augustine Beckwith, "Conversion," *The New Schaff-Herzog Encyclopedia of Religious Knowledge* 3 (1963), p. 263.
44. James, *Religious Experience,* pp. 169-170.
45. See Lewis Rambo, "Psychological Perspectives on Conversion," *Trinity College Today* (April 1980), pp. 4-5 and James Bjornstad, "Cultic and Christian Conversion: Is There a Difference?" *Update* 6 (1982), p. 54.
46. Bjornstad, "Cultic and Christian Conversion," p. 54.

these stages: the *initial* or *preconversion,* signified by the tension and questioning of role and being, including emotions of anxiety and stress; the *crisis,* thought of in terms of conviction of sin, or confrontation with answers to ponderous questions; and the *postconversion* stage where answers are found, relief is felt, release of problems is experienced, and confusion is lifted. The convert feels renewed, redirected, integrated, and fully functioning. This rather sudden climax typifies the religious conversion experience; however, in the more gradual form of conversion (the slow building up of tension, or the gradual growing of faith), many of the same elements of the sudden variety are seen. The usual feelings regarding conviction, surrender, and assurance operate even though they grow to a peak at the decision moment. The decision may not be momentous, but the effect is equally as releasing. And as James suggests, the most characteristic of all of the elements for the religious conversion crisis, and the "last of which I speak, is the ecstasy of happiness produced."[47] The results seem the same.

Emotional Factors

The role of the emotions in causing behavioral change has long been studied. Since religious conversion deals with the core of men and women and changes them so drastically, emotions, too, are factors in experiencing conversion. W. H. Clark, after stating that Freud remarks that beliefs acquired through emotional experiences are removed only by an equally intense outpouring of emotion, proposes the concept of "conversion shock" as the emotional dynamic in the abrupt change.[48] And Robert Mogar believes that the bulk of the research indicates that the intensity of the experience rather than the contents determines change.[49] Even early studies such as James's *Religious Experience* hinted at the dynamics of emotion involved in the change experience. William James, quoting one of Starbuck's correspondents, writes, for instance:

I have been through the experience which is known as conversion. My explanation of it is this: the subject works his emotions up to the breaking point, at the same time resisting their physical manifestations, such as quickened pulse, etc.,

---

47. Ibid., p. 203.
48. Walter Houston Clark, "Intense Religious Experience," *Research on Religious Development: A Comprehensive Handbook,* ed. Merton Strommen (New York: Hawthorne, 1971), p. 533.
49. Robert E. Mogar, "Current Status and Future Trends in Psychedelic (LSD) Research," *Journal of Humanistic Psychology* 5:2 (Fall 1965), p. 161, in his research regarding change and drug use, suggests that the work dealing with crisis-experiences like Erikson's concludes that the personal crisis is not pathological but a critical choice in life demanding a leap of faith which may become the catalyst for an emerging inner conviction or awareness and forthcoming change.

and then suddenly lets them have their full sway over his body. The relief is something wonderful, and the pleasurable effects of the emotions are experienced to the highest degree.[50]

It is important to stress here that the religious excitement brought about by such situations is not conversion; only when it results in a new look at life, as a reintegration of being, a change, does it fulfill the term. Religious conversion is more than the product of nervous instability or the expression of moral need. It is a deep form of change.[51] Perhaps it is here that some distinction should be made between the experience of emotion and the conversion experience. It is correct to say that the conversion experience may be emotional in tone; however this may be caused by the convert's cognizance of the distance he/she is from home. This may cause deep emotional pain, or exceptional exhilaration. The conversion itself is the return, not the emotion caused by any number of forces or situations.

The relationship of emotions to the dynamics of religious conversion has received extensive study. The dynamics of emotion are factors assumed to operate in the experience itself, if not chief causes. For example, there is some evidence that suggestibility follows and is enhanced through the pressures of emotions such as stress. Intense emotion lessens inhibitions and contributes to suggestibility. This is William Sargent's major theme, for he sees religious conversion as the result of a mental psychological abreaction in which the mind is simply overloaded with emotion. And it seems there is evidence that the involvement and excitement that accompanies involvement increases a person's susceptibility to change, especially if the situation requires that participants assume some initiative.[52] The relationship of suggestion and persuasion will be discussed in more detail in the section analyzing environmental and revivalistic factors.

Religious conversion is by some diagramed in a conflict-resolution model. There are conflicts that build up in the preconversion state that strive toward resolution. Since conversion is usually seen in a religious context of some kind or another, the conflict oftentimes centers around values and takes the form of a choice between them. There are mental processes which actively resist change—changes of belief, ideology, behavior, cause, or intention. Thouless suggests that it is this conflict that humankind tends to rationalize. The convert-to-be may rationalize the systems offered, as contrary evidence is presented, as the basis for a new attitude. The conflict may be strong when the person may be unwilling to give up the comforts of certain convictions and

---

50. James, *Religious Experience,* p. 201.
51. See Frederick Morgan Davenport, *Primitive Traits in Religious Revivals: A Study in Mental and Social Evolution* (New York: Macmillan, 1905) for an example of this.
52. Frank, *Persuasion and Healing,* p.112.

to pass through the "unpleasant and insecure condition of doubt. He [she] may also be unwilling to give up the comfort and security he [she] received from membership of the social group to which he [she] belonged."[53]

Salzman considered these conversions brought on through pressures related to conflict to be a regressive type of conversion experience, for it is an attempt to solve the pressing and serious problems in living, or a way of dealing with extreme disintegrating conflict. Regardless of the conflictive base for the change, it is a pseudo solution, and he speculates that it is likely to occur in neurotic, pre-psychotic, or psychotic persons. He, however, is not consistent in suggesting this personality correlate for religious conversion when he adds that it may also occur in presumably normal people when they are faced with major conflicts or insuperable difficulties.[54] The process at work in this conflict model may actually result in normalcy and a better coping with life and therefore be a positive influence for the individual, as Boisen suggests. Salzman is perhaps correct in assuming that if the traits are caused from pathology or psychopathology and result in regressive tendencies, they are not normal. Perhaps only a trained analyst can distinguish between the progressive form and regressive form; I certainly would not want to generalize here.

Conflict stems from many sources: doubt—when the person feels that his or her life seems more of an expression of human interest than divine; stress—when a person feels inadequate and is unsettled within his or her mind; tension—produced from a number of sources (family, the church, one's conscious or unconscious lack). Conflict, then, whether emotional or psychological in nature, actually may precipitate decisions and even encourage them. John Delorean suggests that "foxhole conversions" may be legitimate and even infers that most biblical ones are precipitated by such conflict. He also thinks that when everything you have always wanted and all your dreams are being fulfilled you are not inclined to reassess ultimate values or priorities or to look at spiritual life.[55] When it all falls apart, it makes you take more than a casual look at yourself. He certainly was in a position to make this evaluation.

Conflict has an impact on religious conversion. This has been analyzed by scholars with an interest in the actual psychodynamics of the experience. The term "conflict" is broad as we have seen, and usually refers to some type of emotional turmoil experienced prior to the decision. When one reviews the literature of religious conversion there is little doubt that various psychodynamic factors are evident in the experience. Johnson and Malony identify inner conflict as a source of conversion. Building on Freud's theo-

---

53. Thouless, *Introduction,* p. 104.

54. Leon Salzman, "The Psychology of Regressive Religious Conversions," *Journal of Pastoral Care* 8:2 (1954), p. 75.

55. Havlik, "Trends and Issues," p. 64.

ry of conflict they suggest that such researchers as Robert Thouless and Erik Erikson's crisis model use this theory in their understanding of change. This crisis may be psychosexual in nature, or occur mainly in early childhood and finally be resolved in adulthood. What results in focusing on this aspect of change is a psychodynamic definition of religious conversion.

> Christian conversion may coincide with a state of conflict which is part of both the conscious and unconscious experience of the person. The conflict may coincide with a developmental life crisis, the resolution and process of which has many similarities to the crisis of Christian conversion.[56]

Sargent points out that those who want to eliminate erroneous beliefs and undesirable behavior patterns, and then implant saner beliefs and attitudes are more likely to achieve success if they can first induce nervous tension or stir up sufficient feelings of anger or anxiety in order to secure a person's undivided attention. This action increases suggestibility, and he feels that by increasing or prolonging stress, including physical debilitation, a more thorough alteration of the person's thinking processes will be achieved.

> The immediate effect of such treatment is, usually, to impair judgment and increase suggestibility. . . . When the tension is removed the suggestibility likewise diminishes, yet ideas implanted while it lasted may remain. If the stress or the psychical debilitation, or both, are carried on a stage further, it may happen that patterns of thought and behavior, especially those of recent acquisition, become disrupted. New patterns can then be substituted or suppressed patterns allowed to reassert themselves; or the subject may begin to act or think in ways that precisely contradict his former ones.[57]

This would validate the use of psychological weapons in the attempts by some groups to get change through the use of such things as fasting, chastening of the flesh by scourging, drumming, dancing, singing, music, inducement of fear, lighting incense, drugs. There seem to be many ways to alter normal brain functions for religious purposes as James's nitrous oxide interest testifies. Sargent charges that few sects wholly neglect the role of these emotional psychological stimulants to change.[58]

The role of conflict in religion has biblical imagery. The story of Jacob and the night wrestling match and encounter with God is an example. But this conflict of wishing you were one thing and knowing you are another is severe and produces tension that may find release in the religious conversion experience.

Other forms of conflict and tension are exhaustion caused by the struggle and weakening of the power of the mind to integrate happenings consis-

---

56. Johnson and Malony, *Christian Conversion*, p. 53.
57. William Sargent, *Battle for the Mind* (New York: Harper & Row, 1957), p. 144.
58. Ibid., p. 143.

tently and fear brought on from external circumstances. It is commonly realized that the great evangelists of previous eras, such as Jonathan Edwards and John Wesley, dwelt on the horrors of damnation, while some modern evangelistic movements use more subtle means of producing fear. Many a student of homiletics is acquainted with Jonathan Edwards' famous sermon, "Sinners in the Hand of the Angry God." His preaching has been most unjustly judged by it. Many have read with fear and anxiety the following phrases:

> And though he will know that you cannot bear the weight of omnipotence treading upon you, yet he will not regard that, but he will crush out your blood, and make it fly, and it shall be sprinkled on his garments, so as to stain all his raiment. He will not only hate you but will have you in the utmost contempt; no place shall be fit for you, but under his feet to be trodden down as the mire of the streets.[59]

It is no wonder that Edwards has been accused of confusing God with the devil! Fear arousal of this kind causes great conflict within. A natural human reaction is release in situations like these, a release that religious conversion can perhaps provide. Ducasse suggested that in the intrapsychic conflict, a need for commitment, guilt, and fear were necessary factors for a religious conversion. In addition, he felt that there was a sense of failure involved with the fear, based on the inability to conform to the demands religion made. This inability to conform produced depression, therefore contributing to the tension and anxiety.[60] Salzman adds a twist to this, indicating that while fear is the dynamic involved, he suggests that hate could be the motivational factor to consider.[61] Salzman sees this hate motivation repeated on a smaller scale throughout history in the development of religious doctrines. The mass hysteria caused by thoughts of werewolves and witches not only caused the deaths of werewolves and witches but produced a large number of so-called conversions in the prevailing churches and *into* the ranks of witches as well. The contagious and widespread nature of the conversions during such community hate programs indicated the extent of the hatred and may very well be a strong cause along with suggestion in many conversions.[62]

---

59. Vergilious Ferm, ed., *Puritan Sage: Collected Writing of Jonathan Edwards* (New York: Library Publishers, 1953), p. 374.

60. Christensen, "Religious Conversion in Adolescence," pp. 19, 20.

61. Leon Salzman illustrates this belief in "Types of Religious Conversion," p. 18. He remembered in 1936 a meeting in Canada in which a preacher spent an entire sermon attacking the faculty of a seminary. "They were unfit, not Christians, and so on," and ended the sermon with a call. A number responded and were presumed converted. The dynamics of the call were hate, he suggests, and appealed to similar feelings in the ones who responded.

62. See Ibid. and also see a brief discussion of witchcraft in "Witchcraft," *The Oxford Dictionary of the Christian Church*, ed. F. L. Cross (London: Oxford

It is also believed that especially in the frontier revivals, an emotional stimulus evident in conversions was that of "escape." The success of the evangelistic meetings in early American settlements was that they offered the readiest means for the hardworking pioneer to find an escape from his everyday drudgery into a world of temporary exhilaration; this of course is only speculation, but could be factual if the experience included an active *seeking* for release from the everyday work of the frontier. For like satisfaction of other desires, conversion may fulfill the need for new experience with peculiar intensity and fullness in these kinds of situations.[63]

It would seem then that the presence of an emotional matrix can be significant for the experience of religion. Forces in conflict, stress, tension, fear, anxiety, feelings of intense inadequacy, and worthlessness often precede the crisis. The conflict seems to be a conscious one, even though its sources may find roots in the unconscious conflict which simply adds to the intrapsychic stress. There appears to be a period of growing awareness where the person senses the emotional dividedness of allegiance and dissatisfaction with life in general. This subjective tension nudges resolution. It may take the form of problem solving, or reunification of self, or an experience of a new identity. The next period is one of consideration which comes through an advocate for another faith or belief system. Their climax of the emotional stress is often called the "conversion," but the most significant factor is not the movement but the fact that religion or faith is seen as a resolution. This is the uniqueness of religious conversion. In addition to the emotional, psychological factors, there seem to be additional contexts wherein religious conversion occurs. Among these is the developmental context.

University Press, 1958), p. 1472. Also included are enumerations and chronological outbreaks of witchcraft and the ensuing reformations within the Christian Church.

63. For an excellent study of the revivalism of early America, the cultural, personal factors in its early and rapid rise, see William Warren Sweet, *Revivalism in America: Its Origin, Growth and Influence* (New York: Abingdon, 1944).

Chapter 5

Growth: Factors in Change

"The death of my father left me sad and depressed for a couple of months. But that eventually wore away. And when it did, I found myself completely stripped of everything that impeded the movement of my own will to do as it pleased. I imagined that I was free. And it would take me five or six years to discover what a frightful captivity I had got myself into. It was in this year, too, that the hard crust of my dry soul finally squeezed out all the last traces of religion that had ever been in it. There was no room for any God in that empty temple full of dust and rubbish which I was now so jealously to guard against all intruders, in order to devote it to the worship of my own stupid will."

Thomas Merton

Religious conversion may have emotional causes (triggers) such as conflict, but it is possible that religious conversional change may be particularly predisposed to certain times in the life cycle, during certain stages of development, or be impacted by various situations as illustrated above in the response by Thomas Merton.

Most opinion regarding religious change finds a significant resource in the particularly vulnerable time of adolescence. While this time period is not the only time conversional change occurs, it is, however, a prime time for conflict, identity crisis, searching, reevaluation, and value selection. Religion requires deep commitment and religious identifications are often made during adolescence. It is a time of personalized faith, a time when faith moves beyond the other centers of origination and becomes actually, personally believed and acted on. In addition to developmental factors, there are personality, gender differences, and societal pressures at work to encourage and nudge religious change. These factors as well as the impact of culture and personality provide additional contexts for religious conversion and a rich base

94

for understanding the dynamics of the experience.

Developmental Factors

Adolescence

It has been suggested that adolescence is the most favorable time for religious conversion.[1] It is a unique age. It is a crucial time in the development of the self, and the conflict orientation of that period of time has been observed. And while stress and emotional turmoil seem to characterize the childhood and adolescence of religious converts, this background may not "elucidate . . . the specific processes that may induce a change in the form of a religious conversion."[2] However, based on a study of conversion to a small deviant cult, Lofland and Stark (1969) suggest that a religious "problem-solving perspective" and "seekership" within that viewpoint may predispose a person toward a change in his or her particular religious form.[3] And the results of some investigation underscore the apparent role of stress and anxiety in precipitating deep change of cognitive belief in those already prone to religious conversion by some complex past experiences.[4] Adolescence is obviously not the only time when anxiety and stress are seen, but these seem to appear more naturally here.

Regarding the religious maturity of adolescence, much has been said. The Catholic satirist Alexander Pope in part suggested

> Behold the child, by nature's kindly law,
> Pleased with a rattle, ticked with a straw;
> Some livelier plaything gives his youth delight,
> A little louder, but as empty quite:
> Scarfs, garters, gold, amuse his riper stage,
> And beards and prayer-books are the toys of age.
> ("An Essay on Man," Epistle II, 1. 275-280.)

---

1. G. Stanley Hall and William James, *The Varieties of Religious Experience* (New York: Mentor Books, New American Library 1958), p. 162 ff.; George A. Coe, *The Spiritual Life (New York: Eaton and Mains, 1900)*, pp. 29-55, where he discusses the mental state of adolescence and the religious feelings of youth; Paul Johnson, *Psychology of Religion,* (Nashville: Abingdon, 1959), pp. 81-97, adds an especially good section on the religious development of adolescents; see also Charles W. Stewart, *Adolescent Religion: A Developmental Study of the Religion of Youth* (Nashville: Abingdon, 1967).

2. Chana Ullman, "Cognitive and Emotional Antecedents of Religious Conversion," *Journal of Personality and Social Psychology* 43:1 (1982), pp. 183-192

3. See S. Lofland, and R. Stark, "Becoming a World Saver: A Theory of Conversion to a Deviant Perspective," in *Studies in Social Movements,* ed. B. McLaughlin (New York: Free Press, 1969).

4. Ullman, "Cognitive and Emotional Antecedents of Religious Conversion," p. 192.

It is in the lives of younger youth where wonder and spontaneous religious commitment often occur. These characteristics have described the great religions of humankind and are essential parts of religious conversion. We must note, however, the religious conversions will not all be alike. They will differ according to one's point of personal development. What is it about the development of adolescence that impacts religious change?

First, it is important to look at the moral side of the experience. Using Lonergan's typology of moral conversion, one would argue that moral development is impossible until a higher or more mature state of thinking had occurred. Kohlberg's third or postconventional level of moral reasoning would be a necessity in that case. This stage includes such mature concepts as self-chosen direction, a more universal ethical outlook, and evaluation of options that moves one to ethical decisions. Kohlberg believes that postconventional moral transformation requires enough adult experiences of irreversible life decisions, care, and responsibility to make moral evaluations. A religious conversion of a moral nature demands such maturity.[5] Adolescence is especially significant for the development of moral experience. Morality in its fully developed form is not possible before the time of adolescence if information supplied by Kohlberg and Piaget is accurate. Even if not, however, ethics and morals require a certain degree of intelligence, notably the ability to form concepts and to generalize into categories of thought. Maturity in moral judgment is reached between the ages of seventeen and twenty, according to W. H. Clark.[6] He adds as well that guilt plays a large part in adolescent decision making. Since the human animal tends to move in the direction that will alleviate guilt and the anxiety that is caused by it, religious conversion has for some a close tie with the alleviation of the sexual guilt emerging in young people.[7] Since movement to an autonomous, postconventional morality requires specifically adult experiences, religious conversion with a deeply moral tone would need maturity and life experience that only adults could possibly have. This implies that adults would be the logical age for deeply moral conversion.[8]

James Fowler and James Loder have provided additional insight for religious educators regarding formation and transformation and their relationship to developmental issues. Fowler's contribution tends to be in the area of process and formation while Loder emphasizes the paradox that "no

5. Walter Conn, *Christian Conversion* (New York: Paulist, 1986), p. 29.

6. Walter Houston Clark, *The Psychology of Religion* (New York: Macmillan, 1958), p. 122.

7. Ibid., p. 117.

8. Lawrence Kohlberg, *The Philosophy of Moral Development* (San Francisco: Harper & Row, 1981), pp. 344-372, or see Walter E. Conn, "Merton's 'True Self': Moral Autonomy and Religious Conversion," *Journal of Religion* 65 (October 1985), p. 514.

9. Andrew Grannel, "The Paradox of Formation and Transformation," *Religious*

amount of careful formation can transform."[9] For Fowler, conversion happens constantly in the developing organism itself. As one grows, each modification in interpersonal patterns, decision making, and symbol structures hint at the need for change. These are, for Fowler, what might be described as mini-conversions. Fowler uses an interview technique and has indicated that these shifts in behavior, or symbol structure, often occur in the process of discussion which serves as a trigger for the experience on occasion. Fowler hints that the dynamic of conversion is made up of several epochal shifts in one's orientation and values. Conversion is linear for Fowler, then, and one must look at the developing person through the whole lifespan in order for conversion to be completely understood. Since stage shift for Fowler may come quite dramatically, these "conversions" are often accompanied by disintegration and anxiety. These stage transitions may be called conversion and as each new stage is consolidated, the person grows toward wholeness.[10]

The educational implications of Fowler's work are significant. For example, the impact of earlier images of God and religion often color our perspective and inform our adult understanding of God. This means that care must be given to provide a proper and truth-filled image of God in order for the nature of God to remain consistent within the personality structure of the individual. It is important to realize that by guarding our young their worldview may not be challenged and thus their view of God and religion will be dwarfed. Also, it would become important to note the duration of the conversion possibility itself. All through life conversion can happen. The experience seems to be most logical at the shifts through stages rather than a once-for-all event. Conversion, in its gradual and sudden imagery, merge in Fowler's research.

Mary Ford-Grabowsky has critiqued Fowler's work and pointed out the flaws in his research. She correctly challenges Fowler in suggesting that his model fails to properly define "religious faith in general, and Christian faith in particular."[11] She suggests that Fowler's concept of the person is narrow, and his seven *aspects* of faith express functions of human cognition rather than experiential spirituality. She would rather see a balance brought to Fowler's work through correctives of a more biblical basis for understanding faith experience.[12] Naturally, with this bias, Fowler's understanding of conversion change would be intellectual in focus.

Education 80 (Spring 1985), p. 387.

10. For an excellent discussion of the stage theory of James Fowler as it relates to conversion, see Leroy T. Howe, "A Developmental Perspective on Conversion," *Perkins Journal* 33 (1979), pp. 20-35.

11. Mary Ford-Grabowsky, "The Fullness of the Christian Faith Experience: Dimensions Missing in Faith Development Theory," *The Journal of Pastoral Care* 51:1 (March 1987), p. 39.

12. Mary Ford-Grabowsky, "Flaws in Faith-Development Theory," *Religious Education* 82:1 (Winter 1987), pp. 80-81.

It is also clear from the developmentalist perspective that conversion and development, while clearly distinct realities, are somehow connected. The adolescent and adult crises of identity and development provide the occasion for the necessary existential conditions to occur that may fuel religious change. At various key points in life development and conversion blur. One preconditions the other. Shifts occur in life due to dramatic religious change, and change occurs due to the growth of development and the situations that nurture it. Thus the close relationship between developmental issues and religious conversional change are seen. (See Chart 3)

It was Starbuck's studies that first observed that the incidence of religious conversion was the highest in the age of adolescence. Observing this, he felt that normal religious conversions were therefore adolescent phenomena and recognized that fear, guilt, and depression preceded the reactions. Pratt saw adolescence as a normal period for the experience although he minimizes the violent and sudden adolescent religious conversion experience in suggesting that the entire "moral and religious process of the adolescent

CHART 3: List of studies and relative age-time computations.

Name:	Causes:	Average Age:
Starbuck (1899)	1,265	16.4
Coe (1900)	1,784	16.4
Hall (1904)	4,054	16.6
Athearn (1922)	6,194	14.6
Clark, E. T. (1929)	2,174	12.7
Argyle (1959)	Study of Literature	15.7

period may well be called conversion."[13] Much like Fowler's and the research of developmentalists, early studies often identified adolescence as a prime age for religious change and conversion.

Studies using empirical methods have tended to agree as to adolescence being a prominent scene for conversion.

There have been other studies dealing with numbers of converts, but not dealing specifically with the age of conversion. For example, E. T. Clark in 1929 and Gordon Allport in 1948 found that only about 7 percent of the college population had experienced sudden conversion. These authorities find adolescence the natural time for the experience. However, just how one defines conversion may modify this conclusion. For example, if conversion is termed in its gradual form and includes turning points and times of decisions, later times may be indicated.

Jung in 1933 found that the middle age and after were the prime years for religious concern. His views received some support from Fuerst (1966),

---

13. James Bissett Pratt, *The Religious Consciousness: A Psychological Study* (New York: Macmillan, 1926), p. 122.

who questioned seventy-five subjects over fifty years of age and reported that turning points in general occur at various ages throughout life.[14] Since the studies of Argyle, the American Institute of Public Opinion (AIPO) polled a national sample of Americans on sudden "religious or mystic" experiences, and found about 20 percent of the adults answered affirmatively and could describe such an experience.[15] Using content analysis, five kinds of experience were found: 1) a mystical sense of union with God, 2) a conviction of forgiveness and salvation, 3) answers to prayers, 4) reassurances of God's power, and 5) dreams and voices.[16] This research shows that the experience is not necessarily a distinctly adolescent phenomenon.

Twice-born experiences have seemed to be normal for youth. Probably the most effective longitudinal study ever attempted in this area was by Charles Stewart. His studies led him to spend 1962-1963 at the Menninger Foundation in alliance with the Child Study Project. Here he had the occasion to study youth from a variety of religious backgrounds and with many different variables of growth and nurture as they entered puberty. From this he drew case studies and inferences for a psychology of religious conversion. He points out various developmental factors evident in conversion experience and contributory to its occurrence. In contrasting boys and girls, he suggests each undergo puberty with primary sexual maturation. The menstrual cycle in girls begins between ages eleven and one-half to thirteen, and the first seminal emission occurs in boys between ages twelve and one-half and fourteen. The secondary sexual characteristics such as physique, timber of voice, and auxiliary hair, etc., are paralleled in both the boys and girls. The young adolescent is, in the period immediately following puberty, undergoing changes from his external struggles to the inner conflicts that he feels from his burgeoning sexual drives and the ambivalences he feels regarding his parents. These affect the religious sensibilities.[17] Another significant study in more recent history has been that conducted by Search Institute founded by Merton Strommen. While conversion was not the primary focus for Peter Benson's analysis of adolescence called *The Quicksilver Years,* he does provide information about the centrality of religion for adolescents. In this research the majority of young adolescents reported that religion is "the most important" or "one of the most important" influences in their lives. And while boys attach less importance to religion than girls, young adoles-

14. Walter Houston Clark, "Intense Religious Experience," in *Research on Religious Development: A Comprehensive Handbook,* ed. Merton P. Strommen (New York: Hawthorne Books, 1971), p. 532.

15. American Institute of Public Opinion, Press Release, April 15, 1962.

16. Robert J. Havighurst and Barry Keating, "The Religion of Youth," in *Research on Religious Development: A Comprehensive Handbook,* ed. Merton P. Strommen (New York: Hawthorne Books, 1971), p. 690.

17. Charles William Stewart, "The Religious Experience of Two Adolescent Girls," *Pastoral Psychology* (September 1966), p. 49.

cents are more likely to experience religion as liberating than restricting, thus stretching them to explore alternate viewpoints. Most young adolescents believed that religion had both a vertical focus on God and a horizontal focus on others, justice, and peace.[18] This research suggests that adolescence is a prime time for religious reevaluation and change.

It is obvious that there are religious needs at this time period. In a recent research study called *Valuegenesis,* youth in the Seventh-Day Adventist church were sampled by Search Institute. It was discovered that a little more than one-fifth of Adventist youth (22 percent) displayed what the study is calling "mature faith." This scale is based on Search Institute's mature faith scale developed in their landmark study of Protestant religious education with five mainline denominations. In *Valuegenesis,* it was revealed that Adventist youth are much more likely to display faith maturity than are their peers in those mainline denominations. Adventist youth are comparable to youth in the Southern Baptist convention, which has been quite successful in teaching parents about the importance of faith development in the context of the home and in developing effective congregationally based Christian education programs. Furthermore, Adventist success in nurturing faith maturity occurs among both boys and girls and across racial/ethnic categories. These faith maturity ratings are somewhat disappointing, however, when you look at the percentage of youth who have an undeveloped faith. Adventist youth, like the majority of Protestant youth, fall into the faith type called "undeveloped faith." Faith is least well-formed among ninth and tenth grade boys.

Adults reflect the same kind of pattern. Only a minority of Protestant adults evidence the kind of integrated, vibrant, and life-encompassing faith congregations seek to develop. However, in every age group from the age of thirty women exhibit greater faith maturity than men.

What is emerging in this research is a pattern in which "faith is only partially experienced or lived out."[19] Signals point to a faith that is "on hold," restricted, even dormant. One factor that may account for part of this pattern is the large percentage of mainline adults (67 percent), and Adventist adults (25 percent) and Adventist youth (72 percent) that evidence difficulty in accepting salvation as a gift rather than as something to be earned. Benson argues that from an understanding of grace "comes the freedom that allows people to move out of neutral, to risk."[20] Legalism may be hampering this growth.

---

18. Peter Benson, Dorothy Williams, Arthur Johnson, *The Quicksilver Years: The Hopes and Fears of Early Adolescence* (New York: Harper & Row, 1987), p. 111.

19. Peter Benson and Carolyn H. Elkin, *Effective Christian Education: A National Study of Protestant Congregations Summary Report* (Minneapolis: Search Institute, March, 1990).

20. Ibid., p. 13.

It is evident from this research that for many mainline Protestant denominations faith is not well formed. More than two-thirds of adults say that their faith lacks a strong vertical component, a strong horizontal component, or both. This finding presents the church with a great challenge in its ministry to men especially, in whom a fully integrated faith maturity is relatively uncommon.

Regarding adolescence, Arnold Gesell says:

> As the adolescent enters his teens he *[she]* often recurs to quiet, meditative periods of self-examination. He *[she]* has earnest moments of high resolve and aspiration. He *[she]* begins to define himself *[herself]* by matching *(himself/herself)* with that of other selves. He *[she]* explores his *[her]* potentials in terms of self-chosen heroes and ideals. Thereby he *[she]* gives precision and status to his feelings.[21] *[Italics mine]*

One crucial problem is identifying what kind of adult the adolescent is becoming and what sort of life will provide the greatest satisfaction. In addition, various other developmental tasks affect adolescent emotional growth. First, the adolescent must learn to accept his or her own physique and determine the place of new relationships with age-mates of both sexes; these tasks are social in nature. The social tasks to be mastered in this area are often defined by each culture and subculture and many times develop almost naturally within the subculture.

Second, the adolescent must develop independence from his/her parents and other adults. This area of development finds anxiety running high, and the feeling tones and stress existing in this period prove intense. This sense of independence runs beyond religious feelings and often includes economic, occupational, and intellectual freedom. At this time the adolescent finds that he/she must think of a proper ideology appropriate for later marriage and family life, and values need to be firmly fixed into the mind of the youth, and anxiety and conflict emerge as the concomitant emotions.

Third, in the area of development, autonomy, social competence, identity, achievement, and sexuality other worries and concerns are exhibited. While most young adolescents report no major conflicts with their parents, other dynamics are suggested by research.

• Boys and girls experience similar gains in autonomy between fifth and ninth grade.
• Only a small minority of young adolescents report major conflicts with parents.
• Both boys and girls increase in self-disclosure, empathy, and friendship-making skills between the fifth and ninth grade. In all three areas, girls

---

21. Arnold Gesell, *Youth, The Years from 16 to 96* (New York: Harper, 1956), p. 336.

report more competency than boys.
• Social alienation is highest for fifth graders and is higher for boys than for girls.
• Between the fifth and ninth grades, girls develop a less favorable concept of their own body image.
• At each grade level, girls report higher achievement motivation than boys.
• Thirty-nine percent of fifth graders report "being in love." The percentage rises to 51 percent by ninth grade.
• One in five ninth graders report that they have had sexual intercourse.
• Only about one third of young adolescents report that they have had "good talks with my parents about sex."[22]

Research regarding the worries and anxieties of this age group is equally revealing. They worry about school performance, worry about "my looks," worry about relationships with friends and victimization. Adolescents worry about national issues of peace and justice as well. National issues such as hunger and poverty, violence, and nuclear destruction are significant concerns for these budding intellectuals. Of course the age-old concern about one's parents caps the list of concerns. The research indicates that younger youth worry more than older ones.[23] So the age of adolescence has its share of tensions which lead to insecurity and personal confusion—all feelings that religious conversion can help to erase.

Havighurst continues his developmental task chronology by listing the following tasks for early adulthood, adding possible additional sources for conflict after adolescence, such as 1) selecting a mate, 2) learning to live with a marriage partner, 3) starting a family, 4) rearing children, 5) managing a home, 6) getting started in an occupation, 7) taking a civic responsibility, 8) finding a congenial social group.[24]

The developing adolescent finds that along with physical growth which causes tension in the social sphere, there is budding intelligence, which tends to stimulate and release a new kind of questioning spirit. *The Newson Report* states graphically:

> Boys and girls who used to ask inquiringly, "What do we do?" or "What's that" now commonly react with "Why should I?" or "How do you know?" to much of what they have loved and practiced in the past. They become increasingly aware of the differences of opinion between adults and of the gulf between practice and profession. The borderline between cynical disengagement and constructive questioning is narrow.[25]

22. Benson, *The Quicksilver Years,* p. 33.
23. Ibid., p. 65.
24. Robert J. Havighurst, *Human Development and Education* (New York: Longmans, Green & Co., 1953), pp. 9-41. Adapted from Part I.
25. Ronald Goldman, *Readiness for Religion: A Basis for Developmental*

This kind of questioning about life is further encouraged by the mass media. Television, for example, in the new programing for adolescents, deals with problems thought above and too mature for the adolescent age only a few years ago. Such topics as rape, incest, premarital sex, and drugs are common fare on the tube. The umbrella culture of the times also is reflected in adolescent behavior. The shift in authoritarian respect on the part of youth has provided a focus on personal responsibility. There are basic needs in this period which need fulfilling in order for complete integration with life and reality to take place. The need for security, with its concomitant feeling of freedom, is important to resolve. Status is another factor needing resolution. Youth often live in the worst of all possible worlds, being neither an adult nor a child—seeking to find meaning in life within the social and mental context, but not yet able to be fully integrated into it. Youth also have needs in the area of relationships. Love, for example, is being quested—love that a group, or a tradition, or a belief can provide. Religious conversion may appropriately fill this need. The years of adolescence, from twelve to sixteen, are a watershed in the emergence of an ideological framework for later life.

In M. H. Podd's study of ego identity 134 male college juniors and seniors were interviewed. J. E. Marcia followed with identity interviews covering occupational choice, religious beliefs, and political ideology. "Crisis" and "commitment" were assessed in each of these areas to define each identity status of the youth. The implications of this study are essential to the development of the theses in this book. In essence, the morally transitional subjects were changing with regard to identity issues as well as moral issues. Or stated more clearly, in order to question the conventional morality you must have questioned your identity too. In other words, the adolescent questioning of moral issues and concerns as to what is reality is central to adolescents' identity concerns. Podd suggests as a sideline that morally-conventional subjects have a considerable likelihood of *never* having an identity crisis or an identity questioning at all.[26] It would appear then in relation to the concerns of this book that the adolescent nature to question morally centered things would be directly related to the religious conversion experience, providing there is a similarity in the kind of crisis faced in adolescence. Religious conversion would then provide the framework for crisis in adolescence which contributes to the identity formation of the youth themselves. This relationship provides a unique bridge between religious conversion and personal identity experience.

Religious Education (New York: Seabury, 1965), pp. 161-62.

26. M. H. Podd, "Ego Identity Status and Morality: An Empirical Investigation of Two Developmental Concepts" (Ph.D. dissertation, University of Chicago, 1969), quoted in Lawrence Kohlberg and Carol Gilligan, "The Adolescent as a Philosopher: The Discovery of the Self in a Postconventional World," *Daedalus: Journal of the American Academy of Arts and Sciences* (Fall 1971), pp. 1051-1086.

Adolescence is a time for adjusting conformities and trying to sort out what is to be instituted into one's ideological framework and what is to be rejected totally. Various motivations for change exist within the adolescent. They include: physically, emotionally, intellectually, ideologically, developmentally motivated actions.

Such pressures for change are illustrated in this discussion in the thinking of one adolescent regarding her conversion experience. Notice especially her ambivalence to her true motives, yet the concomitant decisiveness regarding her mother's church. Both factors are evident in this illustration.

> I do not know how to speak of my religious experience in the teens. I had gotten along very well without a "religion" before, but when I was about fourteen there was a series of revival meetings held in the different churches; and going to the Methodist church one evening, more out of curiosity than anything else, I was so frightened by the evangelist's statements as to our sinful condition that I became quite excited and would probably have "gone forward" if I had not had such a decided step now and also for the fact that this church was neither "my father's" nor "mother's church," and I let myself be swept off my feet by the enthusiasm for it. One noon seven of us girls were going home and saying, "I'll go if you will," so that is how I came to "go forward" that night. . . . Later on I very much regretted this "conversion," because if I had been let alone until I could think things out for myself I would have thought "father's church" the one I believed in and really cared for.[27]

Notice above the various contributing factors for this adolescent religious conversion. On careful study, one can see her yielding to emotional needs, group pressure, historical ties, and inner need. Since adolescence is a time when these factors seem to be the most significant, it can be seen why there have been more apparent religious conversions in adolescence than at other times.

Another factor in the adolescent is that of a sort of "timeliness." It is here that the youth senses his or her place in the history of the reality of living. The older adolescent begins to look back to the antecedent sources of the present and think of the future in new terms. This extension of temporal range, this sense of the past and the active attempt at deciphering the meaning of the present makes the youth examine his or her roots. This factor makes adolescence a prime time for any kind of change, including religious conversion. Another factor is the fact that this period of life is one when the youth is an idealist and is preoccupied with utopian reconstructions of society, with a disposition toward the formulation of ideologies. In some this is very pronounced; in others it is delayed or atrophied altogether. Nevertheless it would seem that this would contribute as well to the kinds of decisions religious con-

---

27. Luella Cole, *Psychology of Adolescence* (New York: Rinehart & Company, 1948), p. 370.

version causes and the kinds of intellectual commitments adolescents make.[28]

More generalized statements concerning adolescence and religious conversion were made by the early writers. James suggests, for example:

> The age is the same, falling usually between fourteen and seventeen. The symptoms are the same—sense of incompleteness and imperfection; brooding, depression, morbid introspection, and sense of sin; anxiety about the hereafter; distress over doubts, and the like. . . . In spontaneous religious awakening, apart from revivalistic examples, and in the ordinary storm and stress and moulting-time of adolescence, we also may meet with mystical experiences, astonishing the subjects by their suddenness, just as in revivalistic conversion. . . . Conversion is in its essence a normal adolescent phenomenon, incidental to the passage from the child's small universe to the wider intellectual and spiritual life of maturity.[29]

Starbuck, on the other hand, saw religious conversion functioning in adolescence as a means of shortening the times of insecurity and of bringing the person out of childhood into new life as an adult. Conversion would, then, for Starbuck, intensify the normal tendencies and shorten the period of storm and stress. Religious conversion crisis is equated here with identity crisis even though Starbuck was not familiar with the term "identity."[30]

Identity for adolescence has to do with the perception of the self. Youth spend considerable energy working through their identity, struggling to see if the way they see themselves is really the way they are.[31] The identity issue is further complicated because of the many choices that youth have as they grow up. When this religious change is seen in the light of identity experience one realizes that conversion must be woven into the whole fabric of life. Of particular importance is Erik Erikson's work on the development of personal identity through the resolution of a series of crises. Since conversion is a calling to something new and often different and challenges individuals to probe their lives at its deepest level—that of self-consciousness and a heightened awareness of one's limitations—identity formation and conversion have a natural affinity.[32]

Various explanations have been given to detail the reason for so many adolescent conversions. The unique time of adolescence does predispose

---

28. A more detailed study of the contributing factors in identity development will be in the following chapter.

29. James, *Religious Experience*, p. 164.

30. E. D. Starbuck, *The Psychology of Religion* (New York: Charles Scribner's Sons, 1915), pp. 224, 262.

31. Daniel O. Aleshire, *Faith Care: Ministering to All God's People through the Ages of Life,* (Philadelphia: Westminster, 1988), p. 129.

32. See chapter six for a detailed study of the personal identity theory of Erik Erikson based on his work on personal psychosocial development. For a discussion regarding identity and religious conversion, see Mary C. Boys, "Conversion as a Foundation of Christian Education," *Religious Education* 77 (March-April 1982), pp. 211-224.

youth to the experience of religious conversion more often it seems than for adults. No one today would hold that conversion is totally adolescent, but certainly adolescence as a developmental factor is influential in the timing of religious conversion. The period of youth or early adolescence proves to be a time when individuals may be sensitive to the emotions of religious experience. Awe and wonder are more easily expressed, due to lack of inhibition and culture pressure. Pierre Babin has a unique concern for the adolescent's sensitive period as the right time to develop faith.[33] Religious conversion in this period becomes an identity-forming event, "the act or event in which the young person gives his life a direction and meaning in relation to transcendent values, with a depth of consciousness and decision that put an end to the vacillations of his adolescence and profoundly affect the moral and religious sense of his adult life."[34]

The experience may be identity forming and unifying at a deep level, for the experience is centered at the core of a person. And as Coe suggests in illustrating the feelings of adolescence, there is a vague lack, a general discontent, a feeling of wanting something and wanting to be something that is not clear to one's self.[35] Even though the language used to describe the feeling of religious conversion is strong, a sense of incompleteness, a tantalizing awareness of something as belonging to one's true self but not yet realized in one's self, is evident.

Various psychological theories have ensued to explain the actual occurrence of religious conversion in adolescence. For example, Leon Salzman suggests that it is not difficult to understand why conversion happens in adolescence. It is a period of struggle against authority and an effort to achieve independence which results in hostility, and, for Salzman, religious conversion is release of this hostility by joining a group with which one can agree.[36] James Maloney speaks of regression to the level of infantile trauma in an attempt at some kind of mastery.[37] Charles Stewart related religious conversion with a type of coping exercise wherein the person learns to live in a society where change is expected and not to be feared. And he concludes that there are multiple determinants in the developmental history of each youth which encourage change. Not only healthy or sick temperament, or socio-economic facts, or religious instinct feed into the adolescent idiosyn-

---

33. Pierre Babin, *Faith and the Adolescent* (New York: Herder and Herder, 1964), pp. 111-115, suggests that sensitive period be used to mean the stage in which the subject is inclined to a particular attainment "by virtue of a maturation of the function necessary for this attainment. Thus during childhood there is a period sensitive to learning to speak."

34. Ibid., p. 122.

35. Coe, *Spiritual Life,* p. 50.

36. Leon Salzman, "Types of Religious Conversion," p. 19.

37. James C. Maloney, "Mother, God and Super-ego," *Journal of the American Psychiatric Association* (1954), p. 120.

cratic religious complex. He also suggests that the internalizing experience is not isolated to any one age but appears to resolve inner conflicts better following puberty than at any other time. He points up the sex differences in the adolescent experience in showing that in the female the experience may depend upon her passive reactive patterns, her reflection of others' expectations of her, and her whole sensory apparatus in a global appropriation of reality. The male uses a more active mode of coping—more identification with the religious figure—Christ, pastor, or priest.[38]

In summary, the developmental context regarding adolescence seems to reflect that this period of time in the individual's growth is a time when there is a good possibility of intense change, religious or otherwise. Maturational elements become ready for resolution and the crises of youth provide ready fodder for religious conversional resolution. Granting sexual differences in both, readiness for the concerns about religion in adolescence helps the religious quest in some ways be more evident.

Whether that change is seen in terms of psychological understanding of "oral" issues related to trauma in early object ties, or whether that religious conversion is explained in terms of coping, the variety of the cause is not as significant as the variety of experience and the commonality of this age period. Whether the conversion is brought about by the change from ego-centrality to concern for others, from separation *from* persons to reconciliation *with* them, or from isolation from a community to an allegiance with a new one, religious conversion happens more easily in adolescence due to the sudden handling of emotions, orientation and the need to face one's own identity. It would not be proper to limit the experience to adolescence solely, for along with adolescent concern for change, integration of society with the emerging self-consciousness brings about the opposite characteristics also evident in adolescence, such as a time of carelessness, indifference, and doubt. There is also ample evidence of religious conversion at other ages as well.[39] We have also seen that since conversion of a moral variety

---

38. Stewart, "The Religious Experience of Two Adolescent Girls," p. 54.

39. See ibid. Recent studies indicate that among some revivalistically oriented groups the age of conversion is dropping from the teens down into late childhood. See D. Yoder, *Nurture and Evangelism of Children* (Scotdale, Pa.: Herald Press, 1959); Robert O. Ferm, *The Psychology of Christian Conversion* (Westwood, N.J.: Revell, 1959). Ferm believes the ripe age to be higher and points out that by using college students as their subjects, many of the early studies unwittingly were operating with a truncated sample. In surveys of three churches, Ferm found the average age of conversion to be 43, 46, and 41 years respectively. Converts made by Graham's first British campaign averaged in their middle thirties. Carl G. Jung, in "The Psychological Foundations of Belief in Spirits," *The Structure and Dynamics of the Psyche*, Bollingen Series, Vol. 20 (New York: Pantheon Books, 1960), pp. 301-318, emphasized mid-to-late thirties as a period of moving from an extroverted, external reality orientation, while Hiltner ("Theology of Conversion," pp. 35-42) writes that con-

demands a certain maturity of thought and cognition later ages may be more appropriate for this motif in religious conversion.

This, however, is not to say that religious conversion as we have described it does not happen in the teens. The conversion may be more exciting and have with it more accompanying phenomena, or the conflict may be more readily traceable to normal events of this period of life, but the change is equally as deep as those coming later in life. For adults who have already experienced the trauma of adolescence, religious conversion may be more emotional and cause a more extreme unsettling. To be converted may imply to an adult a total change of ideology, and this makes religious conversion less likely due to the accompanying societal pressure involved. Certainly the more open emotional responses of the teenage years and their ability to establish new allegiances easier than adults are factors in the more common occurrence of this experience in adolescence. Barbara Jones goes so far as to state, and I agree, that from the vantage point of today it seems probable that much of what was called religious conversion in adolescence consisted of conditioned developments expressed in accepted patterns of response, "developments which in contemporary terms might be called identity crisis."[40] These crises, brought on perhaps from the extreme idealism of adolescence or the rather traumatic developmental processes involving all of the areas of a youth's life, including ideological and emotional commitment, tend to be influential forces for the developmental context of religious conversion. For the conversion decision could be an attempt at rationalizing the various forces existing within the youth. It becomes the effective means of releasing youth from an excessive sense of sin by helping them associate with ones who have had the same experience, and through this a sense of community is evolved, giving a sense of fellowship which is equated with "experience." It provides a positive identity, and as Clark suggests, "distracts him from preoccupation with sex by supplying him with a sense of purpose which at its best transcends and includes all other lesser purposes."[41] Thus adolescence is a component relational factor in religious conversion.[42] For Erikson, psy-

---

version is most important, likely, and easily cultivated in the thirties rather than in the early teens.

40. Barbara Eleanor Jones, "Conversion: An Examination of the Myth of Human Change," (Ph.D. dissertation, Columbia University, 1969), p. 211.

41. Clark, *Psychology of Religion,* p. 117.

42. Christensen delineates the component parts of conversion that relate directly to adolescence ("Religious Conversion in Adolescence," pp. 27-28). 1) There are predisposing factors of a specific unconscious conflict plus the adolescent age; 2) there is a conscious conflict related to the unconscious conflict which produces guilt, anxiety, and depression; 3) there is an acute reaction which is precipitated by intensification of the foregoing through participation in a religious meeting; 4) there is withdrawal from others because of a new sense of estrangement and a feeling of unreality; 5) there are feelings of submission which follow in the surrender phase with a sud-

chosocial interpretation of the identity crisis in terms of the value of fidelity argues for an intrinsically moral dimension in adolescent conversion experience. Since one crisis in young adulthood is that of intimacy and religious conversion has the feel of that other-worldly falling-in-love, one might argue that it might be more difficult for conversion to take place later on in youth since they are more secure in their own identity and would have to risk restructuring it and building new relationships in order to experience it.[43]

It would seem then that the developmental phase of later adolescence and early adulthood has special significance for all subsequent personal change. This is the period in which adult identity takes shape, and it is a time of strong enthusiasm and a marked tendency toward an emotional polarization. This time is one of great ideological receptivity and of a high experiential intensity. This is not to say that for an adult, religious conversion will not happen, or to suggest, as Lifton does, that adult change and identity depends upon a specific recapturing of much of the emotional tone which prevailed at the time that this adult identity took shape,[44] but rather that this identity of youth establishes a period when a religious conversion fits into the kinds of decision making, maturing, and conflict that is a part of that period. The relationship between religious conversion and personal identity seems evident from the developmental issues.

Personality Differences

In discussions about the phenomenon of religious conversion the questions always arise: Is there one kind of personality which is more likely to be converted? Are there people who cannot be converted? Are there "anesthetic" types who defy conversion, as James suggests? In answer to these questions, research has been limited. James argues that some people never are "and possibly never under any circumstances could be converted. Religious ideas cannot become the center of their spiritual energy. . . . They are either incapable of imaging the invisible; or else . . . . subjects of barrenness and dryness." He also asserts that in some people their inability for religious faith is caused by intellectual problems which check their natural tendencies toward God.[45]

In other persons the trouble is more profound.

---

den understanding and feeling of elation accompanied by auditory and visual events; and 6) this change modifies his behavior. The analysis is only generally relative, for the factors that cause conversion are only dealt with in the first two stages, those being conflict and its results.

43. Conn, *Christian Conversion*, pp. 26, 27.

44. Robert Jay Lifton, *Thought Reform and the Psychology of Totalism: A Study of "Brainwashing" in China* (New York: Norton, 1956), p. 469.

45. James, *Religious Experience*, p. 167.

There are men anesthetic on the religious side, deficient in that category of sensibility; just as a bloodless organism can never, in spite of all its goodwill, attain to the reckless "animal spirits" enjoyed by those of sanguine temperament; so the nature which is spiritually barren may admire and envy faith in others, but can never compass the enthusiasm and peace which those who are temperamentally qualified for faith enjoy. All this may, however, turn out to have been a matter of temporary inhibition.[46]

George Albert Coe asked this question more directly and felt free to suggest a possible solution. If, for example, you should expose to a converting influence a subject in whom three factors can unite, such as a pronounced emotional sensibility, a predisposition toward automatisms, and a passive sensibility, Coe felt, you might then safely predict the result: "There would be a sudden conversion, a transformation of the striking kind." With this suggestion Coe asserts the relationship of temperamental factors in validating religious conversion. He recognized that this temperamental origin does not diminish the significance of the conversion when it happens. The ultimate test for Coe is, like James, nothing psychological. He notes nothing definable in terms of how the experience happens, but he identifies something ethical instead. He suggests that one can define the experience in terms of the outcome. What are the results? This is the important question for Coe.[47] Coe's findings were not contradicted by a study by Kildahl (1957, 1965), who found twenty sudden converts in theological schools both slightly less intelligent and somewhat more hysterical than twenty matched gradual awakeners. He hypothesized that the converts would be less intelligent and would perceive authority figures as more threatening. The converts would be more hysterical, undergo more depression, and show fewer humanitarian tendencies. They should be, he felt, more conservative. In his study, the converts went from an admittedly irreligious condition to a religious one. Using various testing materials (the Rorschach, ACE, MMPI, Strong, etc.) he found his group to be less intelligent, scoring higher on the hysteria level of the MMPI, but none of the other hypotheses could be supported. It is interesting to note that in the intelligence scales, the mean scores for both groups fell in the superior range, the 74th percentile for the suddens, and the 87th percentile for the gradual group, with only 4.3 percentile points higher than the hysteria scores for the sudden group. It would seem that the suggestion that there is a definite personality correlate for sudden religious conversion experience is not successfully demonstrable here.[48] Kildahl's samples were small and may not reflect the average religious convert, but would seem to indicate that students with sudden conversion experiences fall more often into hysteric

---

46. Ibid., p. 168.
47. Coe, *The Spiritual Life,* p. 144.
48. John P. Kildahl, "The Personalities of Sudden Religious Converts," *Pastoral Psychology* 16 (September 1965), p. 37.

types on a testing scale and tend to be somewhat less intelligent than their counterparts with gradual religious development.

James as well suggests that the candidates for conversion are often in the possession of an "active subliminal self" which results in a high degree of hypnotic sensibility.[49] In 1965 Roberts studied forty-three theological students along several dimensions and found that those who had been converted in the direction of their parents' faith had higher MMPI scores for neuroticism; this was not substantiated in an earlier study by Stanley in 1964, who found a slight negative correlation between sudden religious conversion and neuroticism.[50] A most interesting study done by Wood (1961) and reported by Allison shows that, of twenty-five members [men and women] of the Pentecostal Holiness religion studied, Pentecostalism attracts uncertain, threatened, inadequately organized persons with strong motivation to reach a state of satisfactory interpersonal relatedness and personal integrity. This conclusion, however, would be tempered by the location of the church (deep South) and the nature of the cultural and social beliefs and should not, I believe, be considered sufficient for general use.[51]

Sargent defines those most likely to be converted in terms of Pavlov's typology for his dogs, which in turn is parallel to the Greek typology of the choleric, melancholic, sanguine, and phlegmatic personalities. He notes,

> It is impossible to avoid classifying the human subjects according to basic temperamental types, each of which may call for a different type of physiological and psychological treatment. The stronger the obsessional tendency, for instance, the less amenable will the subject be found to some of the ordinary techniques of conversion; the only hope is to break him down by debilitation and prolonged psychological and physiological measures to increase suggestibility.[52]

Freudian analysis suggests, on the other hand, that sudden converts tend to have unusually greater repressed resentment and hatred toward their fathers or toward authority in general. This, as observed above, is not demonstrated by Kildahl; however, most psychologists and psychiatrists believe that for the more regressive types of religious conversion the personality of the converts is identified by an extreme dependency on strong, omnipotent figures. And God is the synthesized result of this need for authority. This may be traceable among those whose sudden change or gradual shift of center is caused by an imbalance of pathology or neuropathology, but does not hold true to those of the more progressive type wherein the integration proves

---

49. James, *Religious Experience,* p. 193.
50. Clark, "Intense Religious Experience," p. 532.
51. Joel Allison, "Recent Empirical Studies of Religious Conversion Experiences," *Pastoral Psychology* 17 (September 1966), p. 26.
52. William Sargent, *Battle for the Mind* (New York: Harper & Row, 1957), p. 127.

beneficial to the new believer. It seems obvious that there are individuals who have impaired adaptive capacities, but this has not been established for converts in general.

This problem of a commonality in personality correlates is inconclusive because there is surprisingly little work on this problem. The research is complicated by the previous confusion regarding a definition for religious conversion and by the variety of abrupt and gradual conversion experiences. Possible differences in group conversion and individual ones and the concomitant factors in their occurences, as well as the very narrow groups studied, further complicate this area.

James, for example, regarded the sick soul as the most likely candidate for religious conversion, for the sick soul is generally introverted and pessimistic in outlook, taking the problems of life profoundly to heart. He seems to be reminiscent of Kierkegaard's person who is in despair and knows he/she is in despair. But to attribute sick souls to be the type for religious conversion does not seem to be complete enough. Rather, those who are susceptible to suggestion, those who find pressure and anxiety easily, may find religious conversion the way out. But these will not perhaps be progressive in nature and the experience will not lead them to maturity or identity, but rather be a means of coping, as Stewart suggests, or simply be a form of psychopathological reaction.

The only recurring personality correlate is that of susceptibility to suggestion. Other research seems to be marginal in nature except Kildahl's preliminary work which suggests only a slightly lower intelligence and higher hysteria in those with sudden conversions, yet personality as a factor in conversion seems to be a rather marginal conclusion and must be placed far down the list of factors in suggesting a source for the experience.

There is some consensus, however, as to what will prevent religious conversion. For example, most authorities agree that indifference best prevents conversion. A policy of total noncooperation, detachment, and humor seems to be the best defense against induced change. A lack of involvement avoids commitment. However, this is a will-choice, and not a personality characteristic. It is interesting to note that the choice *not* to get involved may be the very emotional stimulus needed to begin the suggestion toward involvement. This paradox is hinted at by Sargent, yet conclusions are not drawn.[53] The opinion that certain personalities exist in converts proves to be little established, other than by mere speculation or opinion; however, research of this sort does seem to suggest that certain types who are more easily swayed by an outside influence may have changed more often.

---

53. Ibid., pp. 107-110, 225-233.

Societal Adaptations

Suggestion

Suggestion and suggestibility seem to be factors within the personality that contribute to religious conversion. However, these are not necessarily thought of as constructs within the personality of the individual. Therefore it is important to analyze the contributing factors for this experience to see what goes into the experience itself from outside the person. Suggestion may be caused by sociological and theological influences. When James speaks of outer influences he refers to their effects on the inner life, yet well before the 1900s the role of unconscious mechanisms was clearly appreciated. Coe described the influence of what he called "subconscious automatisms," well-organized sequences of thought or action that in particular circumstances achieve dominance over the conscious, volitional life patterns of people. He thought that conversion could best be understood as a group phenomenon, where the "gang" impulse was operative in temperamentally passive and suggestive people whose nature favored the occurrence of what he called automatisms. He understood the preeminent role of sexual and aggressive feeling in adolescence, but felt that a temporary proclivity was really needed for these problems to be handled in conversion.[54]

Suggestibility is the product of group pressure, social pressure, style of meeting, concept of belief, intentional manipulation, subtle coercion, and exploitation. Some distinctions between brainwashing and Wesleyan revivalism have been drawn.[55] Brainwashing employs intentional manipulation, whereas revival techniques seem to allow for much greater personal freedom and choice. Sargent concludes that religious conversions are the direct result of one person or group of people working on others with techniques or through group patterns that are geared to cause the kind of desired change in behavior.[56] Research which relates conversion with brainwashing has noticed unique similarities when dealing with the ideological shift in intellectual or coercive motifs in conversion. For example, conversion when produced through excessive influence is usually not a once-in-a-lifetime event. There are often a series of movings in and out of various communities when the motivation for change has a clearly external source. Also, the decisions to join or to become a participant in a new religious movement can be made suddenly, dramatically, or emotionally, "but the most fruitful way to view conversion to new religions is a series of experiments entered into somewhat gingerly. Many join with so-called latent reservations, affiliations are temporary

---

54. Coe, *The Spiritual Life,* p. 128 and on until the end of the chapter.
55. See below, n. 88.
56. Sargent, *Battle for the Mind,* pp. 200ff.

and on trial."[57]

It certainly cannot be denied that certain techniques render aid to suggestion in decision making, but a significant study by R. W. Wilson (1976) assists us here. He found little evidence of suggestibility or dependency as a precondition for conversion to Christianity. Cedric Johnson and H. Newton Malony commenting on Wilson's work indicated that "the psychological process whereby the person may or may not be rendered more suggestible does not have sufficient evidence to include it in a definition of Christian conversion."[58] They conclude by saying that the question of whether the conversion was brought about by the Holy Spirit or through the emotionally charged situation which nurtures a climate for coercive change is a "moot point."[59]

An interesting addendum to the research on brainwashing is in the area of sensory deprivation. Certain trance states and mythical experiences result through sensory overload or denial. This area of research could prove interesting and perhaps aid in the psychological explanation of how the brain functions in these sensorially heavy experiences. It cannot be denied that Sargent's position is demonstrable and that certain fear arousal or exhausting techniques of revivalists raise the level of suggestibility. In this state of mind the subject becomes liable for any suggestion. Hopefully the impulse would not be demonic, yet under these circumstances of complete breakdown as Sargent describes, the person would be vulnerable to even the best or worst intentions. Nevertheless, great and dramatic religious changes occur through these factors.

Culture

We have noted that religious conversion, a form of deep change and an intense commitment to an ideology, seems to be a common experience of humankind, exhibited in varying intensities and lengths. It is conditioned, however, as are any personal experiences, by those things that make a person human, those factors of time, space, culture, society, tradition, place, expectation, genetics, need, and interest. The experience has been suggested as going to the very core of the person and instituting meaningful changes and decisions that are shown in behavior different from that previously exhibited. Yet this experience must be variously understood by the person in time and place. Just as each is defined by beliefs, politics, social status, occupations, education, morality, and interest, so with religious conversion

---

57. Bill J. Leonard, "Getting Saved in America: Conversion Event in a Pluralistic Culture," *Review and Expositor* 82:2 (1985), pp. 120, 121.

58. Cedric B. Johnson and H. Newton Malony, *Christian Conversion: Biblical and Psychological Perspectives* (Grand Rapids, Mich.: Zondervan, 1982), p. 57.

59. Ibid.

these factors are also present. Jones suggests that culture is the filter through "which external influences are received and its function as a mold in setting the lifestyle has long been recognized, and this totality also shapes the religious form which, in turn, is part of the very cultural influence."[60] Since conversions of both religious and secular nature occur within culture and take the shape of cultural norms and forms so the person and the experience are formed by this social, cultural context. The convert is perhaps even conditioned by it and unavoidably unable to eliminate its power in the religious conversion experience.

Take, for example, the effect of the environment on religious conversion. Joel Alland in 1962, in his work on trance state possession, similar in context to conversion, demonstrated how increasing knowledge of the effects of bombardment of the senses alters persons' decision-making faculties. Alland's data are based on observations of the church services of the United House of Prayer for all People, an ethnic church founded by C.E. Sweet Daddy Grace. The trance state consisted of a momentary or prolonged loss of voluntary control over body movement, involving mild body convulsions, prolonged dancing, falling to the floor either with body contractions or remaining still as in a faint. He found: 1) a high percentage of carbon dioxide (due to the heat and stuffiness of the room), which can help facilitate mystic-like experiences by enhancement of the ability to see things when the eyes are closed; 2) the loud rhythmic music with a simple repetitious beat; 3) the otherwise forbidden social dancing except for dancing for God in the trance state; 4) the fasting all day by seekers.[61] Accordingly, one sees a selective reduction of certain stimuli with the aim of producing an altered state of experience. The experience here mentioned is often accompanied by glossolalia.[62] Along with the environmental context is the related influence of ordinary cultural factors.

It has been recognized that in times of general societal unrest, in times of wars, epidemics and the like, more religious conversions can be found. At times of revivals, change in the structure of the group causes certain anxiety

---

60. See Jones, "Myth of Human Change," p. 155.

61. Joel Allison "Recent Empirical Studies of Religious Conversion Experiences," *Pastoral Psychology* 17 (September 1966), p. 26.

62. Allison (ibid., p. 29) also quotes a study by Stone (1963) of a community in the gulf states whose membership was contingent on conversion signaled by a vision. In the narratives of the vision, all the elements of classic conversion were present including primary feelings of being lost or disorganized, self-surrender, and feelings of newness, but the crux lies in the attainment of a vision with definite visual symbols given by God to signify his promise for future help. For final acceptance into membership the vision is made public with the accompanying high emotionalism of crying, marching, and shouting. Stone reported that the religious visions occurred mostly during adolescence and there was considerable backsliding after visions. The content of the visions also contained material personally and culturally related to these people.

in those within the group structure, and for those of less adaptive ability conversion could be a way of rejoining a group or achieving a role within a group. Anton Boisen related the "Holy Roller" movements during the economic depression of the thirties to similar processes "where the personal conversion experience was a passage right to a group membership."[63] It seems then that religious conversion would not be as likely to occur if the culture did not expect it to occur. This may be the reason de Sanctis' study did not reflect many sudden conversions and why he attributes growth to conversion, solely rejecting sudden instances of conversion in his sample, for the theology of conversion was Roman Church which usually does not include the normal possibility for the occurrence in any dramatic form. Wesley finds this to be the case, perhaps, when he writes: "In London alone I found 652 members of our society who were exceedingly clear in their experience, and whose testimony I could see no reason to doubt. And every one of these (without a single exception) has declared that his deliverance from sin was instantaneous; that the change was wrought in a moment."[64]

It would seem then that the particular form religious conversion effects can be the result of suggestion and imitation, which implies that perhaps in other faiths and other countries, although the nature of the change would be the same, the occurrences would be different. James also argues that in Catholic lands where the sacraments exist as a means of appropriating the holy, the individual need for religious conversion is less stressed and therefore less common. For example, culture imposes certain constraints that tend to offset the natural preference for diversity. "A child brought up in the Confucian tradition could possibly arrive unaided at the intricate system of Christian theological beliefs."[65] John Dewey comments correctly in this respect:

> The particular interpretation given to this complex of conditions is not inherent in the experience itself. It is derived from the culture with which a particular person has been imbued. A fatalist will give one name to it; a Christian Scientist another, and the one who rejects all supernatural being still another. The determining factor in the interpretation of the experience is the particular doctrinal apparatus into which a person has been inducted. The emotional deposit connected with prior teaching floods the whole situation.[66]

But it is evident that religious conversion has meaning in various cultural contexts. The fact that in some countries membership in the church or community may be contingent upon having certain experiences indicates

---

63. Anton J. Boisen, "Economic Distress and Religious Experience—A Study of the Holy Rollers," *Psychiatry* (February 1939), p. 185.

64. James, *Religious Experience,* p. 184.

65. Gordon W. Allport, *The Individual and His Religion: A Psychological Interpretation* (New York: Macmillan, 1950), pp. 23-24.

66. John Dewey, *A Common Faith* (New Haven, Conn.: Yale University Press, 1940), p. 12.

that there is for some an expectancy factor evident in religious conversion. It is for some the cultural traditions that bind and form a person into a certain type of belief and therefore shape his or her experience, and since a person is a being who in many ways works from stimulus-response reaction, he or she may want to move within the context of his tradition or group, society or church, in the most anxiety-free way. He or she will want to be accepted in the group and culture, and it is here that the element of expectation is an important factor.[67]

It may be that cultural conditioning is more significant than suggestibility in determining the form that the conversion may take. Do certain highly charged emotional environments cause some kind of reorganization of the human psyche and therefore make people more prone to convert?

It is also important to suggest here that religious conversion seems to be group-related. By contrast, mystical experience tends to be more person-centered. It is a singular, core experience. Primarily, as W. H. Clark suggests, the conversion experience may trigger a mystical response but tends to be socially related, suggesting the unifying function of group or crowd over the mind. It seems safe to say that emotional tensions are heightened, and the individual's ability to succumb to suggestion is increased when in a social setting where pressures are evident. However, as important as culture and society are, they should not be allowed to totally eclipse the internally coherent system of freedom inherent within the person. It is true, of course, that personality is fashioned and expressed in a social milieu, yet it is a self-contained system as well, as Allport suggests.[68] What may be suggested, then, is that the cultural influences and social setting in which religious conversion is found or expected are factors in the expression of the experience.

Revival Crisis

A study of religious conversion would not be complete without some reference to the social setting of revivalism as this forms for many the cultural context of the experience. Since conversions are most often reported during revivals or immediately succeeding them, the focus of attention in this cultural form must be examined. Revivalism will be here used to mean *the*

---

67. It is on this concern that James Bissett Pratt, *The Psychology of Religious Belief* (New York: Macmillan, 1907), p. 153 comments, "The violence of the experience is in part induced by the suggestions of conventional theology and in part is purely imaginary, existing in the expression rather than in experience. I venture . . . at least nine out of every ten conversion cases reported in recent questionnaires would have had no violent or depressing experiences to report had not the individuals in question been brought into a church or community which taught them to look for it if not to cultivate it."

68. Gordon Allport, *Pattern and Growth in Personality* (New York: Holt, Rinehart and Winston, 1963), X-XI.

attempt at manipulating the environment to produce changes in people. This is not to eliminate genuine revival, which is a return to the will of God as perceived by the individual, but this definition means the organization of a setting to heighten suggestion and therefore to manipulate people to make decisions that they normally would not make. This is a process which induces emotionalism rather than response to the emotion which religious experience has. The techniques of the professional revivalist have been broadly grouped into the following aims: 1) securing a suggestive audience by the creation of crowd conditions, 2) still further heightening the suggestibility of the audience by raising its emotional tone, 3) securing from the audience the desired response by suggesting the way to respond.[69]

Understood in its simplest terms and psychological elements, the revival is like a process aimed at breaking down previous inhibitions while involving an image of the self as a great sinner. There is an active role that the leader plays in encouraging release and self-surrender.

The revivalistic approach is based on the premise that all experience of God is the same and each person must come the same way. While the content of salvation for many churches is the same it does not necessarily mean that the method of approach will take the same form. The diversity of people and varieties of experience James talks of so much is often denied in revivalism. There is with this approach a vague relationship of "fellowship" with religious conversion experience by revivalists. The emotional tone of the revival does not make clear the distinction between these two factors of religious life. Fellowship and its ensuing feeling of closeness, presence, love, and concern are not experienced. Fellowship is more often caused by the situation and when experienced unites those involved in religious change. Religious experience, on the other hand, deals in the feeling tones of life and the personal expression of one's understanding of the "Holy" in the life. Fellowship often is created by people and has operating all of the other factors that make community or *koinonia* possible. Revivalism, by contrast, tends to focus on uniting the external factors and confusing the experience with the form of the experience.

The planning and promotion of revival-oriented meetings date back to Charles Finney, whose *Lectures on Revivalism of Religion,* originally published in 1835, is a study of how to sustain pressure, increase guilt, enlarge audiences, and deal with hindrances in the converting process.[70] Historically, the revival appealed to all people within and without the established churches of colonial America. When it was finished it left the citizens of thirteen

---

69. Alfred Clair Underwood, *Conversion: Christian and Non-Christian: A Comparative and Psychological Study* (New York: Macmillan, 1925), p. 202.

70. Charles G. Finney, *Lectures on Revivals of Religion,* ed. William G. McLoughlin (Cambridge, Mass.: Belknap Press of Harvard University Press, 1960), pp. 91-120.

colonies with a new sense of pluralism and a growing awareness of national identity.[71]

The Great Awakening in New England was largely the product of Jonathan Edwards, who was the first to fully document historically and add a theological defense to what was happening. He believed that one must crucify self as the first step to regeneration. A person had to renounce his or her very identity and fall back through all of the previous feelings and conditioned beliefs—back to innocence and even ignorance. It was fear which was the primal mover for Edwards. He saw it as his duty to move his congregation into a crisis which would scare people into changing. Thus he preached terror. Some have equated this process with that of modern psychotherapy which leads patient through the agony of regressive self-revelation.[72] David Williams says,

> Edwards' analysis may have been similar to that of modern behaviorism. But the therapy he advocated was closer to that of Freudian psychoanalysis and post-Freudian "Ego psychology," the rooting out of unconscious sources of "sinful" behavior in the hope that these might be replaced by more healthy inclinations and a new, more healthy identity.[73]

Williams makes a particularly cogent observation regarding religious conversion and personal identity in Edwards' theology.

> Personality, or identity, once established, protected a person from fear. This fear was so great that the mind suppressed all consciousness of it, and yet it provided the negative reinforcement that held the personality together and kept self-love on the throne. The destruction of this identity, what might be labeled today as "identity crisis," was the crucifixion of the self. According to Edwards, such a conversion was the only way for a natural person to get out of self and into, not just another identity, but a space beyond the relativism of human identities, into God.[74]

Much is attributed to Wesley and revivalism. Jones suggests that Wesley formalized the myth of religious conversion as just sudden occurrence and associated it with revivalism.[75] The rise of revivalism, however, is traced to many causes and not just the form of the meeting. In the United States population make-up was a factor. Individuals had migrated, and now they were

71. Donald L. Gelpi, "Conversion: The Challenge of Contemporary Charismatic Piety," *Theological Studies* 43 (1982), p. 606.

72. David R. Williams, "Horses, Pigeons, and the Therapy of Conversion: A Psychological Reading of Jonathan Edwards' Theology," *The Harvard Theological Review* 74 (October 1981), p. 347.

73. Ibid., p. 348.

74. Ibid., p. 351, or for a more complete discussion of this topic see Jonathan Edwards, *Miscellany,* No. 782, in *The Philosophy of Jonathan Edwards,* ed. Harvey G. Townsend (Westport, Conn.: Greenwood Press, 1955), pp. 112-126.

75. Jones, "The Myth of Human Change," p. 168.

without social identity. There was also a new concern about formal religion and a quest for personalization in religion.[76] These factors coupled with the revivalistic approach created a definite kind of spiritual condition, a kind that was not entirely satisfied unless there were some kinds of results. The emotions were stirred to the depths, felt, and decisions demanded.

Windemiller showed the relationship of Chinese brainwashing and eighteenth-century revivalistic techniques. In his exhaustive study he concludes that there are similarities, such as the crisis experiences and problem-solving processes which aid in stable ego identity; the two processes involve emotional upheaval, bring forth changed lives, and rely on group pressures which involve interrogation, confession, organized structure and inclusion of new words, exhaustion, suggestion, doubt, fear, and guilt. The results often are the same as well. Yet the two are dissimilar in content, goals, and motivation since they have basically different worldviews to promote.[77]

Nevertheless, with revivalism came religious conversion. This was due to the format of many revivals. The meeting was designed to lead up to decision and this was the climax of the crisis drummed up during the meetings. This decision paralleled the giving-in phase of the experience. There is, however, nothing wrong in asking for decisions; a prompted time of decision can be a meaningful turning point for lives in conflict. But the springing of conversion suddenly and intensely through a procedured, manufactured manner in the hope of acquiring a *quantity* of conversions may be simply environmental factors at work and the revival technique operating at its fullest potential.[78]

Revivalism, then, seems to be a factor in the incidence of religious conversion. It contributes to the social situation, which in turn affects the individual who encounters the external stress provided. The arousal of fear and anxiety by preaching that humankind is not all they might be, simply increases the potential for stress and allows for conversion to occur. Early investigators pointed to these factors and concentrated on various symbols which arouse emotional images in persons and repetition as additional contributors to change.[79]

Not only do culture or environmental factors add to the incidence of religious conversion, but it would seem logical to infer that there might be some

---

76. William Warren Sweet, *Revivalism in America: Its Origin, Growth, and Influence* (Nashville, Abingdon, 1944), pp. 3-22.

77. Allison, "Empirical Studies," p. 30.

78. No attempt has been made to historically outline and chronologically set apart revivals in history. For more formal discussions of revivalism's impact and approach see Sweet, *Revivalism in America*.

79. See Ames, *The Psychology of Religious Experience*, p.330; Coe, *The Spiritual Life*, p. 146; John W. Drakeford, *Psychology in Search of a Soul* (Nashville: Broadman, 1964), pp. 195-196; and Hadley Cantril, *The Psychology of Social Movements* (New York: Wiley, 1941), pp. 64 and on.

social settings that would reintegrate or return to consciousness some early childhood trauma or early religious commitment which would be brought to the fore through the insistence of another person, preacher, leader, or ideology. These remembrances could bring on the emotionalism necessary for an abrupt or a more gradual change to take place.

Related to this concept are the studies of Helen Carlson who reports on confusional states among college students. These states have a slight relationship with religious conversion in that anxiety tends to have a key part in the change induced by both. She states that "some situations recreating the original trauma was the precipitating event for the confusional state, particularly in the conversion experience."[80] It seems reasonable to suggest that there is a similar relationship between the acute initial feelings of anxiety and the situation that recreates rather vividly memories of past happiness, trauma, or depression and therefore calls back need-fulfilling emotions which in turn give a nudge to the embryonic experience of change.

On the more cynical side, Marjoe Gortner—an Evangelical preacher whose documentary in the late sixties, *Marjoe,* exposed some of the more bizarre forms of revivalistic methodologies—suggests that people want some sort of experience. They want to feel good and be entertained. Revivalism provides a kind of social context for entertainment. According to Flo Conway and Jim Siegelman, Marjoe took pride in his ability to understand and manipulate people. His healing and tongue-speaking episodes were the product of careful, thoughtful, manipulation of crowds.[81]

On the other hand, in a more gradual religious conversion and shift of allegiance that has definite, obvious incubated factors involved, the family plays a large part. Horace Bushnell's concept of nurture is appropriate here, for he feels that sudden conversions in the average family are not too significant and are even superficial, and suggested that for the majority of people the long pull of change was preferable. He attributes to "ostrich nurture" the expectancy factor in religious conversion.

> Again there is another and different way in which parents, meaning to be Christian, fall into the ostrich nurture without being at all aware of it. They believe in what are called revivals of religion and have a great opinion of them as being, in a very special sense, the converting times of the gospel. They bring up their children, therefore, not for conversion exactly, but, what is less dogmatic and formal, for the converting times. . . . To bring up a family for revivals of religion requires, alas! about the smallest possible amount of consistency and Christian assiduity. . . . So they fall into a key of expectation that permits, for the present, modes of life and conduct which they cannot quite approve. . . . Finally the hoped for day arrives, and there begins to be a remarkable and strange piety in the house. . . . The

---

80. Helen B. Carlson, "The Relationship of the Acute Confusional State of Ego Development," *International Journal of Psychiatry* 45 (1961), p. 517.

81. Flo Conway and Jim Siegelman, *Snapping: America's Epidemic of Sudden Personality Change,* New York: Dell, 1978), pp. 50, 51.

children stare, of course, not knowing what strange thing has come! They cannot be unaffected; perhaps they seem to be converted, perhaps not.[82]

For Bushnell, nurture toward conversion was hard, involving truly total involvement by the parents each day, and was closely related to the biblical concept of sanctification. Religious conversion for Bushnell could be caused by too many external factors, and these kept him eternally critical of conversion of the sudden variety. These factors, such as the family, the early childhood experiences, and expectation of the revivalistic approach seem to be additional factors in the occurrence of the experience. But even Bushnell discovered his insight into the gospel early one morning in what some would call a sudden conversion. When his wife awoke that morning, to hear of an enlightenment, "she asked, 'What have you seen?' He replied, 'The gospel.' It came to him at last, after all his thought and study, not as something reasoned but, as an inspiration—a revelation from the mind of God himself."[83]

Psychological Growth

Religious definitions of conversion tend to interpret the process in light of the faith that is being developed.[84] Therefore, stress is often seen as a reason for the process of change to begin. Psychology, on the other hand, attempts to understand *what* is happening and, therefore, often emphasizes the *movement* and its *causes* rather than trying to understand its significance for faith. In understanding the contributing factors in the crisis of religious conversion, some time must be spent dealing with psychology in the process itself, at least those operating in conversion. Some of these processes have been alluded to previously, but what follows is additional material regarding contributing factors in the dynamics of the experience. Some theories only suggest intelligent speculation, others based on research tend to show more reliably the factors involved. A psychological view of religious conversion is descriptive by nature. It is an attempt to understand the process of the change. It attempts to explain the process rather than to evaluate and place value judgments on it. This is in direct contrast to most religious definitions of the term.

Understandings of the psychological nature of religious conversion vary. Sargent, previously cited, alluded to the positive correlation between modern psychoanalytic and psychiatric interpretations which see conversion as psychologically like the process of self-abnegation, which leads to brainwashing. In his discussion he traces the many uses of the psychological

82. Horace Bushnell, *Christian Nurture* (New Haven, Conn.: Yale University Press, 1888), pp. 62-64.
83. Conrad Cherry, ed., *Horace Bushnell: Sermons* (New York: Paulist, 1985), p. 16.
84. David K. O'Rourke, *A Process Called Conversion,* (Garden City, N.Y.: Doubleday, 1985), p. 38.

mechanisms which recondition the individual by causing intense anxiety and strong emotions such as anger, fear, hate, and guilt. This process wipes the "mind clean and allows new concepts to be instituted."[85] Irving Rinder has studied the same process in the area of role change when one self-role is substituted for another through the application of debasement or degradation, according to Earl Furgeson.[86]

Many explanations of the dynamics of religious conversion deal with the ego. Christensen suggests that all religious conversions are simply attempts at a reintegration of the ego's defense systems, some of which succeed and some of which do not.[87] In this description the ego then, in a process of symbolic conscious representation, acts on the unconscious conflict and the suppressed conscious conflict seeking out a solution. Since conflict by definition is a threat to a person, when the resolution comes, there is usually a sense of well-being, elation, and understanding. To the believer the experience is attributed to happening outside of the self.

Those who deal with the pathological implications of this kind of rapid change see in religious conversion a successful attempt at solving problems, real or imagined. If the conflict is not resolved positively and maturely in a religious conversion experience, there might be a retreat into schizophrenia or schizoid states as the magical solution to the problems. This regression type of religious conversion would occur when the inner struggle with authority, independence, hostility, and resentment becomes too great for the normal ego's defensive network, and there is a break. In order to explain the positive integration factors of unity and behavior that often accompany a conversion, individuals of this bent simply apply Freud's understanding of "regression in the service of the ego," which always has a positive outcome aiding maturity.[88]

Oftentimes religious conversion is related to personality reorganization. Boisen felt this way and differentiated between those which lead to maturation and positive results and those which end in some kind of psychosis. Salzman and Sullivan's early paper "Schizophrenia: Its Conservative and Malignant Features" suggests that some sort of pathology is responsible for the experience itself. It seems reasonable to assert that conversion under this framework would result in a unification of the personality on a socially unacceptable basis, rather than on an acceptable one. If psychosis and conversion were alike in their source, the cataclysmic eruptions of acute psychosis and

---

85. Sargent, *Battle for the Mind,* pp. 150 and on.

86. Earl Furgeson, "The Definition of Religious Conversion," *Pastoral Psychology* 16 (September 1965), p. 10.

87. Christensen, "Religious Conversion in Adolescence," p. 25.

88. See Joel Allison, "Empirical Studies," pp. 122 and on, and Charles William Stewart, *Adolescent Religion,* pp. 266 and on, for a more complete analysis of this process.

conversion would be nature's attempts to eliminate the sets and attitudes that hamper growth and effect a reorganization of one's pathology. The difference then between someone being a gifted and dedicated Christian convert or a backward schizophrenic would be the fact that they were predetermined by the character elements which they brought into the crisis of conversion.[89] But to prove this is another problem and has not yet been scientifically done. For the present this must remain a theory.

Bernard Lonergan suggests that moral self-transcendence is the inherent capacity of the dynamic structure of change. Conversion brings the capacity for self-transcendence, he suggests. During the moments of conversion there is religious self-transcendence called, you will remember, that of an other—worldly falling-in-love. Conversion has a threefold psychological result. For Lonergan it includes the attainment of intellectual, moral, and religious self-transcendence. When converted, the person will be in an otherworldly love-state and oriented to the mystery of the transcendent deity.[90]

In addition to those who see conversion as a psychopathological situation can be added those who, rather than theorize concerning the nature of the experience, suggest the psychological dynamics involved. For example, religious conversion could be the interpretation of paired changes in the level of ego-functioning. This occurs first in the form of regression followed closely by a sudden reintegration. It is like other regressions before release, but the reintegration usually is long-lasting. It seems that moving into the area of the dynamics of conversion is more profitable, for in looking at its psychological functioning one does not have to theorize as to the nature of the source, be it pathology or normality. Again Carlson's work on confusional states is helpful here. She suggests that religiosity may be one of the outcomes of the confusional states of youth, and therefore religious conversion reflects normal reaction formation and dissonance theory.

Much of psychoanalysis attributes religious conversion to the realm of simple attempts to handle repressed material seeking consciousness which are within the framework of religious beliefs. It is logical that Freud's theories would then reflect an attempt in conversion to resolve the Oedipal conflict.

Other research ties religious conversion to brain functioning. After lobotomy operations, when the mind is freed from its old straitjacket and new beliefs take the place of the old ones, experiences similar to religious conversions take place. These are simply surgical attempts at organization with-

---

89. H. R. Bagwell, "Abrupt Religious Conversion Experiences," *Journal of Religion and Health* 8 (April 1969), p. 168.

90. James Robertson Price, "Conversion and the Doctrine of Grace in Bernard Lonergan and John Climacus," *Anglican Theological Journal* 62 (October 1980), pp. 341, or see Bernard Lonergan, *Method in Theology* (New York: Herder and Herder, 1972). See chapter entitled "Dimensions of Conversion." Lonergan is considered one of the most important contemporary figures on conversion and religious change.

in the conflict model.[91]

Studies on sensory deprivation and its effects on behavior and change seem significant. A series of studies done by Philip Solomon (1961) have altered the usual patterning of sensory experience by preventing physical movement blocking vision, hearing, and touch. Under such conditions there appears an hallucinatory-like activity.[92] This observation has led to some speculation as to the relationship of sensory deprivation to mental illness. Social deprivation of the psychotic could be creating a situation of perceptual isolation likened to the laboratory experiments. Would religious conversion be a possible result? It would be well for further study in this area of mind functioning. For a study of the circumstances under which changes occur, whether in a group or in isolation, with sensory overloads and stimuli present, or information regarding the patterning caused by groups and environment may yield a rich information regarding the actual process of change within the perception of the convert.

On the whole, however, most seem to agree that actual processes of the mind operate in the change. James's concept of "subconscious incubation," for example, is simply the current concept of repression by which that which is unhappy, painful, or incompatible in the mind and in consciousness is banished into a region called the unconscious. From the unconscious it may influence behavior or conscious processes of thought but cannot be voluntarily made a part of the conscious stream of thought.

One has some choices in looking at the dynamics of religious conversion. Some attribute the dynamics to the realm of the conscious or unconscious. Others look to Jung who would focus on the beyond-individual-consciousness forces of the collective unconscious and its concomitant archetypes in exerting pressure for personal integration or disintegration within the individual. One only has to pick a particular school of psychoanalytic thought and master the vocabulary. Since humankind is a multiplicity of motives, energies, relationships, and yet is still unique, most of these ego functions as well as the popular vocabularies of change could apply under given situations given enough time. Whether one wishes to adopt the concept that the dynamics involved are simply regressions in the service of the ego, repression, abreaction, or sense deprivation, is not the issue so much as the fact that there are many psychological functions occurring dynamically resulting in change. As mentioned earlier, whether or not the divine is operating in these changes is not without possibility or even probability but certainly could be included as a valid additional factor if one wanted to take the position that religious conversion is a deep kind of change initiated by God when properly understood. The sudden kinds of religious conversion may easily be seen to

---

91. Sargent, *Battle for the Mind*, p. 139.

92. Philip Solomon et al., *Sensory Deprivation: A Symposium Held at Harvard Medical School* (Cambridge, Mass.: Harvard University Press, 1961).

have dynamics psychologically oriented and operating. They may have regressive or progressive outcomes. This change is just as deep and devastating in reorganizing and in redirecting the life of the person toward new goals and in giving new motives grounds for being as any other type of change.

Similarities seem to exist between conversion and pathological change. However, these similarities seem to be only in their dynamics. Both dramatic religious conversion and schizophrenic psychosis happen in the psychic life of a person. They occur as a process rather than as static, independent occurrences and seem go through some identifiable stages which move toward conversion or psychosis; the conditions that cause the experiences may be alike in scope and intensity; and the stages in the process of conversion (preconversion state, etc.) seem to reflect the same early stages of schizophrenic psychosis— which are overextension, restricted consciousness, transition events, disinhibition, psychotic disorganization, and psychotic resolution.[93] But even though the stages seem similar, the results may be dramatically different.

Conflict

Another touchstone with psychopathology is in the nature of conflict as it relates to change. (The term conflict refers to the emotional turmoil that is experienced prior to dramatic change, but it is used so broadly that it is often meaningless for our use as a religious category.) Research done with forty converts from four different belief systems and thirty nonreligiously affiliated nonconverts provide insight into conflict and its relationship to change. According to this research, conflict can arise from numerous sources—ambiguity, impermeability of one's belief system, cognitive quest, or emotional factors which may include the perception of childhood relationships with one's parents or childhood stress and trauma.[94] It is quite commonplace that the conversion event may follow periods of emotional confusion and disturbance. Family stress often becomes a factor in causing such anxiety. After reviewing the lives of twelve historic conversions, A. J. Krailsheimer discovered that most had lives marked by tensions or imbalance in family relationships, and all before the age of sixteen. Ignatius Loyola, Blaise Pascal, Armand-Jean de Rancé, John Bunyan, Charles de Foucauld, and Thomas Merton had lost their mothers; William Booth, Edith Stein, and Charles de Foucauld added to that the loss of their father. Augustine was nineteen when he lost his father, and it is well-documented that he had a deep and close relationship with

---

93. Raymond J. Wooten and David F. Allen, "Dramatic Religious Conversion and Schizophrenic Decompensation," *Journal of Religion and Health* 22:3 (1983), pp. 213, 214.

94. Conn, *Christian Conversion,* pp. 182, 183.

his mother; Martin Luther incurred his father's fury by joining the church in young adulthood, and St. Francis had uneasy relations with his father and after his conversion was totally estranged from his family.[95]

It seems then that both the theologians and the psychologists were to a degree right concerning religious conversion—the theologians claiming it as a positive phenomenon, and the psychologists assuming that there very well could be some pathology present in some cases. Both positions acknowledge the actual fact of this kind of deep change. Both positions realize the complexity of isolating a locus for change within the person. The pressure on the early writers about religious conversion, such as James, Starbuck, and Leuba to take a stand on the issue of conversion forced them to make the best conclusion regarding it. Starbuck says, "The ultimate test doubtless will be, does (conversion) contribute, in the long run, in the individual and in groups of individuals, to permanent growth?" The settlement of such a question far exceeds the maturity of the psychology of religion.[96]

Since conversion has become a more central theme for regeneration, there have been observations on more tertiary causes for the experience. For example, some research has looked at the role of folklore to invoke conversional change. It is interesting to note that during the early days of the Hutterite movement individuals imprisoned for their beliefs used singing as a means of conversion by giving personal testimony, while during the colonial period in South America, various Catholic missionaries reworked traditional folk dances, folk dramas, and processions from Africa in such a way as to facilitate proselytization among the local indians.[97]

Trying to understand religious conversion from a psychological point of view is a distinct contribution to contemporary scholarship. Evelyn Underhill suggests that the best way of describing religious conversion is as a gradual and complete change in the equilibrium of the self.[98] The terminology of psychology provides us with an added dimension for our understanding of the process. Johnson and Malony suggest that the behavioral scientists can provide helpful insight through the use of psychological modeling developed from the psychosocial and psychodynamic perspectives. They suggest that a psychological model of religious conversion has "heuristic value." The symbols it evokes are helpful in understanding the dynamic. Culture and conflict are key ideas. The periods of movement involving growing awareness, consideration, and incorporation seem to be generalities observed by behavioral scientists which inform our understanding. "A convert is therefore defined not so much as someone who has crossed a boundary but

---

95. A. J. Krailsheimer, *Conversion* (London: SCM Press, 1980), p. 154.

96. Starbuck, *The Psychology of Religion,* p. 164.

97. Merrill Singer, "The Use of Folklore in Religious Conversion: The Chassidic Case," *Review of Religious Research* 22:2 (1980), p. 170.

98. Evelyn Underhill, *Mysticism* (New York: Dutton, 1961), pp. 176-177.

as one who is moving toward a center, Jesus Christ."[99]

Psychology provides insight into the change from various perspectives. Johnson and Malony evaluate psychology's contribution to this discussion correctly when they add that,

> The *responding person* is described in the biblical terms of repentance and faith. These are behaviors that can be observed by the social scientist. God may have caused the person to change his/her mind and have faith but he accomplishes this by touching the whole person—body, emotions, mind, etc.—in a defined cultural context.
> The *thinking person* responds to the divine call. Cognitive processes are evident as the person has a change of mind toward God, self, and sin. The psychologist can carefully observe and evaluate these cognitions.
> The *feeling person* is observed in response to the divine call. Repentance sometimes involves strong feelings of grief and conflict. The feeling may come during a crisis of identity in adolescence. The question of the adolescent "Who am I?" may find resolution in the assurance "I am a significant child of God" that can come with conversion. The identity crisis and conversion experience are two different actors on the same stage of the person's salvation. Each has its own part, but both relate to the same story—conversion.[100]

In addition to this, it would seem that an outline could be made illustrating the dynamics involved in religious conversion, as well as the contributory contexts of the experience, and triggers to or prestates of the experience itself. Chart 4 is a compilation of this sort. The parts contribute to the whole of the conversion experience. It should be noted that the illustration is not intended to be complete, nor does it show relational factors in any proportional way. Rather, it is used to illustrate the various factors in the conversion process attested to in this chapter, and it can be used as a guide to the totality of the experience. The fabric of religious conversion is knitted to these elements, and the organization of the circles shows the fact that each element is somehow related. None can be seen in isolation; the whole is significant. Just as the emotional context of the religious conversion may be affected by the developmental context, so can the experiential feel be attributed to the social and/or psychological context. The relationship is one of intermixture, and the elements must be seen in their totality, isolated only as one particular conversion is examined. If, for example, the ideological orientation of the convert is to a particular understanding of God, it must be seen in the context of the group or developmental stage of the person in order for it to be properly understood, or if the conversion seems to be cognitive in nature the substantive preconditions or situations might inform its cause.

The various factors that institute a change may be organized, empha-

---

99. Johnson and Malony, *Christian Conversion,* p. 174.
100. Ibid., pp. 169, 170.

Chart 4: The Context of Conversion

The following illustrates the interrelationships of the various contexts which form the fabric of conversion experience.

sized, and even suggested, but the process of the change itself seems to be beyond any type of manipulation and control. Psychological attempts at controlling the process do not seem to be significant in themselves; rather the conditions are what are controlled. Change occurs from within.

It would appear that the process of religious conversion is a movement toward wholeness and integration and includes a decision to deal with the onrushing realities of living. These realities may be ideological, theological, social, or developmental, but they are perceived as real and needing resolution. They come at once through a process of disorientation and through an "experience of gathering together the fragments of the exploded past."[101] One senses forgiveness and mercy which has its source in something else, some *Other* who is not oneself. The convert feels grasped by God. Resolution often occurs.

The fact that integration occurs around a core event, an event that gives meaning to the future as well as to the past and present, is important. It becomes a new way of looking at oneself and at life, and the crisis aids in this integration and direction. The decision gives direction, usually in a theological sense. Its content is usually that of Christian tradition. What is it that makes a conversion religious? What becomes significant is the focus of what the convert is converted to.[102] The return to God is at the core. Often the sense of God's presence is the feeling. In this sense, religious conversion is in its deepest sense a decision involving the appropriation of an "Other," the Christ figure. In Christian tradition conversion marks the beginning of the process of living the Christian life, however perceived, and because decision is an act which occurs in a period of time, it seems sudden, yet as shown may be incubated through conscious or unconscious elements. And as mentioned, in times of crisis persons make major decisions, if only because of the nature of crisis itself. For it is in these times that fate, as it were, is hanging on the line. "Crisis periods have therefore creative possibilities," suggests Boisen. They are periods of change, and they make or break a person.[103] They are crisis periods in a positive sense, a chance for change. This process of change has both personal and social dimensions.

There are biblical examples of how individuals changed and immediately set out doing "good" works. Mary at Bethany and Zacchaeus are prime examples of persons who faced the potential to grow and decided to be different personally as well as active socially. Institution-centered conversion or book-centered change which stresses "truth" to the exclusion of social consciousness falls short of locating the experience of change in the ministry of Christ. Some have argued for a rebirth of incarnate theology which impacted history and still impacts culture today. In conversion we are called to have a "saving faith in the incarnate Christ who came into our world to die for our sins and to show us how to live."[104] The movement toward God in religious conversion involves the whole person. Psychologically speaking, it is integrative for it provides a new mind set (*metanoia*). Our basic loyalty is transferred from ourselves to God, and the ego is stripped of those things that support it and finds completion in God.

Another context of religious conversion is this concern with "I." The ego concerns of conversion are significant. The life centers on such topics as

---

101. Happel and Walter, *Conversion and Discipleship*, p. 9.

102. See O'Rourke, *A Process Called Conversion*, p. 38.

103. Anton Boisen, *Religion in Crisis and Custom: A Sociobiological and Psychological Study* (New York: Harper & Brothers Publishers, 1945), pp. 68-69.

104. John F. Havlik, "Trends and Issues in Evangelism Today," *Faith and Mission* 2:2 (1986), p. 10.

existence, values, traditions, right and wrong, sin, life itself, culture, meaning, and direction—problems whose resolution seems momentous for the person. The direction and result of the experience is centered in a new identity, the identity of a group, person, tradition, ideology, or movement. In any case, however, conversion may mark a shift in social identity and can even invite new views of community as well as perform a shift on the convert's personal life.[105] It provides a place where one fits as well as an ego identity.

The positive results of conversion (those inner-experienced), such as security, happiness, resolve, and direction, to say nothing of the observed completeness expressed by converts, seem to indicate the uniting effect of religious conversion. The sense of unity is due to the emotions of these experiences themselves, as well as to the new unity of ideology that accompanies the decision. The content in the ideology may not necessarily be complete, only fragmented in the beginning, but conversion's advance toward completion involves ideological frameworks which are a move toward unification.

Before a more detailed analysis of the relationship with identity it is necessary to move from religious conversion into the equally fascinating experience labeled "identity." At this point the reader needs to be reminded of the aims of this book. We wish not only to see the function of the conversion experience, and to understand its myriad definitions, but also to see what relationship this has with identity formation and crisis. How are the experiences alike?

Those factors that have a relationship with identity have been stressed; the functional elements as well as some causal contexts have been suggested. Further development of this relationship must await proper understanding of the identity experiences. Nevertheless, at this point it seems reasonable to insist that this profound change called religious conversion is a realignment of interests and attitudes containing beliefs, commitments, values, and that it results in changed behavior. The process is never complete, for people are always in movement, yet it brings an intense change affecting us where we are most affected, at the center of our being, at the core of our lives, at humankind's center.

We leave religious conversion then for the time being, only to return in summary as relationships are drawn.

---

105. From Josiah Royce, "The Problem of Christianity," Vol. 1, *The Moral Burden of the Individual* (Chicago: Regnery, 1968), pp. 109-159, quoted in Paula Cooey, "The Power of Transformation and the Transformation of Power," *Journal of Feminist Studies in Religion,* 1 (1985), pp. 26, 27.

Chapter 6

Identity: The Way to Become

"I walked out to the hill just now. It is exalting, delicious, to stand embraced by the shadows of a friendly tree with the wind tugging at your coat tail and the heavens hailing your heart, to gaze and glory and give oneself again to God—what more could a man ask? Oh, the fullness, pleasure, sheer excitement of knowing God on earth! I care not if I never raise my voice again for him, if only I may love him, please him. Mayhap in mercy he will give me a host of children that I may lead them through the vast star fields to explore his delicacies whose finger ends set them to burning. But if not, if only I may see him, touch his garments, and smile into his eyes—ah then, not stars nor children shall matter, only himself."

Elisabeth Elliot

Throughout history people have asked some form of the following questions: "Who am I?" "Where do I belong?" and "How do I fit?" Times when these questions rise to the top include moments of swift change, social dislocation, or cultural upheaval. These periods of change are present as periods of "dissolution or of new birth according to the particular view of individual values and historical sequences from which they are interpreted."[1] And in history such periods have come at regular intervals. The Middle Ages was a time of childish prepossession. The Renaissance, on the other hand, opened the door for individuality and freedom. Others would single out different periods in the history of the Western world as special times of heightened awareness of individual personal identity. Individuals such as Rousseau, Plotinus, St. Augustine, or Erasmus all hinted at the importance

---

1. Helen M. Lynd, *On Shame and the Search for Identity* (New York: Harcourt, Brace, 1958), p. 13.

of individuality and identity. Discussions about personal identity are not new. The search for identity and change has been so important that it is possible for Erik Erikson to say that the search for identity has become as strategic in our time as the study of sexuality was in Freud's time. "The patient [or person] of today suffers most under the problem of what he should believe in and who he should—or, indeed, might—be or become; while the patient of early psychoanalysis suffered most under inhibitions which prevented him from being what and who he thought he knew he was."[2]

How one answers the questions of personal identity may have more to do with how well one understands the society, culture, and perception of the world in which one lives. The period of today's culture finds this topic especially interesting. It is a time of lawlessness, self-absorption, careful positioning. Some have called it a time of loss of nerve, and age of conformity, a period of cultural chaos, or escape from personal responsibility—although the problem of AIDS and personal financial freedom may be changing that. The liberalism of the 1960s and 1970s has been replaced with a new conservatism and people are again beginning to be labeled as alien, isolated, alone, and depersonalized. All these social pressures blend together to bring the issues of identity to the front. New identities are emerging such as African-American, Latino or Hispanic.

Social science suggests a term which has relevance to those interested in the religious realm. The concept "identity" has been broadly understood. It has been used so much in the past decade it is in new need of refinement. Americans, Afro-Americans, the clergy—yes, even the telephone company— can have an identity crisis. According to a most eloquent spokesman for this concept, Erik Erikson, so can Martin Luther or Gandhi.

We have seen the varied use of this return to God—conversion. We have seen the interaction of its psychosocial elements. Key to this understanding is the self-integration of the conversion experience itself. The by-product of the experience, this response-by-return to God is the knowledge, even self-authenticating knowledge of belonging again to the kingdom of God.

> Praise be to the God and Father of our Lord Jesus Christ who has bestowed on us in Christ every spiritual blessing in the heavenly realms. In Christ he chose us before the world was founded, to be dedicated, to be without blemish in his sight, to be full of love; and he destined us—such as his will and pleasure—to be accepted as his sons through Jesus Christ, in order that the glory of his gracious gift, so graciously bestowed on us and his Beloved, might resound to his praise.[3]

This positive concept of fitting and finding a place among the family of God and in the world, this commitment and resolution of personal conflict in

---

2. Erik H. Erikson, *Childhood and Society* (New York: Norton, 1950), pp. 242, 239.

3. Ephesians 1:3-6, *New English Bible*.

returning to God in conversion, this becoming one of God's own children finds a close friend in the psychosocial phenomenon of personal identity.

The problem is that the term "identity" has many meanings and just as many theories from which concepts of identity are derived. David De LeVita suggests that "conceptual meanings that are valid only at a certain level of complexity may be used erroneously on other levels."[4] Since a concept like identity touches so many fields of study, clarity in definition is helpful, even though apparently difficult. Identity is often presented as a conceptual framework that links the individual and his or her culture closely together.

Sorting out the various definitions of identity and then using their essence or commonalties for extrapolation to the religious conversion experience is difficult, since our concern is more about the experience of personal identity than theories of identity. Only brief treatment of identity theory is necessary. Among the many ideas extant for discussion regarding personal identity are these: the ability to know and experience oneself as having continuity (Eissler); the apparent satisfaction one finds in achieving and playing a role (McCall and Simmons); the idea of separateness from life (Kramer); the interaction of one's view of himself or herself with that of the perception of others (Greenacre); a deep belief in how one fits in the scheme of life (Wheelis); knowledge and experience of an almost mystic true self (Kramer and Wheelis); and shame and anxiety as causes of the experience (Lynd). There are others who use personal identity to simply mean the role one plays (Strauss). Identity can as well be represented by more than seventeen different connotations or focal points.[5]

Writing from an entirely different background than many of those mentioned, Erik Erikson gives us a most detailed framework for identity formation. Although he deals with conversion and its relationship with identity only briefly in his books *Young Man Luther* and *Gandhi's Truth,* his concepts allow for extrapolation to the conversion experience itself.[6] One aim of this book is to do just such a relational observation, and Erik Erikson is a model representative of identity theory.

Personal Identity

An understanding of the term "identity" must be specifically established. Thus far the term "identity" has meant, in a commonsense way, "knowing where one fits." This definition is not so specific as it could be. It does,

4. David J. De LeVita, *The Concept of Identity* (Paris: Mouton & Co., 1965), p.3.

5. A. M. Becker, *"Kindheit, Gesellschaft and Inclantitat," Psyche* 11 (1956), p. 536, or see De LeVita's introduction to identity formation in his book listed above.

6. Personal letter from Erik Erikson, Stockbridge, Massachusetts, October 26, 1972.

however, emphasize the experience of personal identity. This experience may be both instantaneous or gradual, moving through the life cycle, or occurring at a moment. As social psychologists use the term "identity," you sense an organizing concept which is ambiguous, diffuse, and almost as elusive as personal identity itself.[7] For the social psychologists, identity is seen usually as a product of interaction with others in social settings.When we move into its literal derivative sense we move out of the realm of a concept in consciousness to its usage in math, logic, and philosophy.

Looking at the history of this term, as does De LeVita, we see its roots in logic as a controversial paradox. Our interest is in its relationship to people. We are interested not in logic's relationship, but "namely the identity of the human personality, this being the history of the concept of person itself."[8] This personal concept has Old Testament roots. The biblical identity question relates to whom people belong. Exodus 34:33-34 notes that Moses put a veil over his face, a mask, so to speak, when communicating with the people, but when in contact with God, he took the mask off.[9] What is implied is the direct confrontation with the Creator God; all false roles and non-me identities must be shunned and released. It is here we have a unique touchstone with conversion experience. In relationship with God, all false identities are gone. With God, people see themselves in a different way. Real-knowing-who-I-am identity is demanded for change to take place. To build new roles, one must be free of false gods and false roles. In God, or "in Christ" in the Christian tradition or Pauline sense, we find the real knowing-who-I-am-me. The New Testament has numerous illusions to this concept of belonging.

Understanding identity takes us from the science of logic and math through Lock to Hume. But it is interesting to note that a shift takes place during these times, a shift from its roots in the concepts of epistemology ("How do I know that a frog is the same as a tadpole in essence and not form, and therefore has a common identity?") to a more psychological concept, a consciousness approach with psychological, with even metaphysical, overtones. For example, ("I know I have a common Jewishness that transcends my time and space and role in life"—a personal identity, an idea of consciousness and continuity and fit and belonging.) For some, William James is seen as the progenitor of this latter understanding.

James saw the concept of identity helpful in determining his definition. First, he uses that concept of identity which is laid down in the proof of who we are. The substantialist view includes such things which are determinators of our personal identity: name, profession, physical attributes. Second, James

7. Anselm L. Strauss, *Mirrors & Masks: The Search for Identity* (Glencoe, Ill.: Free Press, 1959), p. 9.

8. De LeVita, *Concept of Identity,* p. 13.

9. Ibid., p. 14.

would reason out one's identity by association. "I call the same things mine because they arouse the same feelings in me." This sense of one's things arousing in us a sense of possession not found in things which are not ours locates personal identity in the conscious sensation, almost physical sensation of owning something. James's third sense is purely transcendental. If you want something to possess identity, James would suggest, it possesses *a priori* by the ego.[10] Those three relationships are unique to James: transcendental, associational, and substantial.

Erik Erikson added to this a psychosocial quality in identity's development. For Erikson, the term "identity" finds its roots in Freud. The term itself cannot be primarily attributed to Freud, however. Since Erikson claims a rich relationship with many of Freud's teachings, it does not seem inappropriate that Erikson's usage is clouded with Freudian overtones. When referring to his link with the Jewish people, Freud referred to an "identity" that aimed attention at the rich blending of values and culture which were his heritage.[11] Erikson is quick to pick up on this concept, uniting something in the core of the person with something that is central to the cohesion of the group. He suggests,

> The young individual must learn to be most himself where he means most to others—through others, to be sure, who have come to mean most to him. The term expresses such a mutual relation in that it connotes both a persistent sameness within oneself (self-sameness) and in a persistent sharing of some kind of central character with others.[12]

Erikson has a unique way of looking at personal identity. 1) When Erikson talks of identity, he stresses the psychosocial forces extant in personal development which recognize the importance of society and culture on personality formation. 2) A second important aspect of identity is that person himself or herself. Thus, Erikson stresses ego function in identity. 3) He mentions the series of conflicts that confront an individual as he or she copes with prescribed tasks in society. These conflicts occur in time and age, and are resolved in the person. Therefore, to understand identity one must take into account 4) the mutual interaction between the individuals and the society in which they finds themselves.[13] These four aspects are significant to Erikson's theory. There is then, this dual nature for identity. He defines it as a maintenance of self-continuity and at the same time an identification with something beyond oneself to acquire the essential characteristics of the

---

10. Ibid., pp. 32-40.
11. Erik Erikson, "Identity and the Life Cycle," *Psychological Issues* 1:1 (New York: International Universities Press, 1959), pp. 101-102.
12. Ibid.
13. Mary Howard Dignam, "Ego Identity of the Modern Religious Woman," *Journal of Religion & Health* 6:2 (April 1967), p. 107.

group to which one belongs. To see personal identity in relationship to religious conversion moves the concern for change into the entire life cycle.[14] This is perhaps the most important contribution of the developmentalists. As we move personally forward, we move religiously forward, too.

Erikson, in illustrating identity, builds on William James as an example. "A man's character is discernable in the mental or moral attitude in which, when it came upon him, he felt himself most deeply and intensively active and alive. At such moments there is a voice inside which speaks and says, 'this is the real me.' "[15] Erikson suggests that James uses "character" to describe "identity." Identity, for Erikson, however, must be prefaced with the term "a sense of" for this better describes the feeling tones of the experience itself. In defining identity, we are dealing with a process at work within humans, a process located "at the core" of the individual, and yet also "at the core" of human culture, a process which establishes, in fact, the identity of those two identities.[16]

Identity is therefore usually coupled with the noun "formation" which stresses the processional aspect of it. The formation of identity employs a process of reflection and observation that takes place at all levels of mental functioning "by which the individual judges himself in the light of what he perceives to be the way in which others judge him in comparison to themselves and to a typology significant to them; while he judges their way of judging him in the light of how he perceives himself in comparison to them and to types that have become relevant to him."[17] Erikson claims that this process is for the most part unconscious except where inner conditions and outer circumstances combine to aggravate a painful or elated identity consciousness.

Moving beyond this dual quality of identity, Erikson tries not to define identity too narrowly and sees various connotations for the term itself. There is a conscious sense of individual identity, of striving for some kind of continuity within the personal being. Identity also provides a criteria for the "silent doings of ego-syntheses" and proves a means to provide inner solidarity within a group's ideals and larger identity. Erikson admits that these connotations may be ambiguous to some, but he insists that they do help to circumscribe the problem of identity.[18]

Erikson stresses the dynamic process which is identity. For example, it is not the maintenance of a system individuals have ordered within themselves,

---

14. Mary C. Boys, "Conversion as a Foundation of Christian Education," *Religious Education* 77 (March-April 1982), p. 216.

15. Erik H. Erikson, *Identity: Youth and Crises* (New York: Norton, 1968), pp. 19-20.

16. Ibid., p. 22.

17. Ibid.

18. Erikson, "Identity and the Life Cycle," p. 102.

rather, identity makes possible the maintenance of certain essential features of persons, as well as their society, because the ego is responsible for the continuity of self that began in infancy and remains open to current identification and role change through life. Erikson calls this continuity, this drive for sameness, this congruity at the core of person, ego identity. The identity takes on the nature of a governor for change and is implicit within forces of change for the person.

This sense of personal sameness is what K. R. Eissler developed in his contribution to identity understanding. He suggested that the "self" is an independent structure inside personality. Since not all areas of one's self are accessible for investigation, the assumption seems logical.

Identity, then, becomes the feelings of experiencing one's self as a continuum. While Rapaport and Jacobson argued against Eissler's concept when first proposed, Eissler's concept of a sense of knowing when one is right with one's self and a continuous, real self transcending one's personality carries on James' and Erikson's consciousness approach.[19] At the same time, identity takes on a sense of continuity and integration. We see identity being defined as a sense which involves some relationship with others and personal perception of one's place alongside others and their action with others.[20] While agreeing with this, Soddy adds that identity always has an anchorage in a social matrix.[21] Even Berger and Luckmann see the dialectic between people and their world bringing out one's identity. They occasionally slip into this consciousness concept, seeing personal identity anchored "in a cosmic reality protected from both the contingencies of socialization and the malevolent self-transformation of marginal experiences."[22] It is to some major proponents of persona identity in this latter sense that we now turn.

Hans Mol in his book *Identity and the Sacred* explores the relationship of identity to religion. In defining the term, he considers the various foci of identity. Mol would place identity in a continuum with personal identity on the left, moving to group identity mid-stream, while social identity represents the far right, criticizing any approach which defines identity by excluding the interaction of group and social identity with one's own personal identity. He suggests:

> Personal and social identity very much depend on one another, but there are also numerous possibilities for conflict between the two. Even so, conflict is only one of the many reasons for the fragility of the frame of identity. Death, diffidence, conquest, economic disasters, injustice, and, in modern societies, an excessive emphasis on instrumental values, relativization and over-choice of

19. De LeVita, *Concept of Identity,* p. 105.
20. Ibid., p. 108.
21. Hans J. Mol, *Identity and the Sacred* (New York: Free Press, 1976), p. 59.
22. See Thomas Luckmann, *The Invisible Religion* (New York: Macmillan, 1967), pp. 77-106.

identity foci are some of these reasons.[23]

It is personal identity which most closely correlates with the self-integration of religious conversion or return. Mol, however, who seems to see the whole continuum of identity related in forming one's real identity, would use "boundaries" to define the factors influencing identity and giving it meaning. Identity, on the personal level, becomes that "stable niche" we find ourselves in amid the chaos of a world and an environment. That stable nature of this niche (identity) is what we must defend. As the boundaries deteriorate, so does the definition for personal identity. Similarly, on the social level, "a stable aggregate of basic and commonly held beliefs, patterns, and values maintains itself over against the potential threat of its environment and its member."[24] And identity is again defined by its expected limits out of which sameness and continuity is destroyed. This emphasis on personal identity, with focus on clearly defined, expected boundaries, gives insight into the nature of the religious expectations placed by one's life or community.

Mol's insistence to move beyond clearly defined expectations and roles, which are the product of social expectations, to a more stable, conscious level moves us to believe that identity is more enduring than a galaxy of roles and phases of maturity.[25]

Theologians have long argued that in the religious realm return to God has personal value. When one comes back to God, life is revitalized, reformed, and new purpose and direction often become appropriate responses to this new birth. Religious people who feel alienation or rejection find acceptance through an understanding of the love of God. They move out of boredom to celebration or, in contemporary theology, from oppression to liberation. On the personal level the person who was a nobody becomes a somebody, and life lived alone in solitary reflection becomes involved and interactive with community through the presence of Jesus Christ and is experienced personally through the Spirit of God. The gospel addresses each of these issues in a complete way.

Identity, then, means selfhood, "anchored in a transcendent order symbolized in concepts and myths: less self-conscious than take-for-granted."[26] This stable niche in the whole interchanging complex of interaction is the feeling of identity. Its theological counterpart, religious conversion, provides answers to the same existential concerns. One problem with Mol's understanding of identity is that when we blend the identity experience with the religious experience of identity, namely conversion, as we have seen, we find that religion, and specifically the experience of conversion, does exactly what

23. Mol, *Identity and the Sacred,* p. 65.
24. Ibid.
25. Ibid., pp. 59-60.
26. Ibid.

Mol's understanding of identity does. Conversion is a major source of stability and strength and possesses roles and social mores which provide one's identity itself. His definition as that "stable niche" leads us nicely into seeing conversion as a major identity-forming experience, which is one by-product of religious commitment. Mol, as does De LeVita, likes more sympathy for those who think of identity as "the most essential nucleus of man which becomes visible only after all his roles have been laid aside."[27] It is in this light that Mol can assume that identity defines what a person, group, or society really is. He contrasts this objective designation with morality, which emphasizes more what a group or person does than what a group or person really is. Identity, then, is that which gives meaning to existence and that experience which interprets life.

Mol emphasizes the unique fabric of meaning of identity. Identity transcends, in an almost *superadditum* way, and becomes that which gives a person, society, or group its own unique wholeness; yet groups and societies, yes, even religion, attempt through manipulation and suggestion, coercion and explanation of "truth" to form and pattern and locate individuals' identities. It is in this subtle interplay between the patterning of something in religion and the ability of individuals to perceive personal identity, that identity really emerges, and, as Mol suggests, the individual is often the enemy in this process because he senses a uniqueness and a wholeness which he sees in himself beyond the patterning which is given him in the society, group, or even himself.[28]

Identity: Coherent Sense of Self

Allen Wheelis depends upon phenomenal self-theory and sees identity as a coherent sense of self. He suggests that the sense of self is deficient now. Adolescents' quest for answers to the probing question of "Who am I?" and "Where am I going?" gets no sufficient answers any longer. Finding the coherence within oneself is a challenge facing us all. For Wheelis, the group provides the stability in this world of shifting patterns.[29] Coming from a psychoanalytical background or, as he claims, "from behind the couch," he sees personal identity in a slightly different context from Mol. Personal identity for Wheelis is "dependent upon the awareness that one's endeavors and one's life make sense, that they are meaningful in the context in which life is lived."[30] Personal identity for Wheelis relies on some type of stable value system which is consummate with the conviction that one's values and actions are harmoniously related. Coupled, then, with the sense of wholeness

---

27. Ibid., pp. 143, 144.
28. Ibid.
29. Allen Wheelis, *The Quest for Identity* (New York: Norton, 1958), p. 18.
30. Ibid., p. 19.

and continuity that a value system provides is the fact that with a value system one knows how to choose and then how to act. In interactions with others, in the absence of dissonance between belief and practice, one's personal identity then becomes a creation out of living in congruity with one's values, values which are given and lived by one's own groups. For Wheelis, identity is linked correctly with values. It is found specifically "on those values which are at the top of the hierarchy—the beliefs, faiths, and ideals which integrate and determine subordinate values."[31]

Personality for Wheelis is seen growing and reshaping with each new value and action. Personal identity in this sense is not finding something that had been lost. Personal identity and its sense of presence in the life is created and achieved in this value matrix. "Values determine goals, and goals define identity," claims Wheelis.[32] If this is the case, as Wheelis suggests, then return in conversion to God and the ideological value framework which religion provides becomes an identity function for the emerging self, since Wheelis sees personal identity as being formed socially through instrumentalities which have continuity.

Wheelis quickly cautions us, however, about his views for fear that we overstate religion's function as putting excess emphasis on values in identity formation. He suggests that we may be guilty here of mixing levels of theories and generalizations, rather than looking specifically at structure or existence.[33]

A firm sense of personal identity provides in a most poetic way both "a compass to determine one's course in life and ballast to keep one steady. So equipped and provisioned, one can safely ignore much of the buffeting. Without such protection more vigilance is needed; each vicissitude, inner and outer, must be defined and watched."[34] Return to God in this deep sense of commitment, which religious conversion provides, finds close anchorage in Wheelis's theory.

Identity: The Mirrors of Others

Personal identity is approached by Anselm Strauss as deriving from "judgments of others, and a particular brand of mask or identity is fashioned by an anticipation of these judgments."[35] This position, which stresses the relationship of identity to one's role with others has been seen as a fundamental context for this experience. Others holding this position include Mol, McCall,

---

31. Ibid., p. 200.
32. Ibid.
33. Allen Wheelis, "Psychoanalysis and Identity," *Psychoanalysis and the Psychoanalytic Review* 46 (1959), p. 71.
34. Wheelis, *Quest for Identity,* pp. 21, 22.
35. Mol, *Identity and the Sacred,* p. 58.

Simmons, as well as Greenacre.

Through the evaluations, appraisals, and judgments of others, and by our own judging of ourselves, we mirror the identity expected. Often the role of others is seen as an important factor in becoming what we perceive ourselves to be. Ministers in training during their first parish experience often find their identity totally determined by their expectations and the role models given by the members. The pastor arrives, little expecting to be what others think he or she is, but as the demand comes to be the interior decorator, financial wizard, parish priest, father, mother, prophet, and king, his or her once weak *persona* becomes strong. Implicit roles defined by his or her parish begin to be incorporated into his or her life. The incompetent pastor, now believing that he or she is an authority in the church in areas such as decorating and finance, almost ignores the doctrine of the priesthood of all believers. Later in his or her ministry, these roles, having been reinforced down through the years, show their impact on the pastor's own personal identity.[36]

Strauss suggests that "the masks he then and thereafter presents to the world and its citizens are fashioned upon his anticipation of their judgments. The others present themselves, too; they wear their own brands of masks, and they are appraised in turn. It is all a little like the experience of a small boy first seeing himself at rest and posing in the multiple mirrors of the barber shop."[37]

Religion could play a major role in establishing personal identity, then, especially organized and rigidly structured institutionalizations of religion. A religious sect proposes what will happen as you encounter another in a religious interchange. If it happens, the religious forecasting is validated and the learner has mastered the prescribed steps. His or her identity within the group is already ordered by the group's identity validation or as Strauss says: "Kneel, knight, and receive knighthood." These graduation points, these turning points in one's growth within an institutional program help to establish identity.

With this instrumental function, personal identity is related to the place of group think and group expectations. Certainly others help shape one's vision of personal identity, but identity is the basic sense of congruity rather than mimicking. For Strauss, then, fantasy and daydream become important functions in personal identity formation. Through them you must guess what might happen in the interchange and what the expectations of others might be. One must evaluate the important encounters which have high risk for change. They may even be rehearsed ahead of time, Strauss would suggest.

36. See Lynn Mallery, "Changing Roles of Laity and Ministry," paper presented at the West Coast Religion Teachers' Conference, Walla Walla, Washington, April, 1978.
37. Anselm Strauss quoted in De LeVita, *Concept of Identity,* p. 96.

It is much like a movie director rehearsing a scene.[38]

Change happens when the risk is minimized. Included in relational identity formation for Strauss is a sense in which personal identity is the congruity and continuum of one's nature itself. In clarifying this concept, Strauss uses an amusing illustration.

> We have before us an uncooked egg. We may choose to boil, scramble, or poach it, or make it into a dozen different kinds of omelets. Regardless of the treatment this egg receives, it remains an egg. Some people like their eggs hard, some soft, and some very finicky eaters draw fewer specifications. To the extent that any claim is made that "This egg is not cooked," all this can mean is that in more or less degree the egg is finished. Up to the point it becomes converted into charcoal and is really finished, the cooking of the egg changes in appearance, it is still essentially an egg.[39]

This quality of eggness Strauss would perhaps call ego identity, rather than personal identity, for identity comes basically in the fateful appraisals of others by ourselves.

Other contributors to identity theory add little beyond those already mentioned, save Erikson whose formation theories will be explicated in detail next. De LeVita focuses on the "formants" of personal identity, namely the body, name, and life history, all of which come together to provide one's real self. Yet these approaches provide little additional information to the concept of personal identity other than attempting to explain its philosophical nature.

Modern Views of Identity

Where do individuals living in a contemporary society go to find a satisfactory view of personal identity? Modern individualism has suggested that that answer be found within. Evolutionary theory is deterministic, and the view of humanness which comes out of this perspective is equally self-centered. Determinism suggests that people are subject to the environment and that present and future life are determined by forces beyond control. Human identity is largely seen in terms of the biological, chemical, psychological, environmental, and cultural forces converging on life, forming character and personal viewpoints. Early Marxist philosophy hinted at the alienation of humankind—this alienation was from all of life and especially from the capitalistic industrial system.[40]

Existentialists, on the other hand, provide a different insight into personal identity. We are what we conceive ourselves to be argues Jean-Paul Sartre.

---

38. Strauss, *Mirrors and Masks: The Search for Identity,* p. 66.

39. Ibid., pp. 90, 91.

40. See Erik Fromm, *Marx's Concept of Man* (Frederick Ungar, 1961), pp. 103. 104.

"Man is nothing else but what he makes of himself."[41] This self-oriented, almost selfish approach provided grist for the development of individualism and atheistic self-understanding.

James Davis studied college students who held a self-centered philosophy and concluded that a student typically has "no master plan for his existential quest; he just blunders through, learning to cope by gathering up aphoristic bits and pieces of meaning wherever he can find them."[42] Religion, on the other hand, has always protested those philosophies which focus too much on self. Christians believe that there are answers to the question of identity and meaning through authoritative sources, deep introspection, and new relationships. The Bible, the Old and New Testament, seems to address the human condition and alienation which secular philosophy promoted in a direct and concrete way. It is through relationship with God that real self-understanding comes, and scripture provides the outline and answer. It is through understanding God's will that one gains direction and purpose, and it is through knowing God that the void is filled and mission and action are demanded. Identity in the religious realm is closely related to knowing and finding God. That is why religious conversion and identity have so much in common.

Identity: The Cycle of Life

Probably the greatest contributor to the theory of identity formation is Erik Erikson. His work, already briefly cited, moves personal identity from just a discussion of one's authentic self or the importance of others or roles in identifying one's personal identity to an analysis of the actual formation of the sense of identity. His life-cycle concerns relate so directly to our discussion of religious conversion and the change it brings that more detailed exposition is warranted before we can discuss the relationships of how religious conversion and identity theory interact with religion and theology and biblical concepts of personhood.

Erikson links the identity crisis of youth with specific events in psychosocial history. He does, however, make a unique distinction in definition. Personal identity and ego identity are separated and are often found attached to the term "identity." I find Erikson using these terms rather loosely, which I believe is surely logical, for he is defining a process rather than an object. He usually is referring to the term "ego identity" when he speaks about identity. Personal identity involves the simultaneous perception of

---

41. Jean-Paul Sartre, *Existentialism and Human Emotions* (New York: The Wisdom Library, 1957), pp. 15, 22-23.

42. Skip MacCarty, *Who Am I? A Christian Guide to Meaning and Identity* (Washington, D.C.: Review and Herald Publishing Co., 1979), p. 15, originally from *Clergy Talk* (March 1976).

one's self-sameness and continuity, the mere fact of existing, where ego identity refers to the ego quality of this experience.[43] The simplest definition offered by Erikson is that ego identity is an answer to the question "Who am I and where am I going?" Yet the complexity of identity formation requires a larger and more exacting answer. Ego identity for Erikson is "the awareness of the fact that there is a self-sameness and continuity to the ego's synthesizing methods, to the style of one's individuality, and this style coincides with the sameness and continuity of one's meaning for significant other in the immediate community."[44]

Identity is closely tied to an understanding of the stages of people. Erikson sees eight in all. These stages represent crises that each person has in the process of developing an ego identity. But ego identity itself represents the cumulative product of a person's completion of the first five stages of development prior to and including late adolescence. The first four stages, occurring in infancy and childhood, are characterized by a series of conflicts or crises, as Erikson calls them. Identity is the result of the successful resolution of these stages of crises. While Erikson fails to detail conversion experience specifically, one can infer some conclusions regarding its importance and significance in the formation of personal understanding. As a recentering of newness, conversion forces the person to reorganize himself or herself at the deepest level of self-understanding and limits. In the mastery of each stage and with successful resolution of the crisis in each, certain moorings for identity emerge. In summary, the early crises center in infancy, around the development of trust or mistrust; during childhood, the establishment of autonomy versus doubt and shame; during the preschool age, the emergence of initiative or feelings of guilt; later in the school age, the appearance of industry or feelings of inferiority; and finally at adolescence, the struggle between identity and role diffusion becomes central for the person.[45] To denote the area of conflict, the term "crisis" is used by Erikson. For him it is a "moment of decision between strong contending forces."[46] The crisis that may ensue may happen rapidly; various viewpoints and options may become isolated. Thus the phrase "identity crisis" can be defined in Eriksonian language as a moment of decision between forces pulling for a positive identity and forces suggesting a negative identity or identity diffusion.[47] Identity

---

43. Erikson, "Identity and the Life Cycle," pp. 23 ff, and *Identity: Youth and Crises,* p. 174 ff.

44. Erikson, *Identity: Youth and Crises,* p. 50.

45. Dignam, "Ego Identity of the Modern Religious Woman," p. 106.

46. Erik Erikson, "Memorandum on Identity and Negro Youth," *The Journal of Social Issues* 20:4 (1964), p. 31.

47. The terms "negative identity" and "identity diffusion" or confusion will be defined later; until then, it is significant only to understand them as those drives which would inhibit, deter, or misshape the finding of a healthy sense of identity, as far as the person is concerned.

defined as a process finds itself always changing and developing. "At its best it is a process of increasing differentiation, and becomes ever more inclusive as the individual grows aware of a widening circle of others significant to him."[48] It is a process that begins in the first true meeting of the mother and baby as recognition takes place, yet has its normative crisis in adolescence. Identity has its roots in what went before and in many ways is the decisive event which determines what goes on after.

While defining identity, Erikson is careful to keep a close association with the crisis on the individual and the contemporary crisis in historical context. Each crisis helps to define the next; their relationship is one of mutuality. Erikson spends a great deal of time in *Young Man Luther* on just this point.[49]

Erikson, the psychoanalyst, finds himself critical of his own methodology in asserting that one cannot really grasp the term identity within the psychoanalytic method for it has not developed terms to really understand the environment.[50] This phenomenological viewpoint makes Erikson's intermixing of environment and development most significant and his concept of identity so inclusive. His emphasis on the psychosocial nature of identity, his stress on the interpersonal relationships which mark out the self, are equally aspects of it. Erikson calls identity the personality organization framed through the feedback from others.[51]

Note then that the process of identity is dynamic, as its definition is itself. It is not a static maintenance of a system despite strong forces aiding change, the process that makes possible the maintenance of certain essential features of an individual and his society. This continuity of self-representation is ego identity, and its development is neither passive nor static.[52]

Erikson's major contribution is in his epigenetic principle and identity formation. He postulates that every growing animal has a ground plan of organization from which the parts emerge, each part emerging at its time of special ascendancy until a unified whole is produced. Yet in addition to this inner urge for development, there is social growth and familial growth operating. This implies a kind of determinism in that each psychic event is influenced by those which precede it.[53]

Erikson's methodology has been helpful in the construction of the human life cycle. Various factors are being validated on the cycle itself which make his conceptualization more valid. In this book conversion is seen as vali-

---

48. Erikson, *Identity: Youth and Crises*, p. 23.
49. See Erik Erikson, *Young Man Luther* (New York: Norton, 1958), pp. 14-25.
50. Erikson, *Identity: Youth and Crises*, p. 24.
51. Dignam, "Ego Identity of the Modern Religious Woman," p. 109.
52. Ibid., p. 110.
53. Erikson, "Identity and the Life Cycle," p. 52.

dating identity crisis and thus making his scheme in this area acceptable in theory. Erikson is careful not to place absolutes on his diagram of the life cycle of persons. Identity does not have an age, for it is a process, beginning in infancy, finding meaning in adolescence or late adolescence, and striving to be validated in a period of time at the very end of life called "beyond identity." Erikson does not assign ages, as does Piaget, to his cycle, and he is like Ronald Goldman in allowing variations within the cycle. The scheme then is a broad picture of how life is lived, and his observations, even though clinically colored through extremes in observation, nevertheless are enlightening for consideration and investigation even though limited due to some gender bias. Integral to an understanding of identity for Erikson is his delineation of the life cycle, with its significant eight stages of development. Before attention can be specifically drawn to the most crucial stages for this study—that of identity versus identity diffusion—a brief overview of the other stages is in order to fully understand the general outlook. The life cycle has been alluded to as a major premise for Erikson's work.

Basic to the life cycle is the epigenetic principle. This principle suggests that in each living thing there is a pattern which must unfold, the various parts emerging each with a time of special ascendancy, until a functioning whole is formed. Yet the cycle of life is not an isolated entity. Erikson really speaks of two cycles in one—the cycle of one generation concluding itself in the next and the cycle of the individual life coming to its own conclusion. This concept reflects the dual nature of identity as well.[54]

Living together in the cycle of life is more than just a physical proximity. It means that the individual's life states are "interliving," cogwheeling with the stages of other people. The cogwheeling moves people along as they interact with their life stages. Erikson, in speaking of the life cycle, states, "I have, therefore, in recent years attempted to delineate the whole life cycle as an integrated psychosocial phenomenon, instead of following what (in analogy to teleology) may be called the 'originological' approach; that is, the attempt to derive the meaning of development primarily from a reconstruction of the infant's beginnings."[55] This aspect of involving other elements to affect the development of the person in addition to the past growth problems is a significant contribution to developmental approaches.

Erikson suggests that it is well for all to remember this epigenetic principle—anything that grows has a ground plan—and that each item of the vital personality to be analyzed is related to all the other aspects, each depending on the proper development in the proper sequence of each item. Another principle for Erikson is that *each item exists in some form or another* before its time of ascendancy. He illustrates this principle by suggesting that a sense

54. Erik Erikson, *Insight and Responsibility* (New York: Norton, 1964), pp. 132-133.

55. Ibid., p. 114.

of basic trust is the first component of healthy mental vitality, the first virtue to be established in life, and comes in the first crisis. It is the encounter with the stages of Erikson and their resulting crises which are important for healthy identity; a positive or nearly positive solution to them is important for healthy identity to be formed. Each successive step, then, is a potential crisis. (Crisis for Erikson is not a threat of catastrophe, but must be viewed as a turning point, a crucial period "of increased vulnerability and generational strength and maladjustment."[56])

These stages are not the only factors causing conflict in a person, for they must be understood in the context of time and in the framework of the social influences and traditional institutions which determine perspectives on the infantile past and on the adult future.[57] Thus individuals move from one stage to another as soon as they are able, biologically, psychologically, and socially.

Each of the stages of the psychosocial crisis is balanced by alternative attitudes—one positive, the other negative. Erikson uses the world "versus" (vs.) to indicate the person's struggle between the two polarities. When facing one of these crises, humankind is responsible for its resolution. People can go either way, positively or negatively resolving it. If the positive attitudes outweigh the negative ones, the individuals are moving toward a healthy mental viewpoint; yet they may not, and probably will not, solve the crisis totally on the positive side. These crises and their positive resolution should be viewed as the framework for a healthy ego. The healthy ego develops when the crises are settled positively, and an unhealthy ego develops when the crises are settled negatively.

Erikson emphasizes that first each component of the healthy personality is "systematically related to all others," and that they all depend on the "proper development in the proper sequence" of each criterion; and second, that each component "exists in some form before its decisive and critical time" normally comes.[58]

As previously noted, the ego's role in this process is that of regulator and guide. It can give a feeling of sameness in the midst of the crisis and therefore, like identity, find its function as that of assimilator of media, stimuli, and society, much as conversion functions. Erikson's cycle is closely related to the developmental scheme in that he finds within these stages a phase-specific task that must be solved. His theory defends the concept that *the ego is integrally related to the process of identity formation.*

Erikson warns against the misuse of the cyclic theory, cautioning that there are many who would make a sort of lock-step approach to the stages, to check on the maturity of youth and adult. The nature of the cycle approach

56. Erikson, *Identity: Youth and Crises,* pp. 93, 95.
57. Erikson, *Young Man Luther,* p. 20.
58. Erikson, "Identity and the Life Cycle," p. 53.

is one of unfolding and reunfolding, and those who view it rigidly ignore the fact that the ego in the healthy person must continually reconquer negative aspects as they crop up in life.

It is proposed that by understanding the eight stages of persons, one would understand a great deal about life. By understanding the crises they encounter and noticing the successive conflict resolutions, we would learn a great deal about people's later life. Erikson's centering in on the psychosocial development of persons does not exclude his interest in other kinds of development, such as sexual, cognitive, etc. But he points out that the psychosocial development is a process of conflict and crisis resolution where the other forms of development may very well not be.

It would seem, then, that there are four major insights Erikson provides in relationship to religious conversion: 1) The theory of epigenesis of the ego or the gradual opening up of the process of the personality of an individual; 2) a theory of social relationships important to healthy growth, whereby individuals as they develop incorporate the culture and time-space realities to form their own reality and development; 3) a concept of crisis whereby the person systematically reaches resolutions which verify his or her identity and aid the process of identity; and 4) a concept of ego development wherein identity experiences become an integrative force for the totality of the person and are experienced in crisis with resultant effects.

Since identity proceeds in this cycle of life, the first crisis is very important. Identity for Erikson is formed in a resolution of trust versus mistrust. The basic psychological attitude to be learned at this stage is that "you can trust in the world in the form of your mother, that she will come back and feed you, that she will feed you the right thing in the right quantity at the right time, and that when you're uncomfortable she will come and make you comfortable, and so on."[59] By basic trust Erikson means that there is some sort of correspondence between your needs and the world. Yet to learn to mistrust is just as important. There is, for Erikson, a certain ratio of trust and mistrust in our basic social attitude that is critical. When we enter a new situation we not only are able to trust, but we must know how much to mistrust as well.[60]

Erikson postulates some virtues that are evolved through this stage. Since faith finds its origin in relationships and implies trust in another or reliance upon another, faith is related to the development growth of the person. Hope is vital for the survival of a people, for a healthy identity and is a basic human strength without which one could not exist. In humans, hope is established through the lifelong struggle between trusting and mistrusting, and through these crises hope is reaffirmed throughout life. This is important for our understanding of religious development. Faith is irreducibly rela-

59. Richard I. Evans, *Dialogue with Erik Erikson* (New York: Dutton, 1969), p. 15.
60. Mistrust is used in the sense of a readiness for danger and an anticipation of discomfort and must be learned in the context of the culture to which we belong.

tional in origin, according to James Fowler. It is an "active form of knowing and being in which we relate to others, and form communities with whom we share common loyalties to supraordinate centers of value and power. Faith is an active mode of knowing and being in which we grasp our relatedness to others and to our shared causes as all related to and grounded in a relatedness to power(s) and value(s) which unify and give character to an ultimate environment."[61] This relational nature of faith suggests that one's understanding of faith as well as what is needed in religion in regard to change might be nurtured by these crisis moments suggested by Erikson.

Once established through resolution of relational crisis, hope is a basic quality of experience and is evidenced for Erikson in the enduring belief "in the attainability of fervent wishes, in spite of the dark urges and rages which mark the beginning of existence. Hope is the ontogenetic basis of faith and is nourished by the adult faith which pervades patterns of care."[62] It is this quality in identity faith that is directly related to conversion. Conversion itself produces in a very abstract sense the possibility for the Christian to see beyond.

The sense of trust is established more often by the mothering one, and this qualitative maternal relationship forms the basis for the sense of identity which will later combine a sense of being "all right," of being oneself, and of becoming what other people trust one will become. Constructs of God as the "mothering one" are important here in developing clear conceptualizations of God and God-likeness.

A significant suggestion by Erikson is that there are various social institutions that correspond to the stages he postulates. For the first stage, religion is the corresponding institution. It is religion that synthesizes and socializes the deep crises of life. It is conversion which can confront these crises and through return to God resolve them. Mistrust is the source of evil; and religious traditions and rituals provide a collective restitution of basic trust, which in the mature adult becomes a combination of faith and realism.[63] At this early stage of childhood development, the child, having learned to trust his mother and the world to some extent, needs to become self-willed and take chances with the trust learned. The child must see what is and must experiment with personal will against the wills of others to develop in this stage. Autonomy seems to result from the successful resolution of feelings of

61. James W. Fowler, "Faith and the Structuring of Meaning," in *Towards Moral and Religious Maturity,* ed. Christiane Brusselmans, James A. O'Donohoe, James W. Fowler, and Antoine Vergote (Morristown, N.J.: Silver Burdett, 1980), p. 57.

62. Erikson, *Insight and Responsibility,* p. 118.

63. H. R. Bagwell, "Abrupt Religious Conversion Experience," *Journal of Religion and Health* 8 (April 1969), p. 53, quoting Erik Erikson, "Wholeness and Totality: A Psychiatric Contribution," *Totalitarianism,* ed. Carl Friedrich (Proceedings of a conference held at the American Academy of Arts and Sciences, March, 1953) (Cambridge, Mass.: Harvard University Press, 1954), p. 164.

shame and doubt that show up during this age. Erikson illustrates this shame and doubt, "This is the age when the child begins to blush, which is a symptom of knowing one is being watched (from the inside, too), and is found wanting."[64] An individual who has not resolved this conflict and cannot be autonomous will act inferior all of his or her life. A successful resolution of this conflict will give the child a constant positive feeling. There is in each crisis a ration to be found. Neither positive nor negative is eliminated entirely. This stage comes into prominence during the second and third years of life, according to Erikson.[65]

The two organ modes corresponding to the second stage are retention and elimination which begin to function alternately, not only to the sphincters, but also with regard to all functioning aspects of the child. They teach the child the social modalities of "holding on and letting go." Just as sense of trust and mistrust is related to the parental existence of guidance and faith, so is autonomy a mirror of parental dignity. Erikson advises parents with a child in the first stages to be firm, tolerant, and yet gentle, so the child will learn to be the same.[66]

The principle in this stage is law and order. Erikson suggests the young child should be able to reflect on the dignity and the lawful independence of his parents. Parents who are not able to function autonomously because of societal pressures cannot be expected to build autonomy in their children. The virtue or ego strength Erikson attributes to this stage is that of *will*.

> *Will, therefore, is the unbroken determination to exercise choice as well as self-restraint, in spite of the unavoidable experience of shame and doubt in infancy.* Will is the basis for the acceptance of law and necessity, and it is rooted in the judiciousness of parents guided by the spirit of law.[67] (Italics his.)

During this stage the child must yield to the wills of new individuals encountered. The child runs the risk of yielding. Erikson says that it is the task of judicious parents to honor the privileges of those who are strong in will and still to protect the fact that the weak have rights. This stage will gradually grant a measure of self-control to the child who learns to control willfulness.[68]

In the third stage—locomotor-genital—the Oedipal situation is common and the process of identifying with a strong parental figure is accepted. Erikson adds to this concept the idea that the child is now seeing what kind of person he or she may become. The crisis in this stage is brought about by three developments: 1) the child is learning to move freely and violently within the society and has a larger radius of goals presented before him or her;

64. Evans, *Dialogue with Erik Erikson*, p.18.
65. Ibid., p. 20.
66. Erikson, "Identity and the Life Cycle," p. 70.
67. Erikson, *Insight and Responsibility*, p. 119.
68. Ibid., p. 120.

2) the child's cognitive skills are emerging and providing greater language ability and comprehensive scope; and 3) with the first two developments the child has an enlarged imagination and can visualize roles beyond his or her comprehension. Out of this must emerge, according to Erikson, a sense of initiative as a basis for a realistic sense of ambition and purpose.[69] The major organ mode for this stage is classified "intrusive." This includes intrusion by physical attack, aggressive talking, intrusion into the environment by loco-motion, and a never-ending curiosity. The social mode for this stage is that of "being on the make," and includes the joy of competition, goal making, and conquest. The social influences now begin to be a part of the context of growth, and an exemplary basic family is important for the child to suc-cessfully see initiative established. The society provides identity prototypes that take on meaning.

The ego strength which evolves is labeled "purpose." It is the "courage to envisage and pursue valued goals uninhibited by the defeat of infantile fan-tasies, by guilt and by the foiling fear of punishment."[70] It is through the medium of play that the child develops purpose, for infantile play is a trial uni-verse where the past is enacted and projected on a larger and more perfect future stage. This is a time when marriage and family loyalties are important for it is in these that the conscience of the child finds unity and direction.

This stage appears in the fourth and fifth years of development. The child attempts to resolve the conflict of a sense of initiative and of guilt for not being himself or herself. Here is manifested the mode of intrusion and inclusion aided by ideal societal prototypes. Ego strength and a developing sense of pur-pose are most treasured at this stage.

School age provides new tasks with which to identify. A sense of indus-try is contrasted with inferiority. Since the child has previously had time to play, he or she now sees a sense of industry in purposeful responses. The dan-ger of this stage is that the child will develop the "well-known sense of infe-riority."[71] Feelings of inferiority are developed from a sense of being inade-quate because of a lack of technical ability. The child feels useless.

There is no organ mode for this stage or any succeeding stage. Society meets the need for the child to make things by providing some instruction (school) to learn and master the basic skills of technology. Since this stage involves making things, creativity must be stressed, and it is here that Erikson first notes a danger in this stage of identity development.

> If the overly conforming child accepts work as the only criterion of worth-whiliness, sacrificing imagination and playfulness too readily, he may become ready to submit to what Marx called "craftidiocy," i.e., become a slave of his

69. Erikson, *Identity: Youth and Crises,* p. 114.
70. Erikson, *Insight and Responsibility,* p. 122.
71. Erikson, *Identity: Youth and Crises,* p. 124.

technology and its dominant role typology. Here we are already in the midst of identity problems, for with the establishment of a firm initial relationship to the world of skills and tools and to those who teach and share them, and with the advent of puberty, childhood proper comes to an end. . . . School age . . . identity can be expressed in the words "I am what I can learn to make work."[72]

For men this is the end of the identity development. The experience itself provides enough sense of congruity to establish the technocrat in a comfortable identity. The virtue for this stage is that of "competence." This is related to task fulfillment due to certain specific skills. It is the "free exercise of dexterity and intelligence in the completion of tasks, unimpaired by infantile inferiority."[73] This stage, then, emerges in the elementary school years, brings a sense of industry while avoiding a sense of inferiority, manifests the social modality of making things, and is joined by the instruction provided by skilled others to develop competence in the child's ego strength. For women, a distinction Erikson ignores to a large extent, identity is more personal.

The identity stage is one which we must study more closely, for it offers a major contribution to religious conversion's experience.

With the advent of puberty as a context for identity, the struggle between a sense of identity and a sense of identity diffusion seems to develop, only to reach its major crisis in late adolescence. Since Erikson defines identity in terms of ego strength, which is the confidence that one can maintain inner sameness and continuity and is reinforced by the same understanding about oneself by others, identity is a primary task of this age. The opposite of this would be a sense of diffusion, a syndrome which appears when one is unable to maintain the inner sameness, and according to Erikson, especially in accordance with occupational identity. In general it is the inability to settle on an occupational identity that is most troubling to youth. Those who do not find identity tend to find the resolution to the crisis in diffusion or negative identity. This is Erikson's explanation of Luther's refuge in the monastery, for example.[74]

The social institution which Erikson claims is the guardian of identity is ideology. This concept is not just that people will promote what is the best for others. The youth must convince himself or herself that those who succeed in their adult worlds are responsible for promoting what is the best. Erikson suggests that it is through these ideologies that the "fiber of the next generation is found. . . . Adolescence is thus a vital regenerator in the process of social evolution."[75] The social modality for this stage is that of "being oneself, or not being oneself" and of "sharing being oneself." It is seen that

---

72. Ibid., p. 127.
73. Erikson, *Insight and Responsibility,* p. 124.
74. Erikson, *Young Man Luther,* pp. 12-39.
75. Erikson, *Identity: Youth and Crises,* p.134.

identity concern is the chief problem here.[76] It is here that moratorium needs to be provided by society for the youth to reflect without pressure and to feel out ideological, emotional, and identity relating options. The moratorium concept could be a meaningful methodology for the religious educator and perhaps provide for more gradual growth in spiritual things rather than for the acute, crisis-type changes that conversion often exhibits.

The ego strength which emerges with adolescence is fidelity, which is "the ability to sustain loyalties freely pledged in spite of inevitable contradictions of value systems."[77] Fidelity for Erikson is the cornerstone of identity and becomes important through the process of conforming ideologies and affirming companions. Sharon Parks in referring to Erik Erikson's concept of fidelity suggests, "I propose, then, that the threshold of young adulthood is marked by the capacity to take self-aware responsibility for choosing the path of one's own fidelity."[78] Faith then becomes personal for it is no longer the accumulated beliefs of others. She suggests that when the new "self-aware, critical, yet struggling strength does emerge, I am persuaded that it is an adult strength and marks the threshold of adult faith."[79] Identity experience becomes a prerequisite for faith and a necessary ingredient in religious growth.

As identity is formed the person faces its ascendance in the adolescent years and attempts to resolve the conflict between a sense of identity and its concomitant option, identity diffusion. The youth expresses himself/herself socially by either being himself/herself or not being himself/herself, and by sharing this self with others. Ideologies, the perspectives they throw on life, and the settling influence they have on people become important options as a sense of trustworthiness is formed. One wonders if feelings of low self-esteem have any impact on adolescent identity.

One of the most helpful studies in regard to self-esteem is Merton Strommen's revision of the *Five Cries of Youth*. In it he postulates from research data that one youth in five suffers from a cry of self-criticism, loneliness, and worthlessness. There is a vicious circle here. As seen, one's identity is often reflected back in self-concept. As loneliness results in lack of relationships, so self-esteem is reflected back through lack of meaningful relationships. Research supports the fact that one result of low self-regard is loneliness and limited relationships.[80] The church, with its theology of all-inclusive love, acceptance, forgiveness, and fellowship can meet some very specific self-esteem needs in youth. Conversion, that movement which iden-

76. Erikson, "Identity and the Life Cycle," pp. 91-93.

77. Erikson, *Insight and Responsibility*, p. 125.

78. Sharon Parks, *The Critical Years* (San Francisco: Harper & Row, 1986), p. 77.

79. Ibid., p. 78.

80. Merton P. Strommen, *Five Cries of Youth* (New York: Harper & Row, 1988), pp. 16-30.

tifies and personalizes these religious qualities, can become a significant experience to aid in self-criticism and esteem.

After identity's adolescent crisis, Erikson labels the crisis to be resolved as being "beyond identity." With a yet immature sense of identity the young adult now finds a time to fuse his or her identity with others. The conflicts are between intimacy and isolation—the capacity to commit oneself to partnerships and to remain with oneself and alone.[81] This may be especially keen in young women.

The ego strength developed in this stage is that of love which is a "mutuality of devotion forever subduing the antagonisms inherent in divided function."[82] Since this kind of love pervades individuals, it becomes the basis for ethical action. Because this crisis is significant in the forming of intimate ties in an ever-widening social context, others begin to play a significant part. Here identity is reflected in others and their relationships confirm or obscure identity itself.

The persons in the young adult years find themselves attempting to resolve the crisis of intimacy versus isolation, which manifests itself in trying to find themselves in others and in themselves. The traditional social patterns of cooperation and competition aid in the ascendance of this crisis with the hoped-for outcome of love.

Women seem to experience the developing identity differently, however. Carol Gilligan hints that identity may develop after intimacy rather than before. The diverse sexual dissimilarity makes it important. She asks the question, "About whom is Erikson talking?" Her question is important and her answer equally compelling. Erikson's work seems based on the male child. And Erikson only slightly recognizes the differences in male/female development. He suggests that there should be a filling of the "inner space" of a woman. Perhaps this is identity experience for the female. Gilligan on the other hand suggests that, "while for men, identity precedes intimacy and generativity in the optimal cycle of human separation and attachment, for women these tasks seem instead to be fused. Intimacy goes along with identity, as the female comes to know herself as she is known, through her relationships with others."[83]

Gilligan correctly criticizes Erikson and his observations of the differences in sexual characteristics, yet she notes that his life-cycle stages remain unchanged: "identity continues to precede intimacy as male experience continues to define his life-cycle conception."[84]

The seventh stage for Erikson is generativity versus stagnation.

---

81. Erikson, *Identity: Youth and Crises*, p. 125.
82. Erikson, *Insight and Responsibility*, p. 129.
83. Carol Gilligan, *In a Different Voice* (Cambridge, Mass.: Harvard University Press, 1982), p. 12.
84. Ibid.

Generativity as a crisis simply means that man is so made up as to demand to be needed or else he will suffer the mental "deformation of self-absorption, in which he becomes his own infant and pet."[85] It is here that the psychosocial stage of generativity finds its source. Parenthood for Erikson is the first generative crisis, but it is broadened as a general form of being needed and knowing how to fill the needs. Generativity is "the concern in establishing and guiding the next generation."[86] Generativity includes the concepts of creativity and productivity, but is not to be solely associated with either of them. Without generativity, the person becomes self-absorbed or stagnated and is useless for himself or society. Stagnation is often expressed through a regression to a pseudo-intimacy which may be quite obsessive. Generativity has a peculiar relationship with the life cycle for its goes directly back to the first stage—that of establishing a sense of basic trust, or a belief in humankind itself.[87]

The social modalities for this stage are "to make be and to take care of."[88] These are expressed in the home, in the division of labor, and in a sense of shared householding. As to the institutions which reinforce generativity and safeguard it, Erikson claims that all institutions by their very nature codify the related ethics. For it is "generativity itself" which is a driving power in human organization.[89]

The virtue that emerges with generativity is care. Care is "the widening concern for what has been generated by love, necessity, or accident; it overcomes the ambivalence adhering to irreversible obligation."[90] As adults need to be needed, so, for the benefit of one's own ego and for that community itself, adults require the challenge that stems from what has been generated in the past and from what now must be guarded, preserved, and eventually transcended.[91]

It seems, then, that the person faces the ascendancy of this conflict in the middle years in attempts to resolve the crisis of generativity versus stagnation, which manifests the modality of making be and taking care of. All social institutions by a kind of generative ethic develop the virtue of caring.

The final stage of development is validated by the crisis of ego integrity versus despair or disgust. Integrity is not easily defined, and Erikson points to some attributes of this stage of mind to clarify it. It is first the accrued "assurance of its proclivity for order and meaning—an emotional integration

85. Ibid., p. 130.
86. Erik Erikson, *Childhood and Society* (New York: Norton, 1963), p. 267.
87. Erikson, "Identity and the Life Cycle," p. 97.
88. Ibid., p. 166.
89. Erikson, *Identity: Youth and Crises,* p. 139.
90. Erikson, *Insight and Responsibility,* p.131.
91. Ibid.

faithful to the image bearers of the past and ready to take, and eventually renounce, leadership in the present." Second, it is the acceptance of one's one and only life cycle and an acceptance of realizing that there are no substitutions at this point in the cycle. Third, it means then a new and different love of one's parents, free from wanting them to be different or wishing them to be different. Fourth, it is a sense of oneness with men and women of the past which creates feelings of dignity and love. The social modality in this stage is like Tillich's "courage to be" in the face of the paradox of being and not being. For it is to be, even though one has been, and to face not being itself. The wisdom that can be found in social institutions feeds this stage, and prepares the person to face death. The virtue which emerges is wisdom, which is for Erikson "the form of that detached yet active concern with life bounded by death."[92]

Since Erikson's input on identity formation is so massive, I believe there are criticisms that must be suggested regarding his research and theory. For example, one may raise questions as to whether the epigenetic principle can be validated at all. It is much easier to validate psychosexual theory than this, for in dealing with the psychosocial realm suggestions as to the relationship of culture and society can only be assumed but cannot definitely be proved regarding the actual empirical effects. But Erikson must be complimented in using his scheme as a pattern and suggestion rather than a basis for empirical observation, for he sees the ego as a construct and it is useful for the sake of illustration—as long as he is not found simply playing a word game with abstract functions.

One major objection voiced here which parallels the study of conversion is that both Erikson and many researchers studying conversion phenomena study individuals who deviate from the norm. Surely one learns much from studying abnormal development, but how much more could be learned from examining those in peak health. Maslow criticizes this also and indicates that psychologists should seek to find the healthiest, maturest, and most actively productive persons to learn about normal development.[93]

We might criticize his cycle itself in its tendency to isolate individuals in an escalating approach to living, making others view people with a mind to analyzing which stage they are in. Erikson, however, suggests the cycle not be used as a scale, but rather as an "indicator" of development.

Religion and Identity

Older people often look at the identity struggle as just an intragenerational problem. Youth accuse the aged of unglueing the world and leaving a

---

92. Erikson, *Identity: Youth and Crises,* p. 140.
93. Abraham Maslow, *Toward a Psychology of Being* (Princeton: Van Nostrand, 1962), pp. 5-35.

world of unstable patterns. Yet personal identity is formed *within* the context of unstable patterns, even crises, as we have seen in Erikson. What emerges in conversion could be a stable pattern, a context out of which life begins to be ordered. During this struggle identity is beginning to be formed, too. It should be noted that identity has a close relationship with religion. In general, religion identifies us as children of God; the situation in which we find ourselves—we are a people in need of saving. In religion we find out where we belong—in the family of God. Through religion we learn how to belong to God—through commitment. We learn how to relate to others by loving, caring responses. Finally, in religion we focus on our future—identity with God.

The biblical sense of a plan of salvation, wherein humankind is seen struggling back to God, helped by God, at home in God's care are recurring themes in scripture. The account of the fall of humankind in Genesis emphasizes the need to return to the God who gives identity and fulfillment, and the eschatological theme of Ezekiel, Daniel, and Revelation suggests that restoration of men and women in God's image after our pilgrimage in a sinful world is really an identity function. The story of the early Christian workers in the book of Acts and their struggle to find out who they really were focused when they were finally called "Christians." They followed Jesus. Being "in Christ" and preached in "His name." These are unique identity themes.

St. Peter in his attempt to walk on water sinks mercilessly until he looks to Jesus in trust to find a new direction. The symbolism is noteworthy. Jesus, for Christians, becomes the one who gives direction and purpose in life. The story of Mary and Martha explores these same issues with regard to relationship with Christ. The true follower is one who has his or her priorities straight.

Identity themes in religion are not new or only located within the Christian tradition. In Hinduism this issue has always been basic. Hinduism sees the only real goal for humankind as reuniting with Brahman in a close identification, that through yoga we might be reunited with our divine essence.[94]

Richard Fenn suggests that, "Religion inevitably grounds identity in unchanging symbols and so redresses imbalance between adaption and stability, differentiation, and integration."[95] Religion fails if its adherents cease to provide a meaningful system which transcends life itself and becomes the fabric of choices and values. One way to determine religion's success in the world is to observe the deep, ultimate values which it generates and creates. Likewise, personal experience with God must provide and generate

---

94. F. H. Ross, *The Meaning of Life in Hinduism and Buddhism* (London: Routledge and Kegan Paul, 1953), p. ix.

95. Richard Fenn, *Journal for the Scientific Study of Religion* 17:1 (March 1978), pp. 67-68.

and reflect real values if it is to have this stabilizing effect and sovereignty in the life which Christianity claims.

I remember hearing Paul Irwin claim that religion and the church fail if they do not encourage disciples to develop critical thought and to shape a vision of life that can provide intelligent dissent. Religion's main function is providing a vision of what might be in a world learning how to become.

Hans Mol would even suggest that one might look at a church's effect on attendance to see if it is meeting the identity needs of its membership or not.[96] Religion, however, is a very general term and often just means the thing your life revolves around. In this general kind of category, such things as football, hockey, even stamp collecting can become religious issues. But in order for religion to really be "religious" there must be a sense of an "other" there, almost in the sense of Otto's concerns about the "holy." There is, however, another relationship which is significant and that is the function of theology in the identity process.

Theology and thinking about God are close allies of the identity theory. The doctrine of God in most traditions includes allegiance to the being or "other" which we worship. The object of devotion transcends us while, at the same time, it is immanent within us. The doctrine of God in the Christian tradition invites us to consider the necessity of God as being revealed clearly in the history of the world in tangible ways.

G. Ernest Wright emphasizes this aspect in his profound book *The God Who Acts,* when he suggests, "This (Christian) community exists and finds its true life in its responsibility and living relationships with God and its Lord."[97] Other allusions to the quality of personal identity in religion are found in the Pauline image of the "body" of Christ with Jesus as the head and the Johannine images of the quest in response and commitment to God. Persons and God become one, so to speak, in union together as humans share with God. Humankind participates in an almost mystic way with the purposes of God, and therefore life becomes ordered.

The Old Testament does not carry these New Testament themes; however, the personal identity found in relationship with God is a common Jewish theme. For example, the concept of "community" and "corporate personality" reflect this. In the Old Testament God is seen as the One who can recreate the community of Israel. God does it through a renewed covenant, one of peace and not war or dissension. The reason humankind could be at peace was that they were in relationship with God. The God of Israel was always conceived as a person, and "there was no surer way of deepening our own personality than fellowship with the Greater One."[98]

---

96. Mol, *Identity and the Sacred*, p. 82.

97. G. Ernest Wright, *The God Who Acts* (London: SCM Press, 1964), p. 98.

98. H. Wheeler Robinson, *Corporate Personality in Ancient Israel* (Philadelphia: Fortress, 1964), pp. 28-29.

It was characteristic that the national unification of Israel would be generated and even maintained by its identity with God. The knowledge of being a part of prophetic consciousness kept Israel's identity and does, even today, in contemporary Jewish communities. In the world there is always a need for people who will be strong to inner motives, who will be true to right and truth which they sense has been revealed to them, and with this intense commitment to their purpose in life comes identification with the One who gives them direction. Through obedience to the "true calling" one participates in the identity of God. When one disobeys (sins) in the biblical sense, the result is separation from the one true person who models life, and in a sense loss identity is the result. Or, as Paul Tillich claims, "Sin is primarily and basically the power of turning away from God. For this reason, no moral remedy is possible. Only one remedy is adequate—a return to God."[99]

New Birth, Future, and Identity

God becomes the "eternal now," *nunc aeternum,* who meets humans where they are, and as they are, and does not ask for a kind of moral goodness as proof that it is deserved. Rather, God encounters men and women and gives freely a peaceful presence and purpose in human estrangement. Resting in God through faithful response brings God's identity to humankind's empty life.

The new birth concept in scripture provides a New Testament allusion to this process of identification. Nicodemus is pictured in John 3 waiting to engage Jesus with theological possibilities.

"Surely you are a teacher. How else could you do what you do?"

"Verily, I say unto you, unless a man is born from above, he will never see God's kingdom."

"How can that be?" came the ruler's response.

Nicodemus approaches the question of new birth as does any analytical thinker and tries to identify rebirth in a physical sense. Jesus shows him his belief problem and suggests that through water and spirit one is reborn and participates in heavenly things. If, in the water allusion, baptism is referred to, we have a beautiful symbol of personal identity here. Death, burial, and resurrection become the New Testament means of participation with Jesus and, by extension, with God himself. But more probably the water reference is that of human birth—of breaking the water. Physical birth is contrasted beautifully with spiritual birth. Just as one must be born into this world, one must be born into the "other" world. Jesus adds to the belief in Christ as the final step of securing salvation. Jesus provides existence and meaning with his concluding speech in John 3:16, "For God so loved the world that he gave his only begotten son that whosoever believes in him shall not perish

---

99. Paul Tillich, *A History of Christian Thought* (New York: Harper & Row, 1968), p. 127.

but have everlasting life." If you want the kingdom, Nicodemus, you need to believe in God who provides you both models of identity, and a means of attaining the unrealized.

The apocalyptic allusions to identity resolved abound in the New Testament. One striking instance of a new identity is found in Revelation 22. Those that endure, and "wash their robes" presumably in the blood of Jesus, gather with him on the banks of the river of life and "bear his name." They are called to be like him in character, identity, and mission. The new name given to the saints at this glorious event is inscribed on stone, "I will also give him a white stone with a new name written on it, known only to him who receives it."[100] The new name is to be permanent. It will identify complete victory over sin and identify the saint as one of God's own.

New Testament apocalyptic is filled with identity issues. For example those who don't follow God are given a new identity—a mark—and it is of the beast rather than of God. Their manner, actions, and lifestyle reflect evil rather than good. While, on the other hand, those who follow God are sealed. They, too, receive a mark of victory, of belonging. Adventist theologians argue this may be the Sabbath symbol, a day that marks belonging to and rest in God. Others argue that this is a symbolic identification with a God who saves. Either way, the illustration is clear. Belonging and commitment are special, and God recognizes this identification as a part of the proper Christian response to the gospel.

Within the definitions of personal identity we have obvious correlations with religion's function. Personal identity as "that stable niche" reflects personhood in relation with the stable, knowing God. Since personal identity seems anchored in a transcendent order symbolized by religion and God-consciousness, personal identity finds a close friend in identity itself. As others look at the coherence within one's sense of personal identity reflected by values and purposes, choices and important symbols, religion and God-knowledge generate personal identity. Reflecting opinions and masking and/or mirroring one's role bring the personhood of Christians in relationship to a personal God to the front. With the expectations religion offers and within the understandings of theological implications about God, men and women see where they fit and what is of real value in life. They can grow and respond in a comfortable way. We understand how we fit because our relationship is in God, so to speak. Even within the crisis of growth situations, the cycle of personal and ego identity relate to religion. Opportunities to grow, or in Sherrill's terms, "shrink back," provide opportunities to become stable and self-wise in knowing who we are in relationship to God. The question still remains, however: What is the experience like? How is it experienced?

---

100. Revelation 2:17 (NIV).

Chapter 7

Identity: A Context for Faith

"I was brought up Church of England, you know, and baptized, and then at Marlborough I suddenly decided I was an atheist and refused to be confirmed. I used to think that religion was hymn singing and feeling good and not being immoral and always having a high moral tone and really rather priggish. Until . . . I remember one summer bicycling about in Cornwall and coming to a church, St. Irwin, in North Cornwall and meeting the vicar there who was a nice eccentric, and he said, I suppose you think religion is hymn singing in the chapel at Marlborough. And I said—Yes. And he said: Well—read this . . . Arthur Machens' **Secret Glory,** *which suddenly showed me there were the Sacraments, and then I became very interested in ritual, and everything like that, the one fundamental thing is that Christ was God. And it's very hard to believe—it's a very hard thing to swallow. But if you believe it, it gives some point to everything and really I don't think life would be worth living if it weren't true."*
John Betjeman

Coming home to God, or religious conversion marks the beginning of a new life. Like John Betjeman's experience, coming to God through conversional return "gives some point to everything." Identity, like the result of the conversion process, does not bring a quantity to life, but a quality that pervades experience. Personal identity and in a deeper sense and at a more conscious level, ego identity, are influenced by factors not entirely unlike those of conversion experience. Identity is influenced by many factors, molded in the life spaces of individuals, and formed by the cultural context. More specifically now, we focus on the crisis decision in identity. When contrasted with the conversion experience, there are significant parallels.

One of the products of religious conversion is new beliefs and values. Identity often results in values which include religious ideas and, therefore, a close relationship with religious experience is evident. Religion provides for youth and adults a theology (ideology) and a resource for the development of peace among humankind.[1] Erik Erikson even hopes religion can provide a means for bringing out the best in humankind and a world image "sustaining hope" for youth and for the weak.[2]

Religion's role is that of guarantor for the parents' faith, so that youth may reflect from their parents what is meaningful and right. Since personal

162

identity, according to Erikson, first deals with a sense of basic trust, it is this trusting quality in parents' lives which, through interaction with youth or growing children, provides the identity tags for religious growth, and through these stable identity tags promotes return to God for the child of God.

The first step in the religious conversion process is the parental gift of providing the kind of faith which so permeates personalities that it reinforces the child's sense of basic confidence in the world's trustworthiness. Through parenting the first hint of personal identity and conversion begin.

In this change process, however, desire to be recognized becomes very important. Personal identity demands knowing who one really is. Being known by God is just as important. The first step in both processes of change is to become recognized. Erik Erikson states it most beautifully:

> In the Judeo-Christian tradition, no prayer indicates this more clearly than "The Lord make his face to shine upon you and be gracious unto you. The Lord lift up his countenance upon you and give you peace"; and no prayerful attitude is better than the uplifted face, hopeful of being recognized. The Lord's countenance is apt to loom too sternly, and his Son's on the cross to show the enigmatic quality of total abandonment in sacrifice.[3]

One major role of religious conversion and by extension religious experience is to promote basic trust, which is simply the childlike trust developed in the first stages of life. Two things happen when one comes face to face with God in personal conversion. First, one learns what it means to trust someone outside of yourself, and second, the opposite stance can be taken as well—mistrust, doubt, and shame, the counterparts to true trust and faith—may be experienced. As new ideologies are formulated, new theologies begun, new beliefs practiced and pondered, the grappling with doubt and mistrust merge into faith and promise. It was through this grappling that Martin Luther finally believed who he was and what it was he was to eventually believe. Religious conversion's confrontation of the person with ideologies and theological presuppositions fulfills this need as well. Erik Erikson again posits that in some periods of the history of the world and in "some phases of his life cycle, [persons need] (until we invent something better) a new ideological orientation as surely and as solely as [they] must have air and food."[4]

There is, in religious conversion, a tone of conviction essential for personal identity, the same conviction and tone that exists in the identity-forming crisis. This conviction gives Christians a sense of community and a feeling of

---

1. Erik Erikson, "Identity and the Life Cycle," *Psychological Issues* 1:1 (New York: International Universities Press, 1959), p. 142; see also Erik Erikson, *Young Man Luther* (New York: Norton, 1959), p. 22.

2. Erik Erikson, *Insight and Responsibility* (New York: Norton, 1964), p. 153.

3. Erikson, *Young Man Luther*, p. 118.

reality and the resultant strength of conviction aids in solidifying personal identity. J. N. Zvomunondita Kurewa suggests:

> Conversion means turning to Christ and identifying with him; it also means community solidarity around Christ. In other words conversion to Christ means that a new convert takes his or her place with other members of the community around Jesus Christ. As a matter of fact, the most authentic way for anyone to express identity with Christ is to share Christian solidarity with those gathered around Christ.[5]

Think of the implications to pastors, pastoral facilitators, religious educators, and even parents. The church can become the major means by which personal faith and trust is understood and experienced. Capitalizing on the relationship of trust, religious educators and pastoral facilitators can clarify their own mission. They can begin to realize that not only does religion touch the ideological makeup of participants but it strengthens and augments personal religion through communal support and in return enhances personal faith and trust. Religious conversion in return aids in personal identity formation through this function.

There may be a danger in stressing only the feelings of conviction as important. When religion no longer provides hope and meaningful relationships within the community of faith, it will end up lost in delusion, addiction, and lost ethics. Religion at this point will just be fostering illusions, empty promises, and probably fantasy.[6] Since return to God is usually accompanied by this relational component, religious conversion moves individuals closer to those relationships which build up self-identity and conceptualization of one's task and mission.

For many today, a personal religious experience may not be related to identification with a deity. Personal devotion has taken over where formal religion has been inadequate. The secular ideologies become pillars upon which to reflect the past and around which to organize individual faith. Paralleling religion, these secular ideologies tend to counteract and promote a sense of alienation and their own positive ritual and "affirmative dogma." They "do not hesitate to combine magic with technique by amplifying the sound of one voice speaking out of the night, and by magnifying and multiplying one face in the spotlights of mass gatherings."[7] With so many ideologies demanding attention it is important for religion to be as devotional as possible and at the same time to be personally fulfilling. Since identity and conversion often reorganize one around a new center of reference, they are important experiences to facilitate.

One of religion's major roles, then, is to provide a framework of ideolo-

---

4. Ibid., p. 21.

5. J. N. Zvomunondita Kurewa, "Conversion in the African Context," *The International Review of Missions* 68 (1980), p. 164.

6. Erikson, *Insight and Responsibility*, p. 155.

gy, as well as to give one an experiential knowledge of deity out of which feelings and emotions grow. The pastoral facilitator, religious educator, or counselor may wish to use the normal identity experience as a springboard to assist individuals to find meaning in religion as well as find significance in their own personal lives.

Conversion and Identity

Two specific studies by Erik Erikson are especially helpful in seeing the relationship of personal identity with religious conversion experience. Erik Erikson's *Young Man Luther* and *Gandhi's Truth* explore both religious conversion and personal ego identity. These two books deal with the development of identity through the life cycle of two historically great individuals. Insights as to how their identity and culture become internalized to produce historic personages are given. Erikson for one does not try to define the experience of conversion; neither does he try to delineate its source other than to suggest the normal mental growth in this change. He simply treats the experience as real and a means for change in their lives.

Erikson contrasts Paul's conversion with that of Martin Luther. He suggests that Paul's was a kind of *heroic* conversion. Paul was neither too young nor provincial, was of cosmopolitan origin, in public life, and not a Christian. He was a deputy prosecutor for the high priest's office, "engaged fully: breathing out threatenings and slaughter" in the mission of prosecuting the Damascan Christians. His conversion on the road was not only immediately certified as being "of apostolic dimension by God's independent message to Ananias; it also immediately became equivalent to a political act, for Paul, the prosecutor, took sides with the defendants whom he committed to bring to justice."[8] In addition to stressing the definitive kind of change conversion is, Erikson contrasts Luther's conversion with that of Paul.

> There is only one similarity between Luther's experience and Paul's which can be formulated only by somewhat stretching a point. The two men, at the time of their conversions, were both engaged in the law, one as an advanced functionary responsible to the high priest, the other as a student owing obedience to the father. Both, through their conversion, received the message that there is a higher obedience than the law, in either of these connotations, and that this obedience brooks no delay.[9]

Both were shaken by an attack that went to the core of their experience, affecting both body and psyche. The religious conversions of these two men show the same intensity. Both were "thrown to the ground" in more or less psychological states. Some would like to attribute the symptoms to epilep-

7. Ibid., p. 127.
8. Erikson, *Young Man Luther*, pp. 92-94.

sy for Paul. But they both testify to the dramatic turn-around which conversion provided. In one case, however, Paul had been prepared for some kind of a change of mind, in the "kicking against the pricks" statement, for example, which the New Testament indicates. But for Luther, there was a more intrapsychic conversion. Erikson states that Luther never claimed for himself that he had heard or seen anything supernatural. Luther only claimed that "something in him made him pronounce a vow before the rest of him knew what he was saying."[10] One confirmation of his changed life was that of the validation of significant others, and "Martin can claim for his conversion only ordinary psychological attributes, except for his professed conviction that it was God who had directed an otherwise ordinary thunderstorm straight toward him."[11]

Many would attribute the causes of conversion to psychological occasions, but in so doing would not belittle the sincerity of Luther and the meaning for life that these decisions had.

The change in Luther's life committed him to being *monos,* a "professional monk among many."[12] In fact, the real issue at this time was whether Martin should go home to face his father after his conviction; thus, the conversion to become a monk was to provide him a moratorium in which to find himself, as well as a negative identity as a solution to the problem of diffusion. The feelings Erikson describes as exalting in identity formation have already been illustrated; these he sees illustrated in the preconversion state of young Luther.

Gandhi's coming to himself had different circumstances. The situation in the train station is often cited as precipitous to his identity experience. What followed that event was advocation of a nonviolent position.

One factor already mentioned as an element of conversion is sincerity; both Luther and Gandhi were certainly sincere. The conversion experience is unique for its total psychosocial involvement which, according to Erikson, is significant even if you attribute it to inspiration or to temporarily abnormal behavior. The uniqueness of these experiences is that they gave a decisive inner push to a youth in search of an identity within a given cultural situation and provided the ideological commitment which is so necessary for fidelity and identity to be developed and experienced. Perhaps if we were looking specifically at a woman's conversion here we might conclude something slightly different regarding the causes; however it seems that the return and movement to an ideology may cross sexual boundaries. Coming to oneself comprises a generic source for any change—even religious conversion. While there are significant differences in how moral reasoning occurs between

9. Ibid., p. 93.
10. Ibid., p. 94.
11. Ibid.
12. Ibid., p. 93.

males and females these differences may be in responses to teaching methods rather than to moral reasoning specifically.[13]

Another area which could be explored is the area of women's studies and their impact on conversion and identity formation. Some have suggested that one influence would be the kind of experiences which assist spiritual growth and identification with religion itself. Kathleen Fischer has written a unique book which is aimed at those who work with women in spiritual direction and retreat settings. Her work, *Women at the Well,* describes two topics of significance for our concern of conversion and identity. She identifies both spiritual direction and models of Christian growth as areas of unique female identity which must be considered when attempting to understand the female perspective. She describes women's experiences which are authoritative and need to be realized as possible revelatory events when understanding religious change. Her feminist perspective suggests that such factors as mutuality in relationships is important in contrast to dominance and submission and because feminism centers on relationships in a unique way. This would suggest that models and role-taking for women have a different focus than for men and suggests that both the content and the context for women may be uniquely different.[14]

The question for those interested in identity is not whether religious conversion is valid in terms of theological truth but whether it is a part of an identity experience or can be contributory to it. We can say affirmatively that this is so. The religious conversion experience provides a turning point in the life of the young person or older adult and answers the questions raised when individuals face the problem of just what they are going to give their lives to or for. Through religious conversion's experience, an all-embracing goal is obtained and focused, around which the experiences of life will be grounded and interpreted. And in adulthood, identity experience still finds a home. Many adults express their reorganization to a new way, find ideology which directs their inner life, or experience crisis which determines movement and redirection. Identity and conversion seem to have some touchstones.

The outcome of identity experience does not have to be religious, but in the cases of Gandhi and Luther it was. Religious conversion leads to an eventual formulated faith either implicitly given or endowed to the youth through adults.[15] For the Christian, religious conversion implies a God direction, and it is here that the biblical scholar parts with the psychologist. Theologians are often more interested in the ideological formulations devel-

---

13. James E. Plueddemann, "The Relationship Between Moral Reasoning and Pedagogical Preference in Kenyan and American College Students," *Religious Education* 84:4 (Fall 1989), p. 519.

14. See Kathleen Fisher, *Women at the Well: Feminist Perspectives on Spiritual Direction* (New York: Paulist, 1988).

oped after conversion than the processes that create it or in understanding the movement in decision itself.

Although Erikson is quick to judge many conversions and God-oriented decisions as being a part of pathology, he also feels that many decisions for religious values are a means of finding identity by first perceiving God face to face as through a glass darkly, then emerging to the full light of God's presence.[16]

Identity Experience

The identity crisis is simply a normative process and is the psychosocial aspect of adolescing according to some theorists, Erikson included. The time-space when identity decisions are the most experienced is thought of as the period from adolescence to the early twenties. This stage cannot be passed without identity experiences specifically occurring which will determine the youth's later life. The experience is considered normal and even necessary for the youth to determine his role.

The identity experience is a normal crisis characterized by more reversibility or transversibilty than would be found in more psychotic crises which are characterized by a self-perpetuating tendency, by an increasing amount of energy for ego defensive purposes, and by feeling of intense psychosocial isolation.

Some have called the major identity forming experience a "crisis" which occurs in that period of the life cycle when the young person senses a need to find out for himself the central core experiences of his being, some central perspective and direction, some "working unity out of the effective remnants of his childhood and the hopes of his anticipated adulthood."[17] The youth is detecting through the crisis some meaningful resemblance between what he believes himself to be and what he is aware others judge him to be. James Loder suggests that these moments need to be seen as sources of new knowledge about God, self, and the world. They can be seen as the progenitor of strength which can deal creatively with the various experiences of crisis and nothingness which come at us in contemporary life.[18]

---

15. Erikson, *Insight and Responsibility,* p. 140.

16. Erikson illustrates this face-to-face relationship in his analysis of a youth who was among a small group of patients who came from theological seminaries. This youth had developed symptoms while attending a Protestant seminary in the Middle West where he was training for missionary work in Asia. He had not found the expected transformation in prayer; he needed to see God validate his direction. The need was manifested by an anxiety dream in which a face horribly unrecognizable thus seemed to echo, according to Erikson, his patient's religious scruples. Erikson diagnosed the man as troubled and with a desire to see God in order to provide him an identity. This need for divine recognition may be at the base of some conversion experiences. See Erikson, *Insight and Responsibility,* p. 65.

Think of the implications for pastoral ministry if this is true. Pastoral facilitators and religious educators can learn to be sensitive to the crises in their members' lives and plan their ministries around the regular recurring cycles of personal concern. These crises may arise out of the give-and-take of living, family relationships, personal change, growth, situational differences, cultural shift, or personal isolation and personality. In any case, the religious professional can use these situations of crisis which form the basis of self-introspection (identity) and develop methods and caring models which nurture religious life and provide answers to the tensions of personal conflict. Through growing self-understanding (identity) the members of our congregations might learn what centering on God is all about in personal life. Religion is often seen as only an answer to problems, but now religion can be seen as providing direction and personal fulfillment and goal orientation in moments of identity crisis or ideological confusion.

Crisis and Identity

Gordon Allport suggests that a crisis is a situation of emotional and mental stress which requires some significant alterations of outlook within a short period of time. Some of these alterations of outlook frequently involve some kind of change in the very structure of personality. The results may be progressive or regressive in the life as others perceive it, yet in crisis a person cannot stand still; that is to say, that person simply cannot put this traumatic experience into any familiar or routine categories or understand it by any habitual mode of adjustment.[19]

The movement in crisis is usually toward resolution. Youth must either find themselves separated further from their childhood moving toward adulthood, or find themselves moving backward to earlier levels of adjustment which may be experienced in disorganization or dropping out. Adults, too, are moving forward and reflecting backward. Their faith includes both a forward movement and backward glance. These backward movements may result in perceived hostilities and defenses. The youth may become a thorn in the flesh of the teacher, parent, dean, or pastor; the adult may want to return to a simpler, more fulfilling lifestyle, yet the crisis may not become stabilized until after months of disorganization.

17. Erikson, *Young Man Luther*, p. 14.

18. James Loder, *The Transforming Moment* (San Francisco: Harper & Row, 1981), p. viii, or see Andrew Grannell, "The Paradox of Formation and Transformation," *Religious Education* 80 (Spring 1985), p. 390, for an explicit discussion contrasting James Fowler and James Loder's concern regarding transformation and formation.

19. Gordon W. Allport, "Crises in Normal Personality Development," *Contemporary Adolescence: Readings,* ed. Hershel D. Thornburg (Belmont, Calif.: Brooks/Cole, 1971), p. 394.

A person is never "an adult adult, was a childlike child, nor became an ado-lescent adolescent without what Piaget calls conflict—a matter to which I would give a more normative and developmental status by calling it cri-sis."[20] The crisis in identity is not a catastrophe; rather, it should be used in a medical sense where it connotes a crucial period in which a decisive action of movement is implied or is even perhaps unavoidable. These crises occur in human development sometimes more noisily when there are new needs which meet internal or perceived prohibitions, and they occur more quietly when the needs are simply a yearning to match new opportunities.

There is a dynamic picture of the movement within the developing ego of youth, and in this way, during identity's crucial period, adolescents through crisis must find identity or be led to a possible sense of role confusion, according to an Eriksonian model. Conversion—the return to the family of God—becomes a vital identity-forming experience. The identity experience itself becomes the *sense of contending forces striving for resolution.*

The source for identity has an unusually simple explanation for Erikson albeit couched in pejorative masculine language. "Before Darwin the answer was clear: because God created Adam in his own image, as a counter-play-er of his identity, and thus, bequeathed to all men the glory and the despair of individuation and faith. I admit to not having come up with any better explanation."[21]

These crisis moments of decision when identity is realized or at least identity formation begins occur for some rapidly when various choices and paths are clearly seen and decided upon permanently. At the same time a gradual sense of crisis in personal identity can be seen, too. These moments of decisional change reflect those of earlier times and the successful work-ing through of the major epigenetic crisis. Yet the experience itself is defined as a sense of divergence and discomfort with decisions resolving the crisis. Therefore the decision emphasizes the point of resolution and directional change.[22] Thus we often think of identity crisis as being at one point in time. Of course, this raises the question of gradual versus sudden in the identity cri-sis. We have already seen that all change may take time, but the decision or resolution can be experienced in a moment. Thus identity and religious con-version have similarities here too.

Another aspect of the identity experience is an intense *need for devotion.* This is an aspect of the identity crisis which moves to establish a meaning-ful worldview, one that can be believed in, to which youth can commit, in which satisfaction can be sought.

In their late teens and early twenties, even when there is no explicit ideolog-

---

20. Erikson, *Insight and Responsibility,* p. 138.
21. Erikson, *Identity: Youth and Crises* (New York: Norton, 1968), p. 40.
22. Erikson, *Young Man Luther,* pp. 41-45.

ical commitment or even interest, young people offer devotion to individual leaders and to teams, to strenuous activities, and to difficult techniques; at the same time they show a sharp and intolerant readiness to discard and disavow people (including, at times, themselves). This repudiation is often snobbish, fitful, perverted, or simply thoughtless.[23]

For pastoral facilitators and religious educators here is rich ground out of which to build a foundation for worship and devotion. If one response to finding oneself is that of intense devotion, worship can become a major means of providing meaningful movement to religion as an answer to questions of identity confusion. Adolescents especially can be nurtured through the worship and life of the devotional community. After all, for the first time in their development they have the cognitive resources to understand and evaluate what is happening, and their emotional life is important in a new and vital way. Worship, which is an affective activity, touches this aspect of a youth's life in a meaningful way. Since youth are often inquisitive about their faith, their worship often involves questions which force the congregation and pastoral staff to make sure that the worship practice of the church meets personal needs. Devotion may not just be public in nature. Daniel Aleshire suggests that spiritual life needs nurture too:

> Adolescents are capable of spiritual genius. Therese of Lisieux was fifteen when she entered the Carmelite order. She died at twenty-seven, leaving a legacy of spiritual sensitivity that was recognized by her canonization in 1925. Mary, when she gave birth to Jesus, and David, when he seized faith and faced Goliath, were both adolescents by contemporary American standards. Many American church youth may be more interested in MTV than exploring the parameters of classical Christian spirituality. But there are young people in the churches who possess a passion for God, who have an emotionality that is venturesome, who have a spiritual hunger that lingers after the Mass is said or the worship service is over.[24]

Ideology and Identity

It is during the time of adolescence and youth that ideologies play a role in identity formation and provide the contents for devotion and commitment in the experience. Ideologies offer to the members of this age group simple but determined answers to exactly those vague inner states and those urgent questions that come through the identity experience. Ideologies serve to "channel youth's forceful earnestness and sincere asceticism, as well as its search for excitement and its eager indignation, toward that social frontier where the struggle between conservatism and radicalism is most alive."[25] You will remember conversion's relationship to ideology. One does not

23. Ibid., p. 42.
24. Daniel O. Aleshire, *Faith Care: Ministering to All God's People Through the Ages of Life* (Philadelphia: Westminster, 1988), p. 141.

return unless he or she returns *to* something. The individuals healed by Jesus were invited to go on "the way"—with the obvious implications of discipleship and understanding of "the way."

When we ask existential questions about being—and we seem to ask them more intensely during this period of life than others—it is easy to see the role that an intense belief system has for identity experience. In an attempt to solve "being," ideologies provide answers and resolutions to the quest for meaning in life and provide a stabilizing resolution to the experience expressed in the crisis of identity.

Openness to relatedness with others and the search for self-identity are not two distinct problems either. One finds identity in relationships to others for it is here that one notes one's own identity as it is reflected in others. In *The Experience of Faith* I postulate that one of the earliest situations where faith is seen is in the reflected faith life of others.[26] Early conceptualizations of what it means to be religious are often determined and modeled by others.[27] Another quality of identity perception is due to others' feedback. This may be why for the Christian "Christlikeness" is an important goal. Often it is heard that until the people reproduce the character of Christ in their own lives, the worth of Christianity will never be seen.

Pastoral facilitators and religious education professionals already know the importance of modeling in ministry. Youth pastors recognize that their style of ministry teaches more about God than explicit instruction in any religion class or preaching situation. Parents are often surprised to find out that their own children are growing up to be exactly like them in regards to their values and behavior. We also know that a climate of warmth encourages self-esteem, and it has long been recognized that youth with low self-esteem need a community or group where they can sense acceptance and cooperation.[28] It is in the local congregation that young people gain their impressions about what the larger church is like. The members are crucially important and are presumed to be representative of all religious people, and their pastor of all pastors. Thus it is important that we understand how both the wider church and the local congregation are viewed by their various constituents. In the Effective Christian Education study, *thinking climate* was found to be among the strongest contributors to mature faith.[29]

We also know that self-esteem is best associated with purpose in life and direction. These identity factors and facts only tend to support that one's

---

25. Erikson, *Young Man Luther,* p. 42.

26. See V. Bailey Gillespie, *The Experience of Faith* (Birmingham, Ala.: Religious Education Press, 1988), pp. 110-124.

27. Helen Merrill Lynd, *On Shame and the Search for Identity* (New York: Harcourt, Brace, 1958), p. 241.

28. Merton Strommen, *Five Cries of Youth* (New York: Harper & Row, 1988), pp. 38, 39.

identity and perception of need for religion are related.

The Experience of Identity

Another expression of the experience of personal and ego identity is the *feeling tones of the experience* itself. It seems that the crisis is expressed in similar terms as is the religious conversion crisis. There is a pre-state demonstrated by anxiety and conflict. The following quotation, used before in part, will demonstrate the feelings some see surrounding identity.

> I have called the major crisis of adolescence the *identity* crisis; it occurs in that period of the life cycle when each youth must forge for himself some central perspective and direction, some working unity, out of the effective remnants of his childhood and the hope of his anticipated adulthood. . . . He must detect some meaningful resemblance between what he has come to see in himself, and what this sharpened awareness tells him others judge and expect him to be. . . . In some young people, in some classes, at some periods in history, this crisis will be minimal; in other people, classes, and periods, the crisis will be clearly marked off as a critical period, a kind of "second birth," apt to be aggravated either by widespread neuroticism or by pervasive ideological unrest. Some young individuals will succumb to this crisis in all manner of neurotic, psychotic, or delinquent behavior; others will resolve it through participation in ideological movements, passionately concerned with religion or politics, nature, or art.[30]

Noted here is graphic portrayal of *conflict at the core of being,* a conflict with anxiety at its base seeking solution in alternative views about self and life. Its intensity is demonstrated to have both neurotic and healthy results. Erikson illustrated a preidentity state in his analysis of Martin Luther's major crisis. He describes Luther's general mood before he became a monk as *tristitia* (or excessive sadness). The feelings came to Luther before the thunderstorm, when he had been slowly slipping into a melancholic paralysis making it hard to continue his schooling and marry, as his father had urged him to do. During the thunderstorm, he felt intense anxiety, feeling hemmed in and choked up. Erikson suggests that Luther's use of *circumvallatus,* meaning in Latin "all walled in" is significant to describe the intensity of the emotions before the identity-forming experience.[31] This constriction of the whole life, in which there is no particular way out except through the giving up of a previous lifestyle and all earthly future for the sake of total devotion to a new form of living, depicts an extreme identity struggle for Luther and illustrates the kind of feeling tone associated with the preidentity experience.

---

29. Peter L. Benson and Carolyn H. Elkin, *Effective Christian Education: A National Study of Protestant Congregations Summary Report* (Minneapolis: Search Institute, March, 1990).

30. Ibid., p. 14.

Gordon Allport adds to Erikson's insight a list of statements that describe feelings existing before resolution of a conflict in young adults. These typical statements of crisis feelings illustrate a sense of lostness and despair-seeking-solution.

1. I feel I have been dragged into something against my will.
2. I feel like a rat in a maze.
3. I was to be a law unto myself, but cannot. It seems suddenly that the decisions I make must be valid for the rest of my life.
4. The lives of the past and the life of the future seem suddenly to be at cross purposes.[32]

Even though apathy may be experienced while going through these crises, it is only a mask for anxiety deep within.

We have seen that the causes of identity conflict are many—the physiological revolution of genital maturation including feelings of uncertainty about adult roles and a search for some sense of continuity and sameness inside the person. Many causes find their source in events outside the person. Illustrating, Erikson cites a crisis in Gandhi's life which precipitated identity formation and caused anxiety about himself. The crisis was in the middle age of this great man and is used as an example of a significant time when Gandhi solved his identity crisis. The experience happened in the railroad station of Maritzburg, South Africa, when the lawyer made a trip and was ejected from the train because he insisted in traveling first class even though he was recognized as a "coolie" or "colored." At this point, brought on by external circumstances, he abandoned his shy self and, literally at once, radically committed himself to his political and religious destiny as a leader. Even though Gandhi was nearly fifty years old at the time, the individuals he gathered around him were at their identity peak and found in him fulfillment of their ideological needs, and his views became a part of their identity structure.[33] His conversion, so to speak, was precipitated by the crisis situation at the rail yard.

Culture and Identity

Another outside influence effective in causing identity conflict is the *relationship of culture*. Sociologists cite cases of social transportation and cultural deprivation through transmigration as causes of identity conflict and suggest that these anxiety-filled situations aid in people finding their place in life. They suggest that there is a danger in any period of large-scale uprooting and

---

31. Ibid., pp. 2-39.
32. Allport, "Crises in Normal Personality Development," p. 396.
33. Erik Erikson, *Ghandi's Truth* (New York: Norton, 1969), p. 47.

that this exterior crisis will upset the natural ascendancy of inner concerns and pose a traumatic conflict which needs resolution. When people lose their roots, roots that must be firmly founded in the life cycle, roots that "are nourished in the sequence of generations, [they lose their] taproots in disrupted developmental time, not in abandoned localities."[34] This transmigration is a collective crisis and results in the production of new and very intense world images. Oftentimes, these images demand sudden assimilation of the new, and wholeness and initiative are shattered. Wholeness and initiative are attributes of identity and are, therefore, damaged in the moving in a very deep way. This sense of "rootlessness" has a deep effect and causes identity anxiety to be pronounced, while a knowledge of belonging permeates the religious conversion state by contrast.

Internal Sources of Identity

There are additional *internal sources* for identity crisis and the feeling tones that correspond to the experience as well, and they are reminiscent of religious conversion crises. Luther again is a good example. Three or more distinct and fragmentary experiences for Luther which gave impetus for his identity can be cited. Some receive these qualities in one explosive event, Luther may have had many. They are physical paroxysms, a degree of unconsciousness, and automatic verbal utterance, a command to change the overall direction of effort and aspiration, a spiritual revelation, and a flash of enlightenment which was as decisive and pervasive as a rebirth. The thunderstorm had given him a "change in the overall direction of his life, a change toward the anonymous, the silent, and the obedient. In fits such as the one in the choir, he experienced the epileptoid paroxysm of ego-loss, the rage of denial of the identity which was to be discarded. And later in the experience in the tower, which . . . he perceived as the light of a new spiritual formula."[35] Here significant inner struggles are delineated. It is significant to note the experience developing even if we would deny the ego involvement. The development is from disunity and lack of identity, through events and inner struggles that provide impetus for unity and commitment, and to the surety of a new formula for inner peace. Thomas Merton, on the other hand, found stress in contemplation of the world. In solitude he became deeply aware of the world's needs. In fact, it was through contemplation that the needs of the world became present for him. "It [contemplation] does not hold the world at arm's length," he said. A genuine life of solitude was for him a positive way to interface with the world. From these experiences he began to act and speak out for social causes and to understand love in its fullness.[36] The parallels with religious conversion are obvious.

---

34. Erikson, *Insight and Responsibility*, p. 95.
35. Erikson, *Young Man Luther*, p. 38.

Another internal cause for the crisis is the existential fear or dread which causes a quest for the promises of identity. The ego drive of wishing to be known along with crises that stem from intellectual challenges are factors in conflict as well.

In summary, then, the experience of personal identity crisis finds in it the feeling tones of anxiety, depression, fragmentation, and concern for internal unity in the face of crises brought on through inner ego needs, outer cultural circumstances, and age-specific task fulfillment.

Regarding the identity experience itself, then, there is often in the pre-stages of the experience a morbid, often curious, preoccupation with the conflicts that arise from early identifications and the successful working through of these identifications. Identity experience has a moment of decision or, more accurately stated, resolution, where through outer, inner, cultural, psychical, or even negatively worked-through identifications, a kind of giving up is experienced. This giving up is expressed in the finding of identity and the realization of one's place in the cosmos or, in a smaller sphere, finding meaning in one's decisions and position in life. Adolescence seems to be the stage wherein the ascendancy of this kind of crisis becomes prominent, and the resolution of the crisis tends toward a faith that is true to oneself and others and toward the ego result most desired in healthy adulthood. But these feelings of frustration or anxiety may occur at any age.

Moratorium

The setting for identity and its ensuing crisis is postulated as a kind of moratorium or time of reflection according to Erikson. The completion of ego identity takes place during this period, and it is a time permitted by society for a youth to experiment about his identity and major decisions in life. Since societies know that youth change rapidly even in their most intense devotions, they should actually seek to give them a moratorium, or a span of time after they have ceased being children but before their deeds and works count toward a future identity. Erikson uses Luther as an example again of one going through such a moratorium. In Luther's time, for that society, the monastery was for some one possible psychosocial moratorium. It was

> one possible way of postponing the decision as to what one is and what one is going to be. It may seem strange that as definite and, in fact, as eternal a commitment as is expressed in the monastic vow could be considered a moratorium, a means of marking time. Yet in Luther's era, to be an ex-monk was not impossible; nor was there necessarily a stigma attached to leaving a monastic order, provided only that one left in a quiet and prescribed way—as for example, Erasmus

36. Stephen Happel and James J. Walter, *Conversion and Discipleship: A Christian Foundation for Ethics and Doctrine* (Philadelphia: Fortress, 1986), p. 7.

did, who was nevertheless offered a cardinalate in his old age. . . . I do not mean to suggest that those who choose the monastery any more than those who choose other forms of moratoria in different historical coordinates (as Freud did, in committing himself to laboratory physiology, or St. Augustine to Manichaeism) know that they are marking time before they come to their crossroad, which they often do in the late twenties, belated just because they gave their all to the temporary subject of devotion. The crisis in such a young man's life may be reached exactly when he half-realizes that he is fatally overcommitted to what he is not.[37]

This moratorium seems to be built into human development itself.[38] And like all the moratoria in human developmental schedules, the delay of adulthood can be lengthened and intensified to a forceful and a fateful degree by the culture. It is in this period that youth find time to experiment with various ideologies and quest for a ready niche in society. As youth see more clearly toward the close of this moratorium they are able to bridge the span between infantile and childlike actions and meanings and become adults. Identity discovered through this experience aids self-conception and society's recognition.[39] Society also plays a role in this intermixture of moratorium and culture. It has a responsibility to recognize more than just achievement in a person; it must validate relationships to the whole society. This kind of recognition aids the ego in the tasks of adolescing. Recognition maintains the ego defenses against the newly vitalized impulses and consolidates the most "conflict-free" achievements in preparation for a job, resynthesizing the previous childhood identifications in life with the demands of society.[40]

The adult role in this moratorium is that of guide or advisor who corrects or confirms the youth. Implications for pastoral facilitators and religious educators and pastors are evident. The adult role is that of guarantor of faith. At all times, however, youth must feel that they are the ones making the choice. Personalization of faith always comes when decisions about eternal things can be made personally. Attitudes youth find in adults validate adult guarantor roles as well as affirm in the youth some sort of consistency as they emerge from necessary inner confusion. Think how crucial it must be that young girls in the church have positive "role models" who illustrate the nature of God in both word and deed and who hold office in equality with their responsibility. Tragically, men have been the sole beneficiaries of such pastoral models in many congregations.

The age-old concern of "who is Sally playing with," is real. Others do impact us in areas of our spirituality, and for those whose identity is still being found, this modeling becomes crucial. It is especially significant when

---

37. Erikson, *Young Man Luther,* p. 43.

38. Erik Erikson, ed., *The Challenge of Youth* (New York: Doubleday, 1963), p. 10.

39. Erikson, "Identity and the Life Cycle," p. 111.

40. Ibid., pp. 111-112.

it comes to role expectations and gender identification. We often model sex roles which impact identity. Here Kathleen Fischer's work is especially important for spiritual leaders, who tend to be men.[41]

Role Experimentation

Identity theory, you will remember, suggests the great importance of role experimentation in the formulation of a sense of identity. In addition to feelings of certainty and identity knowledge, role taking is a very important factor. Orrin Klapp suggests, "The student of identity must necessarily be deeply interested in interaction, for it is in and because of face-to-face interaction that so much appraisal—of self and others—occurs."[42] Role experimentation is simply the experimentation, so natural in adolescence, when various roles are tried on to see which fits. This quest for a role congruent with the emerging identity of the young person is a positive factor in identity formation.

The larger the field of choice in this role experimentation, the more possibilities for personal identity seem to emerge, and conversely so as well. Both men and women of example are needed. If no choices exist for oneself, a negative identity, or so it could be called, would be manifest. The experimentation which engages youth is neither logical nor systematic. Youth find joy in rather abrupt and challenging roles—which are not typical. Religious workers and pastoral facilitators may find a challenge here. One concern would be that of channeling the roles and experimentation through ritual, initiations, and confirmations.

One problem for the adolescents who are trying to find identity is the fact that if they pick a particular role, they run the risk of commitment to that role. These premature commitments do not prove to be as permanent as those which are developed after a long struggle with various possibilities. The long-term nurture of a church community, youth group, club, or congregation can prove helpful in providing both identity and encouraging return to God through religious conversion.

Negative Identity

If we use the life-cycle model in the formation of a healthy identity, the opposite function of identity might occur, and that is called negative identity, which simply means youth may take on the identity of everything he or

---

41. Fischer, *Women at the Well*, pp. 110-200.
42. Orrin E. Klapp, *Collective Search for Identity* (New York: Holt, Rinehart and Winston, 1969), p. 44.

she has been told *not* to become. When youth are not allowed to experiment with various roles, they often adopt a negative one and assume its identity. Negative identity is not only a component of an unhealthy identity, but is also a *solution* to identity diffusion, at least for Erikson. When individuals seem confused or faced with the crisis of not knowing themselves and how they fit, and the sameness and congruity that comes from identity is not present, a confusion or diffusion may be the result. It is here that a youth who has no identity seeks one, even in negative terms and thus becomes someone for a while, even if he or she may not remain with this identity. Many a sick or desperate late adolescent, faced with continuing conflict, would just as soon be somebody totally bad, even dead, than be not quite somebody.[43]

The roots of this conflict, even though often occurring in the stage of adolescence, have their beginnings in the third stage of the life cycle in the time of initiative versus guilt, according to Erikson. Negative identity seems to be the result of the failure of a developing initiative and the dominance of guilt in this stage of the cycle. As individuals experience identity, sometimes the opposite effect occurs. Some theorists have suggested the term "identity diffusion" as the term used to describe the feeling tone for this crisis of adolescence. It is the splitting of the self, the loss of the central core of one's being, the real loss of a sense of identity. Other theorists would simply explain this as identity confusion. Confusion about one's identity is not an orderly thing. In this process there is a loss of center. Factors that contribute to this identity kind of confusion, then, seem to be the same as those which function in identity for some. The key role is played by the acts of mutuality occurring in the developing ego. For example, there should be some type of mutual recognition between the youth and their peers in order for them to find their own identity, as we have mentioned earlier in our discussion of identity theory. The role of adult guarantor is very important, not only for the ideological feedback and exemplary role that this person may fill, but for the youth's own identity to be personally established. The youth must see themselves or herself in relationship to mature people who can treat them with mutual respect and recognition. This gives one's own sense of personal worth validation, as well as watching one's own personhood in the interaction of life itself.

Jere Yates suggests some factors that should exist for a role modeling and recognition to occur: "1) A youth must be free enough from past problems to choose the important person or group, 2) there must be a person or group who is interested in the kind of youth that he actually is, and 3) cultural conditions must allow the two to meet."[44] Yates also suggests that when this mutual relationship does not exist, then confusion will set in. If a society finds its youth being just what the representatives of that society tell him

---

43. Erikson, *Identity: Youth and Crises*, p. 176.

he is, he has no real personal identity, and this sometimes will lead to great confusion and diffusion.[45] This role of others and the pressures they exert for change is significant for conversion as well, for the factors seem to be correlated.

Most writers spend a great deal of time using adolescence as a major context of identity. The previous elements of identity, the ensuing identity crisis of diffusion, the adoption of negative identity, and the development of the results of identity formation itself, both positively and negatively formed, show the centrality of adolescence for the time of formation. This context is a time of faith development for youth, and this context may be perfect for religious conversion to come to the front. It is certain, however, that religious conversion may provide an answer to identity confusion through its central focus on God as the primary cause.

Identity and Adolescence

For most theorists, identity formation and the time of youth go hand in hand. It is the last stage of childhood, completed only when childhood tags vanish and are subordinated in a social and competitive apprenticeship with peers. For women this time may be later, but is still related to one's relationships with peers and significant others.

Many youth reflect this tension and quest for identity. As the adolescent context for religious conversion reflects the same thing, many look for the "right choice" in these years. The identity quest is part of an important emotional agenda, for the youth is confronted with images of self that are very different from those which were perceived earlier. The identity quest is further complicated in our own culture because of the many choices one has to make.

> When a society tells someone, "You are this gender, this race, this social caste; therefore, you will do these things for the rest of your life," that person may have to deal with feelings of entrapment but not with the problems of identity. On the other hand, when the society says, "You can work at whatever occupation you choose, marry whom you want, live wherever you want, hold to the values and style of life you choose—as long as your choices do not infringe on others' rights," adolescents must struggle with a myriad of options and may have trouble deciding who they are.[46]

Youth are involved in many emotional, cognitive, behavioral issues. It

---

44. Jere Yates, "Erikson's Study of the Identity Crisis in Adolescence and Its Implications for Religious Education" (Ph.D. dissertation, Boston University, 1968), p. 123.

45. Erikson, "Identity and the Life Cycle," *Psychological issues* 1:1 (New York: International Universities Press, 1959), p. 123.

is not uncommon for them to struggle with life or to have ideological conflicts regarding altruism or to be emotionally intense. Youth respond to these conflicts through both testing and conformation. Their cognitive development likewise impacts their religious concerns. The budding abstract ability allows theological insights to make sense now, and home and family, siblings, and peers take on new significance in both positive and negative ways.[47] The social climate of school, work, and church make their impact, too.

Like Hamlet, the answer to the famous "to be or not to be" reflects youth's concerns. Hamlet is the normal, introspective youth trying to sort out life, free from his parents, facing a larger framework of ideology not yet his own. Hamlet believes that in his choices he will form the past and the future. Here is a man caught in an identity crisis conditioned by his age. The age of youth is ripe for indoctrination.[48]

As new ideologies pose values, youth are organizing them. It is commonly thought that three factors influence ideological choice—opportunity, leadership, and friendship; all these are available during youth. Drives which are being unleashed in youth strive for order. An opportunity must be made for the choice to be given. Pastors, teachers, and church workers must help give presence and credibility to the ideological choice. Close friendships and ties should be there for new ideologies to be formed. For this reason, if identity confusion exists, some striving for order and harmony is inevitable.

Religious experience for youth, however, is not entirely expressed cognitively. In fact, one critique of James Fowler's work on faith development is just that. Many have challenged his interpretation of the results rather than his research itself. Fowler's concepts remind one of his predecessors Piaget and Kohlberg. He seems to have a bias toward cognition, consciousness, and the ego and to neglect the deeper levels of personality formation and the self. Mary Ford-Grabowsky argues that faith is a function of the deeper levels of personality and, like Jung, looks for a broader basis from which to examine the phenomenon of faith. Reflecting on the Pauline understanding of humanness, she sees the "outer and inner" man as symbolic for the "eyes" and "ears" activated in the faith experience. "Faith knowing demands the involvement of the deepest part of the Self," according to Grabowsky, and only in depth interviews can this contrast become clear.[49] This means that more than just ideology is being formulated. She argues that any complete theory of faith development would include the following: 1) a confessional aspect, and 2) transtemporal dimensions; 3) an emphasis on the self rather than the ego, and 4) the place of sin and evil in the schema of faith.[50] This broader understanding of faith development supports our concern about identity as

48. Kenneth Keniston, *Youth and Dissent: The Rise of a New Opposition* (New York: Harcourt Brace Jovanovich, 1960), pp. 3-27.

46. Aleshire, *Faith Care,* p. 129.

47. Ibid., pp. 130-139.

48. Kenneth Keniston, *Youth and Dissent: The Rise of a New Opposition* (New York: Harcourt Brace Jovanovich, 1960), pp. 3-27.

a key element in motivation toward commitment. Identity issues encompass more than just ideology and translate into more existential and emotional issues—for example one's sense of belonging.

One curriculum issue that could be addressed from an understanding of identity's impact on life choices is that of heritage. In the religious development of youth, as in the formation of personal identity, some sense of history is important. The call to return to one's "roots" parallels the need in personal identity formation for a place where one is significant in time. In religion, becoming a part of God's "plan" meets this function in identity. When youth find their place in time, life becomes relevant again. Knowing where one fits historically and personally is crucial to a growing knowledge of who I am. All religions have history. Knowing one's heritage often gives birth to a sense of "presence." They know who they are because they are a part of a movement, a stream of time, a denomination with a beginning and a development. Those movements which interpret their past as having been "led" by God, or directed by some sort of prophetic voice, provide even richer history out of which meaning can grow. This may explain the psychological significance of canonization in the Catholic tradition, or the chain of command through the presidents of the Mormon religion, or even the need for prophetic guidance in many other denominations. Even though in youth this concern for history is evident, there is at the same time confusion and indecision about one's real place in history. This sorting out becomes a by-product of the identity confrontation of the conversional change.

There is a psychological dynamic operating in adolescence. There is an innate quest in adolescence, a "search for a new and yet a reliable identity," and it is manifested in the endeavor to find, define, overdefine, and redefine oneself and others through ruthless comparison, coupled with the quest to test the newest possibilities in all areas and to challenge the oldest values. Role confusion takes place only when the resulting self-definition becomes difficult and the youth counterpoints rather than synthesizes sexual, ethical, occupational, and typological alternatives and is often driven to decide definitely and totally for one side or for the other.[51]

Inner identity is important for youth, and this is when feelings of wholeness and progressive continuity occur. Perhaps in this inner identity one finds his closest kinship with the actual phenomenon of religious conversion itself, for through it wholeness and progressive continuity become a key factor in uniting to the family of God.

---

49. Mary Ford-Grabowsky, "The Fullness of the Christian Faith Experience: Dimensions Missing in Faith Development Theory," *The Journal of Pastoral Care* 41:1 (March 1987), pp. 39-47.

50. Mary Ford-Grabowsky, "Flaws in Faith-Development Theory," *Religious Education* 82:1 (Winter 1987), p. 80.

51. Erikson, *Insight and Responsibility,* p. 92.

Erikson's graphic description is appropriate to describe this mood. He likens this time to a natural uprootedness in human life. Like a trapeze artist, "The young person finds himself in vigorous motion. He must let go of his safety hold on childhood and find himself reaching out for a firmer grasp on adulthood, depending for a breathless interval on the relation between the past and the future, on the reliability of those that he must let go of, and reach out to those whom he feels may receive him."[52]

Adolescence is a time, then, for searching, seeking answers to identity itself, a time of major identity crisis in the concluding stages of childhood. It is a time favorable for indoctrination and for the ascendancy of drives—sexual as well as ideological. Adolescence is a time for historical irreversibility which may lead to a standing off and a questioning of history. It is a time for finding a reliable identity through synthesis of occupational and ethical choices. Adolescence provides a search for wholeness, totality, and progressive continuity as well as to the answers and questions of normal uprootedness in the life of the youth. But along with this is a need in the identity quest for an ideological stance that provides answers to existential questions, the real questions that plague adolescents. While adolescence is not the only time that religious conversion might occur, it does prepare the ground for conversional change in a most unique way. While adolescence is not the only time when such crises might occur, it certainly provides a rich context out of which identity can be resolved. It is a rich time to focus on both identity and conversion issues.

Relational Observations

These two experiences, religious conversion and personal identity, have a unique relationship. People change after religious conversion, and people change after finding out who they are in the experiencing and sensing of their own identities. One might say, then, that religious conversion experience and identity experience are alike, even perhaps the very same in fact. All religious conversions have as a chief component identity concerns. Not all identity experiences are obviously religious in nature, however, but religious conversion is an identity experience. It is this way because: 1) both the experience of religious conversion and identity are centrally associated with change in the lives of individuals; 2) both experiences are concerned with the changing of behavior and with the result of a changed frame of reference. Ethical implications follow changed mental constructs. 3) These two experiences affect the very center of awareness in a person. Religious conversion accomplishes this through a basic change of viewpoint and a forthcoming commitment to a "way" or ideology. Personal identity experiences succeed

---

52. Ibid., p. 90.

through the successful resolution of crises and the resultant virtues and values formed in the process, through interaction with individuals and with society and its norms. The result of both experiences is that of a change at the center of one's life. Religious conversional change finds humankind in a new "way," when people "fit" in God's plan. Identity change may create a new sense of integrity when one knows he or she has chosen right and is complete. Individuals perceive its "rightness" through the mirrors of others in role response. The former may proceed from the latter.

Religious conversion has a deep, integrating effect and influence on the personal attitudes, values, and feelings about oneself. Personal identity experiences likewise integrate feelings of wholeness and sameness in individuals. In religious conversion, this sense of integration comes at the resolution of the crises conflict, or the postconversion stage of the conversion crisis. In identity experience it seems to come, I believe, through the resolution of the crisis of identity itself. Identity experience appears to be the strongest when there is opportunity for strong, even life-involving decisions. In religious conversion as well there is a laying on the line of the life at a crossroads-type decision-making event. This integrating, ultimate, focusing experience is innate to both experiences and gives direction for the future role and beliefs of the young person.

Religious conversion and identity deal with similar issues. For example, religious conversion provides a sense of trustworthiness by suggesting an ultimate "One" or "way" in whom or in which one can rely. Conversion fosters identity through community identification and the focusing on personal goals; and it cultivates integrity by developing faith in someone outside oneself.

While identity experience stresses integration of life with the world, religious traditions indicate that wholeness and completeness come in community with the world. The one who seeks God finds complete rest and wholeness in the knowledge that God is his or her God, and the peace and reconciliation which come from knowing this provides religious motivation in the world. The community of the saints so pictured in 1 Corinthians 11 and onward suggests that the body of believers has a purpose. The purpose is to be a model of "God-disclosure" as the expression of one's belonging to the Body of Christ. Each one is an essential part of the united body of Jesus. So as the youth or adult finds himself or herself through the identity experience or through the biblical model of identity—religious conversion—and as the New Birth occurs and men and women are given spiritual capacities, the community becomes the major place pronouncing one "fit," thus giving personal identity through association, acceptance, and support. This acceptance leads to action and Christian mission. Churches which fail to see the importance of personal identity for their ministry miss the great personal value of the church itself in the twentieth century.

Religious conversion has a primary relationship with the deep issues which encourage identity. It is not a relationship in actual time, but in the type of issues that it can deal with. Erik Erikson suggested that one does not successfully move through to the next identity issue and, therefore, to a healthy identity unless one successfully deals with the various stage-ascendancy issues. This is important in the relationship to religious conversion, for with the latter experience in a moment of thorough, gradual decision making, one may rework the previous unsuccessful stages and emerge on the positive side.

Both experiences may have roots within the conflicts of adolescence and, therefore, with role experimentation too. Adolescent role-taking and rejecting of roles allows for rapid change of viewpoint and provides for increased conflict. Adolescence is a major time when identity, frustrations, and change take place most rapidly because of environmental, psychological, emotional, and cultural development. I believe that the same parallels and factors are widened in religious conversion. It is in youth that the first questions are encountered regarding ultimates in life, and the concern for personal future begins. These questions find answers in both religious conversion and identity questing. Experimentation in roles and ideology becomes prominent in this period and allows for observation and acceptance of new worldviews. A resolution for ideological and role confusion is found through religious conversion and through resolution of identity problems. At this time, issues must be resolved regarding a meaningful future, solutions which these experiences provide. A unique intensity of emotion is apparent at this same time due to genetic, environmental, and societal pressures. Change often occurs at a rapid pace.

Since personal identity rests on the foundation of trust, autonomy, initiative, role modeling, a coherent sense of self, etc., the identity crisis may become a normal experience in adolescence and intersect with the growing ideology of a youth. Since the identity crisis in adolescence, the later identity issues faced by women due to intimacy demands, and even perhaps we might add the midlife crisis during the adult years, are times for ideological confusion, it would seem that all these identity periods would be ripe for religious conversion. Studies on church growth even seem to suggest this. People who leave religious organizations after having been converted to them seldom return during the very first years. Their reasons for staying away seem too obvious, perhaps, and they have not had time to restructure their own ideology. However, after fifteen years or so, many come back to their original belief systems, many during midlife crisis. New ideology is being formed, and, therefore, new chance for change occurs.[53] Conversion is, in the words of Charles Curran, "the central moral message of Jesus."[54] If so, this means that conversion may be the generator of ethical decisions and begin the divine-human relationship that makes the walk of faith clear and its action focused.

The religious conversion experience and the experience of identity both have this important feeling tone and crisis sense. Crisis feelings include a sense of dividedness, disunity, and increased tension. As with any decision, there is a certain amount of anxious unrest before resolution. In identity crisis, however, there is a unique difference, which suggests as well that identity experiences do not necessarily have to be religious in nature. There is in the confusions and tensions of identity experience no sense of sin per se, unless shame and guilt, may be taken as its precursors. As the two experiences actually blend in religious conversion, sin and salvation, good and evil, shame and sinfulness, freedom and joy all participate in the resolution. The similar feeling tones of the two experiences, that of positive resolution, with its sense of unity, organization, and postdisaster utopia, suggest the identity function in religious conversion. Through the experience of religious identity, life has new meaning, direction, and purpose, and the person experiencing religious-identity-conversion has a new place in life history—yes, even salvation history, through his or her return to God.

In identity experience and in religious conversion experience there is an intensity of feelings toward commitment. There is always sincerity in this commitment. The identity function of religious conversion sends the individual through strong feelings of anxiety or confusion, of giving up, or surrender to ultimates. After the crisis is over, tension is related and feelings of unity begin. Sincerity is evident. The resulting commitment is usually new. For identity experience alone, it may be an intensely committed belief in oneself, while religious-identity conversions produce commitment to God. Deep commitment exists in both.

When we look at the two experiences themselves, both are framed, molded, and shaped by the actual manifestation of conflict and tension. These factors always exist in the midst of crises. The question being resolved aids in the magnitude of the experience itself. "Who am I?" "Where am I going?" and "What is there in life for me?" are existential questions with conflicts and tension. These questions themselves are the kind that fashion turning points. They provide movement toward maturity and the answers become identity tags in the movement toward God. There is, however, slight similarity in the way extreme identity experience and acute religious conversion experience are physically manifested. The physical manifestations that accompany religious conversion experiences do not seem to be duplicated in most identity crises. When the identity crisis takes the shape of conversion specifically, then there are similarities, for the experience is a part of each.

---

53. Research done in church growth patterns conducted during 1977-78 in the Southeastern California Conference of Seventh-Day Adventists.

54. Charles E. Curran, "Conversion: The Central Moral Message of Jesus," *A New Look at Christian Morality* (Notre Dame, Ind.: Fides, 1970), pp. 25-71.

Religious conversion and personal identity experience deal with existential questions. Yet religious conversion, even though usually framed in a more open religious context, since it is a decision for God, provides the same kinds of anchorages that positive identity resolution provides. These answers sometimes seem to be accompanied with struggles and intense anguish.

Religious conversion may become a more negative identity decision for some, or a kind of retreat for others. Since the formation of a negative identity is a means of resolving the confusion of identity in negative terms, in order for conversion to be a negative function of identity its content must contain those identities that are the opposite of that which the youth wants to become or was told to become. This is probably not a genuine religious conversion, but perhaps we could call it a counter-conversion, implying that it is not a positive thing but is brought about by manipulation and impulse; it is a reaction rather than a choice responding to inner needs or the pleading of an ultimate Being. This also takes into account that some religious conversions are easily explained through external causes, through the experience of reaction, pressure, revivalism, emotionalism, or peer pressure. These may not provide lasting answers to the questions of life and identity. This does not in any way imply that a change does not occur, but change is not evidence of genuineness; it is simply a validation that movement has taken place within the center of a person. For religious conversion to be a negative identity there must be an incomplete understanding of one's identity. There may even be a kind of pathology or a high tendency toward suggestion in this counter-conversion. As understood here, conversion relates more favorably with identity formation than with negative identity formation. The possibility exists, however, for religious conversion to function in such a way as to be a reaction against rather than a movement toward. And since conversion is viewed as a means of solving intense identity-like conflict, the possibility exists for it to evidence itself as a negative identity in some cases.

Religious conversion could even be a kind of identity moratorium. It may provide a time for the youth, or the adult for that matter, to experiment with ideological directions and their implied role definitions. For religious conversion to be part of a moratorium it must be viewed not so much as a movement and an experience as a commitment to an ideology or intensely held position. This, you remember, is a part of our working definition of religious conversion. It is in this respect that the conversion moratorium permits basic life decisions, yet across time after the basic commitment to God for possible determination and experimentation. Eventually, however, the role will become plain, and the youth will continue to mature. Religious conversion viewed as longitudinally occurring over a long period, has a much closer relationship here than conversion viewed as rapid and decisive. The actual functional relationships of religious conversion to identity formation are many. The functions these experiences perform are observable. For example, each experience provides through resolution or decision many of the same results.

Through religious conversion a sense of faith is established, by the convert's faith-leap. Something or someone outside oneself is presented as being available, and hope is encouraged. Religious conversion implies an ideological framework, and integral to this framework is "hope." By accepting the something or someone outside as able to sustain you and solve the dilemmas of life, hope becomes a factor in consciousness.

The products of identity resolution have religious overtones. Hope is nourished by faith generated in the convert's decision to trust God. Purpose is nourished through the childhood play in identity formation, and in the decisions due to conversion adults often find life direction. The individual finds a unifying purpose in accepting and yielding. Erik Erikson's fidelity, as one of the virtues and products of identity formation, finds reinforcement when the decision made in religious conversion allows for new loyalties, freely pledged, in view of alternative or contradictory value systems. The intensity of commitment usually accompanying the conversion strengthens feelings of fidelity. The biblical concept of love is shown in the community of faith provided by these as the new convert joins for fellowship. Here sharing is developed as an additional strength seen in identity as well. Care is in the conversion experience through the totality of change and the concomitant ideological framework, which usually is religious and probably is humanitarian.

Wisdom, that detached concern with life itself in the face of death, is planted through the commitment of conversion. Religious conversions commit one to a direction, to a grappling with existential questions whose answers promote wisdom and peace in later life or old age. In addition to the above function, the experiences themselves are alike and must be viewed as blended in that both religious conversion and personal identity allow self-certainty to be developed through role experimentation. The religious convert finds a new role for himself or herself; that role may be different in its demands. Religious conversion experience produces identity itself, then, and it is perhaps here that we find their closest relationship.

A major role in the religious conversion experience that cannot be overlooked is its function in identity formation itself. The religious conversion experience is a calling to something new, something reorganizing and integrating on a deep level of consciousness. Conversion causes heightened awareness and acute perceptions of danger to the self; therefore, a heightened coping activity within the mind ensues. It causes a desperate search for resources by which to meet the needs so vividly experienced with the sole purpose of providing newness—new ideologies, new perceptions, new achievements, new commitments. Religious conversion brings to sharp focus a person's role in crisis and awakens and mobilizes resources for resolution of the tension produced through sin. Religious conversion provides a new and unusual opportunity to deal with life in a fresh and creative way and therefore the religious conversion experience has as its prime function to provide a sense of wholeness and continuity with life. This is an obvious correlation with the identity theories. It may provide a group identity and even a historical identity, if the experience comes with a supporting group. It is possible that conversion functions in terms of the ego processes, too. Since the ego functions as a regulator and guide to the crisis experience and is at the core of the decisions and their resolutions—providing sameness, integrity, and continuity in spite of change—so religious conversion functions as a regulator resolving conflict and providing continuity and congruity. Both experiences seem to make use of this function of the ego. Granted, religious conversion includes an element of the supernatural working through the natural process, but this aspect is hard to observe and probably even harder to explain or understand.

Religious conversion, like identity, fills the intense need for devotion. It is this aspect of identity crisis and conversion which forms the basic drive toward establishing a meaningful worldview. This need for devotion in individuals allows ideologies which promote devotion to play major roles in determining identity and provides the content for its formation itself. Ideologies offer simple but determined answers to those vague questions caused by both crisis and conflict. The religious identity experience of conversion is a fulfiller of this ideological need.

Personal identity experience, then, is a context for faith. Religious conversion as an identity-forming experience provides the moment for faith to begin. Why people chose God in religious conversion is hard to explain, but at least one such reason is that religion contains an answer to life's questions. And since we are postulating that religious conversion is a means for experiencing personal identity, the factors that influence identity also influence conversion.

Society and culture impact on the way the struggle for identity is perceived, much as religious society and religious culture prepare youth for religious resolutions to life's problems in conversion. For example, common patterns of upbringing acceptable in one particular culture may produce individuals who have shared specific areas of vulnerability and predict certain kinds of identity formation. Religious conversion, likewise, is influenced by culture, group pressure, revivalism, even by possible personality correlates which make for susceptibility. For those whom religious conversion can readily be traced to vulnerability, there may even be a correlation between failure to successfully fulfill the crisis stages of identity formation and then experience a religious conversion as a counter-conversion or a form of negative identity.

In addition to cultural and societal influences that shape the experience, there can be added psychological, emotional, gender, and developmental contexts for both experiences. The same factors that aid in successfully completing the epigenetic cycle for Erikson could well be operating in the religious conversion experience, too. For example, peer pressure, group identity, societal norms, and an adult guarantor's suggestions and influence would have a positive or even a negative correlation to the experience in the same way each of these influence inner and outer change through identity.

It would appear that there is a primary relationship, then, between the contexts of both experiences as they appear in the developmental, emotional, psychological, and societal milieu of life.

There are obvious areas, however, where no relationships can be observed in these two experiences, and only tertiary similarities can be postulated. For example, I believe that conversion cannot be totally equated with identity experience, partly due to the limitations of the definitions themselves. Sudden religious conversion stresses a specific moment or decisive time of change. Personal identity experience has been suggested as being a process beginning with birth and ending at death. Adolescence and youth are prime ages for intense struggle and resolution of many identity conflicts, and so during this time religious conversion as an identity function may occur. If identity is seen as a lifelong process, largely unconscious to the individual and his society unless a more radical confusion or negative identity or moratorium occurs, it has its closest relationship, then, in the more gradual form of religious conversion, whose changes in the religious life happen almost imperceptibly. In this context religious conversion would have a close relationship with identity. Here then is the obvious contrast. Religious conversion tends to show up more often in the form of a crisis moment with rapid resolution and is like the crisis of identity experience but not like the process of identity formation itself. Therefore, religious conversion is a means of acquiring an identity—not the identity process per se, but only one small part of it.

The identity experience is subtle and unconscious at times; when the crisis and confusional states of identity are more openly felt and resolved there is a more open parallel with conversion. Yet one cannot eliminate the real sense of "religious" always present in religious conversion. The presence of the "holy" is significant for conversion to be meaningful; without this it becomes just an identity experience. Perhaps the differences are as significant as the similarities in this case. Only if through the intense struggle of identity formation would the participant in this struggle attach some subjective religious quality to the experience could an identity experience be construed to be totally equated with religious conversion experience. A person going through this kind of experience attaches meaning of a religious nature to it. He would do better to change his so-called identity struggle to the religious conversion struggle to eliminate definitional confusion. Conversion must, therefore, be thought of as a kind of identity experience. It is safe to suggest, I believe, that all conversion experiences are identity-related, but obviously not all identity experiences are religious conversions. Religious conversion is a subheading for identity in this specialized sense.

Summary

What can be concluded, then, is first, religious conversion experiences and identity crisis experiences involving a resolution of crisis constitute means whereby individuals may radically change at a deep and meaningful level. These changes affect the basic self, for they affect ideology, behavior, and ego processes, which are the core of a person's being.

Second, there are many functional relationships between religious conversion and personal identity formation in the areas of ego strength genesis, identity formation itself, ego processes, ideological satisfactions, and role experimentation.

Third, in the constituent dynamics of religious conversion and personal identity experiences, similar relationships exist as to the fundamental nature of the crises experienced. These include similarities in the general feeling tones, constructs of the crises, content of the crises, decisions, and the obvious resultant functions of integration and congruity.

Fourth, regarding the context of both, parallels exist which verify the assumptions posed. As in religious conversion, identity experience has a similar context in developmental and emotional need fulfillment. The ascendancy of adolescence in both experiences is most significant. Both experiences deal with need satisfaction, age, problem orientation, and maturational development during the troubled time of questing.

This identity quality of the religious conversional change hints at the importance of recognizing that knowing God personally through religious conversion is identity producing. Personal identity is a beautiful biblical theme. God works through people "called by name" to be used in the task of revealing God's character to the world. Churches, synagogues, parishes, and fellowship groups cluster around a common identity. Interaction within and through fellow pilgrims focuses identity, sustains it, gives it a purpose and a coherence to life. The apostle Paul suggested a boldness that allows the one "in Christ" to come into the very presence of God. The confrontation for those with hope and trust and a sense of oneness with God would be fraught with fear and dread without this new-found identity. Yet we enter into God's presence in scripture because God has given us a way of access. In the Christian context we find new identity now through Christ's death.

Practical Considerations

The process of religious conversion and the development of personal identity have practical impact. For example, if identity issues are a natural part of the life cycle, the church might make a greater impact on believers if its ministry at significant ages centered on those needs that nudge identity. And if religious conversion is a way of resolving identity issues, the evangelism of the church could become more personal and directly impact the lives of people.

Practical considerations of the close relationship between personal identity and religious conversion have implications for pastors, religious educators, pastoral counselors, religious workers, and parents. For example consider the following areas of ministry and religious education:

1) *Church curriculum:* The development of curriculum in the church has a varied history. The causes for change in what is taught are often driven by cultural shifts or by denominational concern. For example, I know of a denomination which had initiated a comprehensive study plan for the entire adult population of the church in North America. The curriculum was to include a complete exegesis of all the biblical books during a ten-year cycle. During the course of study, about year five, certain denominational priorities erupted to impact the curriculum design. Theological controversy over righteousness by grace and certain eschatological interpretations caused the headquarters to interrupt this orderly progression and institute study of specific doctrines to stem the growing theological fragmentation. The curriculum was being driven by content and culture rather than by the needs of the learner. Needs-oriented curriculum planning would have prevented this roller-coaster shift in emphasis. Identity issues which can be resolved in commitment through conversion could have been considered when the curriculum was designed and implemented. This would represent a needs-driven curriculum that might move toward commitment. Included in the topics for consideration during the curriculum cycle might be such things as material for divorced parents, women's concerns, community problems, political issues which the church can impact, and environmental areas of neglect. These needs-based curriculum modules would lead the church members to a clearer understanding of their purpose in life, their role in community development, enhance self-esteem through that focus, and through these identity areas assist commitment both personally and institutionally.

2) *Pastoral counseling:* Church workers interested in the personal dynamic which occurs in the counseling situation could be benefited by an identity focus, too. The moments when identity issues seem insurmountable, the times when refocusing is needed and mission clarified can be opportunities for the professional to suggest that religion may provide answers to these basic unsettling crises and questions.

3) *Pastoral planning and worship:* Pastoral facilitators and liturgists can use the relationships between identity and religious conversion to prepare significant devotional and worship experiences which both model God-like-

ness and provide affective touchstones with the divine. Since both experiences center on major directional shifts, and encourage both sincerity and devotion, commitment and heightened awareness of God's presence in one's life can be facilitated through careful liturgical planning.

4) *Religious instruction:* The implications in this area of church life are significant as well. Those who plan activities and develop methods of interpreting the faith history and faith life can help. What methods are the best suited to encouraging resolution of personal identity issues and will focus on the religious answers to life-significant questions? How can the outreach and modeling of the church community be changed because of the relationship? What content is best suited for what age group because of the significant identity and conversional issues which are beginning to emerge?

Answers to these questions are explored in the next chapters.

Chapter 8

Conversion: Identity and Religious Instruction

"Man [woman] is not liberated from his [her] old nature by imperatives to be new and to change, but he [she] rejoices in the new which makes him [her] free and lifts him [her] beyond himself [herself]. Where repentance is understood as a spiritual return to the evil and rejected past, it deals in self-accusation, contrition, sackcloth and ashes. But when repentance is a return to the future, it becomes concrete in rejoicing, in new self-confidence, and in Love."

Jürgen Moltmann.

Pastors, religious workers, pastoral counselors, and religious educators often think of their impact on others. Sometimes we overestimate our power on others, but more often we forget that impact. Since religious feelings seem so mystical, so other-worldly, and often are so ethereal we lose heart and fail to recognize the significant role each of us plays in others' religious commitments and change. Somehow we believe that the Holy Spirit will make up the difference in our inadequacies and provide for those to whom we minister that which we are unable to provide. As James Michael Lee points out, this "blow theory" of religious instruction is an incomplete model of how people learn about God and depreciates the role we have in the process of change.[1]

The process of change, through religious conversion with its religious motivation or through identity with a more secular source—or a seemingly secular one—gives new meaning to life. Identity formation—meaning-mak-

---

1. James Michael Lee, *The Flow of Religious Instruction* (Birmingham, Ala.: Religious Education Press, 1973), p. 42.

ing—shapes cognitive, affective, moral, and religious dimensions.[2] These experiences move us out beyond the now and point us to the future, as Moltmann suggests. Making or assisting change in people is also costly. As Robert Kegan says, "Growth involves a separation from an old system of meaning. In practical terms this can involve both the agony of felt meaninglessness and the repudiation of commitments and investments. To the educator the first can be experienced as frightening, the second as offensive; both as alienating."[3] Personal identity and religious conversion as experiences of change force us to see the way to help, to clarify the methods to use, and focus on the meaning of our personal existence. Those insights may be painful to see.

Guiding individuals to God is at most exceptionally difficult, and teachers of religious values have been confronted with a most complex task, confused in its content, and little understood in its process.

One outcome of religion, of course, is change, and this is a purpose implicit within the religious educator's and pastoral facilitator's task. Change in experience and in behavior toward God is the outward manifestation. Shift in values, worldview, and commitment is the inward goal. The religious educator, pastoral facilitator, and pastoral counselor have, however, a number of factors in their favor as the educational/theological task they initiate, especially when it comes to the specific task of aiding change and growth in religious values.

First, religious instruction is an intentional activity. It does not happen by chance or in isolation, and because of this specific goals must be targeted and precise methods employed which enhance the possibility of change. While it is obvious that such values as commitment, faith, love, and hope are important, everyone who has ever explored the process of value formation realizes that at some point the learner must be in charge of the learning and responsible for eventual internalization of those values.[4] After all, how does one learn to cherish someone else's values? Therefore, commitment and reorganization of one's worldview can be significant curriculum concerns. Emerging from the *Valuegenesis* research among Seventh-Day Adventists are some forty-one characteristics of families, congregations, and schools that are associated with faith maturity and loyalty to the denomination. Both national research and *Valuegenesis* have shown that the *effectiveness factors* are additive. That is, the more a congregation, family, or school or college have them in place in adult or youth ministry, the greater growth in faith maturity. In the

---

2. Robert Kegan, "Where the Dance Is: Religious Dimensions of a Developmental Framework," in *Toward Moral and Religious Maturity* by Christiane Brusselmans and James A. O'Donohoe (Morristown, N.J.: Silver Burdett, 1980), p. 438.

3. Ibid., p. 439.

4. Lucie W. Barber, *Teaching Christian Values* (Birmingham, Ala.: Religious Education Press, 1984), p. 93.

Protestant study it was discovered that the effectiveness factors were associated with growth in faith maturity even though the average time adults
and youth spend in formal Christian education programs and events is fairly minimal. Even when youth or adults spend as little as fifteen to twenty
hours per year in Christian education, exposure to effective programs produces
greater faith growth than exposure to less effective programs.[5]

Both the substantive content of faith and the structural process of the
educational experience seem to be powerful forces in teaching in the classical
sense the insight and knowledge of theology, but also in allowing personal
insight to emerge from the arena of experience. Both ways of learning are
powerful, and the two combinations produce a higher faith growth than any
one or either alone according to Benson.[6] These *effectiveness factors* include
such things as: *family practices* which engage the young in helping projects
and in family worship; *mother's religiousness*—the amount of time that she
talks about her faith with the child; *father's religiousness*—the amount of time
that the father and child talk together; *support*—the way that family life is
experienced as loving, caring, and supportive; and in areas of *control*—wherein the family enforces behavioral standards that are life-affirming and assists
in educating the young about life-threatening activities. *Valuegenesis* identified additional congregational *effectiveness factors* that are intentional too.
These include: congregational *climate* issues and effective religious educational programing. School factors related to faith maturity and denominational
loyalty include: *religious programing* and *faith talk* by the teachers as well
as a *caring and supportive climate* in which the school spirit is high and
discipline is perceived as fair.[7]

In this research we discovered that of the forty-one possible effectiveness factors a young person could be exposed to through intentional religious education programing and careful family involvement, only 75 percent
of the youth experienced seven or more of them. In addition, only twenty-six
of these factors were experienced by less than 50 percent of the youth. That
suggests that in grades nine to twelve, you find 53 percent of the students with
high faith maturity and high loyalty have experienced at least three or more
of these factors in congregations, home, and school. So simply by increasing
the number of factors in all three venues, students might slowly develop a

---

5. Peter L. Benson and Carolyn H. Elkin, *Effective Christian Education: A
National Study of Protestant Congregations Summary Report* (Minneapolis: Search
Institute, March 1990), p. 53.

6. Ibid.

7. See Peter L. Benson, Michael J. Donahue, V. Bailey Gillespie, C. Thomas
Smith, Stuart Tyner, Steve Case, *Valuegenesis Document C: A Study of the Influence
of School, Church, and Family on the Formation of Faith Involving Youth, Parents,
Teachers, Principals, and Pastors in the North American Division of the Seventh-Day
Adventist Church—A Summary Report on Faith, Loyalty, Standards, and Schools*
(Minneapolis: Search Institute, 1990).

more mature faith and deeper denominational loyalty. Instruction which has a target and purpose is needed if the opportunity to return to and find identity in God is to be increased.

Next, the religious educator works with individuals who are seeking identity and change. Self-understanding takes time, but the fact that the learner is moving toward change aids the process. All the movements which accompany conversion may occur. Lucie Barber correctly suggests that the action-reflection model is an instructional method to consider in value education, and, since personal ownership of values is the goal for the religious educator, commitment to the long haul is important.[8] And, since the learner's own development is moving toward personal identity, instruction in religion can capitalize on this interest in a most unique way. Educators talk of "teachable moments" and "readiness for learning" as factors in the retention of learning and the perdurability of the transfer of educational content. What better time to instruct in the fundamentals of faith than when individuals are cognitively ready, emotionally concerned, and attitudinally focused on outcomes that impact their whole life and future. If commitment to God is a desired outcome of the learning process, and the conversional model of change contributes to an emerging self-understanding, religious instruction must take into account the readiness for religion which identity experience or its religious counterpart, conversion, offers.

This innate quest in people can be built upon by the religious educator and pastoral facilitator. It seems logical, then, to look at the obvious implications for those engaged in Christian nurture and faith genesis.

The process of religious education is difficult to clarify, as already mentioned. According to Lewis Sherrill, it "is the attempt, ordinarily by members of the Christian community, to participate in and to guide the changes which take place in persons in their relationships with God, with the church, with other persons, with the physical world and with oneself."[9] This type of education is defined by the unique type of content and process born of the tradition involved in the lives of others.

Like William Bedford Williamson, I once believed religious education to be a very easy subject to talk about—simply a process whereby the learner of any age is taught in the setting of the Christian faith. I now realize this simplistic approach is naive, if not presumptuous.[10]

How do you understand a process that is developmental, age-specific, and theological, not to mention religiously experiential? To understand the process of religious education is to understand the mystery of the atonement. St. Paul himself uses pictures to describe it. In allusions to its forensic,

---

8. Barber, *Teaching Christian Values*, p. 93.

9. Lewis J. Sherrill, *The Gift of Power* (New York: Macmillan, 1955), p. 82.

10. William Bedford Williamson, *Concepts and Language in Christian Education* (Philadelphia: Westminster, 1970), p. 32.

moral, and personal nature, he suggests that it is like a law court, a slave market, and a temple.[11] He uses other symbols to hint at its significance. He calls God's people to become children, to be reborn, to enter into the new creation, to participate in another exodus, and to enter into Sabbath "rest." The process is supernatural, the direction is redemptive and freeing, and the nomenclature is symbolic. Religious education is a process like that. It can be defined in the same theological context as atonement, for its purposes and goals are equal. Just as the process of ministerial training is to instruct in skills, tools, and theology to enable God's people to be instruments in dispensing God's grace to a lost/saved world, so the ministry of the religious educator and pastoral facilitator is to dispense God's grace within an educational setting, be it the church, parish, or schoolroom. This enabling process requires focus on religious change, attempts at reorganization of self, development of relevant content, and exciting new methods, just as any other kind of education does. Because it is a redemptive activity, it is conversional in nature and mission.

At this point, I could begin a long defense and definition of the educational setting, but that would bypass the main purpose of this chapter. In this brief suggestion I only want to remind that learning takes place everywhere, and the educational setting for religion cannot be limited to the school, church, home, Sunday school, pastor's study, youth program, or local fellowship. Religious education's primary function involves instruction and involvement in all of life itself: in life situations religious educational concerns, religious identity, and personal identity issues. Williamson concludes that the "only answer to religious education and the church's attempt at trying to define theologies, personnel for an activity, or programs often described as instruction is development of content material selected as important and relevant to the particular Christian group, with appropriate methods and for purposes and ends designated by the group."[12] This is obviously limited in approach. Therefore, religious education includes indoctrination, but in addition it includes the process of life change. One model which attempts such age-specific change-oriented education is the educational system promoted by Barber in her book, *Teaching Christian Values*. Here she attempts through backward progression to approach the teaching of change as an attempt to teach Christian maturity. She hopes that through evaluating the contributions of others (sixteen to twenty-eight years), learning evaluation skills (twelve to fifteen years), perceiving the talents of self and others (six to eleven years), and in discovering talents (two to five years) will provide a system which moves people toward maturity in their Christian life and utilizes more than just cognitive methodology.[13]

11. Romans 3:24-26.
12. Williamson, *Concepts and Language in Christian Education*, p. 37.
13. Barber, *Teaching Christian Values*, pp. 206-209.

If the essentials of the Christian faith are to be assimilated, its tenets must be internalized and education and pastoral ministry will use as its methodology implicit freedom to choose positions, for through indoctrination may come commitment, but only if presented in the light of God's free love. So, while listing the aims of this religious education process, certain theological priorities come to the front. Some priorities seem to stand out:

1) Actual growth in the church is an important by-product of the religious educational task.

2) Developing in persons the capability for religious responses to life and enhancing the divine/human encounter as well as explaining religious truth become key goals.

3) Development of the learner-teacher relationship becomes key in learning religion.

All of these issues find some kind of focus in religious conversion and identity function, as well. How, then, does understanding the close relationship of identity formation and religious conversion affect the teacher-learner-God relationship? How can religious instruction for the school or parish be enhanced because of the connection between personal identity and religious conversion?

Intergenerational or Questor-Guide Relationships

Religious instruction is first enhanced by improvement in the teacher-learner relationship. Identity issues which surface have religious significance and are grappled with in a context of a community whose values become instrumental in leading growing persons through acceptable and confirming roles.

The student should be understood as questor. Eager expectation about the life of faith can be validated by a community of faith. Since religious conversional change and identity experience is nurtured by what is perceived and expected by the roles that are chosen, importance must be given to the selection of the guides whose encounters with questors of identity can be validating and affirming. Encounter situations should be a concern for the body of believers. For as the youth engage with adults whose identity is secure, within this encounter the perceived values will enhance their conversion and verify the church's meaning.

Concern for identity needs by leaders will aid in this process of change. Religious conversion as an identity anchorage can be understood only through teachers who fully comprehend the experiences the youth are going through during their crises.

Since religious conversion seems to be an experience which, through manipulation or coercion, may lead to a negative identity, it would be well for youth leaders, pastors, religious educators, and youth to function together as units, sharing roles, faith experiences, and mutual identities, rather than as adults trying to manipulate youth to convert or to "have" an experience. Exploration of intergenerational ministry could begin this process. Pastoral staffs, religious education faculties, and religious teachers should encourage an *intergenerational context for faith building*. When all generations can share in the interchange of Christian ideas, responsibility, and worship, the symbolic meanings of faith become relevant to the questor—through the guide.

Intergenerational Religious Education is the descriptive definition for what churches and synagogues have been trying for decades. This attempt at directing worship and learning in a context of multigenerations provides a unique model for religious learning and growth within the body of faith. People who learn through their "in-common" experiences, who share "parallel-learning" experiences, and experience what James White calls "contributive-occasions" and "interactive-sharing" learn more clearly about their identity and therefore vision their faith more directly.[14] People identify their own role and function through interacting with various age groups. The activities that are shared provide a "critique of the notion of their self-sufficient, autonomous individuality."[15] This intergenerational aspect of learning provides unity and healing in a congregation who finds themselves broken and isolated. In addition, "the church/synagogue becomes more nearly what it was intended to be and what it vows to be, namely, a living/learning/faithing people of God."[16] After all, the journey of faith is not one which is done in isolation but is always one which is involved with others. Intergenerational activities enhance personal identity development.[17]

There are additional growth benefits from intergenerational religious education. For example, the leadership becomes focused toward a purpose—thus self-esteem is enhanced. Those who direct the programs must "call forth the creative best in people" and this means that they will be forced to explore options that members feel are important and through this process the identity of others will be enriched.

Therefore, it would seem in this intergenerational context, more effective teachings of the values of religion in life and society could be done. Many evangelical churches have learned this lesson. Bill Bright of Campus Crusade for Christ suggests, "We have to model what we believe. If we want our children to be soul-winners, they need to see it in our lives. We can also expose them to other people who are good models, people who are not only living attractive, radiant lives, but who are also witnessing for

---

14. James White, *Intergenerational Religious Education* (Birmingham, Ala.: Religious Education Press, 1988), pp. 26-29.
15. Ibid., p. 250.
16. Ibid., p. 251.
17. Ibid., p. 96.

Christ. We can do more through teaching than through preaching, more through example than through demands."[18]

By realizing the identity potential of return to God through religious conversion, the church family creates an accepting atmosphere of trust, hope, value, faith, and even trustworthiness. Youth would, I believe, be more free to select a positive direction for their lives rather than to experience counter-conversion and a possible negative identity reaction if they regularly experience this type of acceptance and belonging. Tragically, people all too often do not sense this kind of acceptance in church. It is often more clear to youth that people would not only die for what they believe but that they would kill anyone who does not see it the way they do!

If we use an attitude of kindness, openness, rich in intergenerational experiences, *creativity* would emerge in the local educational setting of the church. Creativity is an expression of freedom, an expression of an individual finding his or her own way, so necessary to relating to God.

Many students would like to try new things and be creative but sense an aura of disapproval from adults who view this creativity as "obstreperousness" or "rebellion," because the creativity may result in something "different." Even though the goal is to develop creativity on the basis of freedom, teachers often feel threatened by these divergent thinkers, and creativity is hampered. Many educators may agree that individuality is desirable and even express the necessity for it, yet when it actually takes place (for example, in a religion class by a challenging new exegesis, or a new method of evangelism) we, as teachers rather than as guides, feel threatened by the directness and new insight that this creative person insists upon showing. It is a strange paradox, indeed. When one seeks for God in the life and makes a free response, he or she is able then to choose and return to God; yet we often stifle the freedom to choose by coercion and mold the setting wherein the choice is to be made. When creativity does show up, it differs in style or arrangement from our typical views. Charges of heresy are often shouted, as we ourselves fear a challenge to our position. Youth perceive it as suppression of personal identity and individuality.

Oftentimes youth view the religious educator as another parent. The questors see themselves in a kind of supremacy game with the educator, trying to achieve personal identity and answer the question "Who is in charge here?" However, with this concept prevalent in some youths' minds, the teacher who fails to guide and be sensitive to the quest in process closes the door to an identity resolution or even to a religious commitment. So often the teacher verifies who is really in charge and holds the authority in the class setting. There will be no doubt in youths' minds just what they must do or learn in order to beat the system and emerge victorious, for the teacher, pas-

18. Bill Bright, "Be What You Believe," in *Parents and Teenagers* by Jay Kesler (Wheaton, Ill.: Victor Books, 1984), p. 329.

tor, or religious professional will let it be known who is the fount of truth. A pseudo-intellectual guessing game ensues with the youth trying to guess his or her identity by proper questions and answers. Adults leading individuals toward free identity choices must concern themselves with some of the following issues. Good intergenerational approaches which foster creativity must include:

1) *Openness for questioning.* One of Christ's greatest teaching devices was the honest question. An atmosphere of freedom existed for people to approach Jesus to question him regarding his own mission and message. Earnest seekers after truth must feel open to express frank and deep questions. Creative questions may be the springboard to great insights otherwise left unexplored and a permanent change.

2) Religious educators must in the relationship *reflect the God they too seek,* rather than direct the focus to themselves. This approach will eliminate the ego-tripping of many religious educators who promote their own views as the only truths to be grasped.

3) *Avoidance of "preaching the truth"* to others will result in individuals who have found truth for themselves. Exploration of religious literature and scripture will be invited rather than prescribed; therefore, the truth perceived by the young questor in identity formation will be his or her truth, and personal faith will begin to emerge. Strommen suggests an "incarnational theology" and a renewed sensitivity to those with low self-esteem if religion is to be learned and lives changed. He notes that a rules-oriented religion which low self-esteem youth often tend to accept, must be exposed as practical atheism by contrasting it with a gospel of affirmation and grace.[19] Just being cognizant of the problems generated by poor relationships is not enough according to the research data provided by Search Institute. "It is the empathic and warm relationship of a concerned person" that makes the difference, according to Strommen. The research concludes, "Clearly increased adult interest and attention make a measurable impact on the lives of youth."[20]

4) Intergenerational workers will *listen to counter arguments* and facts without fear of losing the identity seeker. A classic social psychological experiment done in 1949 by Lumsdaine and Sheffield showed that when a belief is so widespread in a society that various individuals have no opportunity to encounter contradictory evidence or opinion, the belief will yield to strong persuasive attacks at a much later date. This is because the individuals have no occasion to develop resistance to counterattack. The principle can apply to our work with youth in the identity quest. Youth respect sound arguments from guarantors who know their beliefs and respect personal commitments but will learn in a more committed way when they are able to

---

19. Merton P. Strommen, *Five Cries of Youth* (New York: Harper & Row, 1988), p. 38.

20. Ibid., pp. 37-40.

be themselves and ask their own questions. As Paul Irwin has suggested, "The church fails its youth if it lacks spirit, but it fails them equally if it does not encourage the discipline of critical thought in shaping vision of life that can provide intelligent direction."[21] It would seem that more effective teaching of values of religion and society could be done by realizing the identity potential of the conversion experience and by providing an atmosphere of trust, hope, and fidelity in which youth could select the direction of their lives rather than causing counter-conversion, as we have called it, and forcing youth into a possible negative identity.

Adults in their relationships with youth should also provide proper moratoria for role experimentation itself. If the experience of conversion becomes a possible moratorium for dealing with the issues of living in this negative sense, adults should respect this aspect of the religious conversion process.

Since historical processes are vitally related to the demand for personal identity in each new generation, and since religious conversion is a means of entering into the collective community of faith in a given tradition, proper, clear, and determined understandings of the historical perspectives of a personal role and place in history and a collective role in society will aid in avoiding identity crises based on failure to know where one fits "in the scheme of things." Religious conversions—turning or returning to—would be easier if a clear understanding of the historical sense was elucidated by leaders in the church and school. Relationships are crucial: "The anthropological condition of religion is to be found in the 'dialectics' of individuals and society that pervade the processes in which consciousness and consciences are individuated."[22] Again in this dialectic, we affirm regularized status passages or "coaching relationships" which build new bridges in identity.[23]

5) Pastoral workers and religious educators could move individuals toward change through the use of methods which *stretch the imagination*. Jesus used such methods to encourage change and to move the disciples and his followers to a deeper understanding of the message of the kingdom. The message of the New Testament was not simply ideological, it was existential—it met needs, filled hearts, moved people beyond, opened up new futures, and reoriented lives. The call to change (conversion) and the invitation to become a member of the kingdom (identity) were at the heart of Jesus' preaching. Happel and Walter understand the purpose of Christ's parable teaching that way. They suggest that this mode of instruction helps encounter the world

---

21. Paul B. Irwin, *The Care and Counseling of Youth in the Church* (Philadelphia,: Fortress, 1975), p. 61.

22. Thomas Luckmann, *The Invisible Religion* (New York: Macmillan, 1967), p. 78.

23. Anselm L. Strauss, *Mirrors and Masks, The Search for Identity* (Glencoe, Ill.: Free Press, 1959), p. 100.

through a new way of looking at things, "but only on the condition that we are willing to shift our attitudes."[24]

The biblical imagery of change is not only to be found in the parables of the New Testament. There are numerous figures of speech in the biblical record which stress the deep shift in allegiance, the identity-forming allegiance, which God wants for the children of God. Such images as "being made alive" (Rom 4:17), "union with Christ" in death and resurrection (Rom 6:1-11), "called" to be a new creation (1 Cor 5:17), "dying to self" and rising again in Jesus (Rom 6:2-8) are all hints at the centrality of the conversional message in the Bible for Christians. Each allusion points to personal meaning and fulfillment and offers an identity along with salvation.

Identity, Values, Conversion, and Content

There are implications in this close association of religious conversion and the identity crisis for those who design curriculum materials and are concerned with the actual content of religious learning. It is important here to define content in its broadest sense, perhaps using James Michael Lee's definition which includes the actual process of education as content itself.[25] This kind of content must thoroughly reflect analysis of the emotional forces that the contents engender in the lives of those with whom educators come in contact. It has been said that the content itself should include a personal view of the individual problems of youth so the content will be "facing a face rather than merely facing a problem."[26] An awareness of the conflicts that cause experience to be expressed are important here.

Resolution of the conversion crisis of identity will, as mentioned before, generate values as a possible product. One primary function of religion is that of value genesis. People who know where they fit and who have a new ideology within God's family have a fresh hierarchy of values, it seems, which aids in the assessments and choices of life. One objective content, then, in religious experience is values. The test of how effective the return to God is, how real one's real identity with God and God's followers has become, is evidenced by how well-maintained and long-kept those values are. A gradual shifting of values, a slow erosion of their motivational thrust, or a rejection

24. Stephen Happel and James J. Walter, *Conversion and Discipleship: A Christian Foundation for Ethics and Doctrine* (Philadelphia: Fortress, 1986), p. 12.

25. See James Michael Lee, *The Content of Religious Instruction* (Birmingham, Ala.: Religious Education Press, 1985) for a complete discussion of the various contents of religious instruction. His work includes a discussion of the varied texture of religious content that has an impact on the conceptualization and the experience of God. His schema identifies nine substantive contents of religious instruction. They are: product, process, cognitive, affective, verbal, nonverbal, conscious, unconscious, and lifestyle.

26. Erik Erikson, *Young Man Luther* (New York: Norton, 1958), p. 17.

of the group's values could be a measure of how deep the quality of the new religious values and identity is. When religion no longer is the progenitor of values for its adherents, the religion is idolatry or, worse, hypocrisy. Values find sanction within the theology, culture, commitment, and values of adult guarantors as well as within the relationship with fellow pilgrims.

The religious educational setting is a primary time when this content of religious instruction is at the front. In the encounter of people moving toward God, values are prominent. If one would believe Ivan Illich, "School systems in general have as a primary focus the shaping of man's vision of reality."[27] If this is true of the so-called secular school, what depth of concern should the religious education enterprise have for developing proper values?

Since the work of pastors, religious workers, and religious educators is in that direct process of guiding the development of others, it is by nature involved in value building and curriculum creation. From the moment someone suggests the music to be listened to at an evening meeting to the method whereby discipline is meted out, religious education has the responsibility of sharing values. The sum total of all of the learning experiences constitutes the curriculum.

Much has been written regarding how values are generated and transmitted. Religious educators and pastoral facilitators must come to grips with the value generation of commitment and the processes which encourage commitment and change. Such methodologies as cooperative learning projects, building community, participatory decision making, storytelling, problem-solving methodologies, clarification, and choice-giving strategies for learning are some which could be explored in the religious setting.[28] Participation in values issues forces youth and adults to make choices, all of which move one to self-understanding and change.

Most recent major researchers in the field of value education at some time refer to Philip Jacob's 1957 study. Jacob's approach, designed to examine values and their transmission in higher education, found, in brief, that no specific curriculum patterns, no model syllabus for social science, no pedigree of instructor, no wizardry of method had much impact on values and their formation. Only two significant factors were hinted at that I believe are pertinent to our work: 1) Values changed within the distinctive climate of a few institutions; and 2) values changed through a relationship with and the personal magnitude of sensitive teachers.[29] Research since the Jacob's report has taken two directions. Agreement with his results sent scholars in search

----

27. Ivan Illich, *Deschooling Society* (New York: Harrow Books, 1970), p. 68.

28. Thomas Lickona, "Democracy, Cooperation, and Moral Education," in *Toward Moral and Religious Maturity*, ed. Christiane Brusselmans and James A. O'Donohoe (Morristown, N.J.: Silver Burdett, 1980), pp. 488-515.

29. See Philip Jacobs, *Changing Values in College* (New York: Harper & Row, 1957).

of extracurricular influences on values. Examples of these were the home, peer groups, and value-laden experiences. These projects yielded little fruit; however, some significant findings came from those who researched peer-group pressure. Changes for some students seemed to occur under this influence, with dormitory living tending to influence some negatively. This research was done in a secular environment, yet a parallel study within religious educational settings would prove an interesting project.

More fruitful, however, than the peer group studies have been those pursuing Jacob's clue that a few institutions held a climate which pervaded the whole institution and thus influenced students' values most. Surely this is not just a trick of fate or something that has just happened! This "climate" is the result of careful planning. The facilities of schools most effective in value changing were ones united in instruction, purpose, and mission. Those with a clear sense of direction became the instigators of change in students' lives and provided the framework whereby identity could be greatly enhanced. Both the effective religious education research and *Valuegenesis* research validates the importance of climate on values and faith maturity.

This is a clear call for self-appraisal, recommitment, and unity within religious educational settings. The century that found such growth in media, communication, and world concerns stands speechless unless recommitment to a purpose and reevaluation of personal involvement with the mission of God become key points again in our view of the religious educational task. This value in religion is an important concern for the religious educator.

Perhaps we have been living with the myth that because we believe intellectually in the best values they will be passed on to those we meet, somehow, someway, by someone, sometime. Evidence seems to contradict this assumption. The process of value formation and value transmission is a project that must be incorporated into the very philosophy, methodology, instruction, and curriculum of school, church, and home.

In any religious education situation, then, attempts should be made toward an understanding of our purposes. It is through clarification of one's purpose, task, and mission (identity) that values are clarified and change can come. It is this identity task that relates personal religious conversion experience to identity function

At a school board meeting I attended, while individuals were stressing the importance of using innovative curriculum materials, a question came regarding what affective and cognitive objectives were incorporated into the board's thinking of this new material. Most either did not know the meaning of the words, or ignored altogether the relationship of method to objectives. If little time is spent in clearly understanding our common mission in the world, aimless wandering will be the result and identity will never be formed. The tragic aftermath of our meanderings will be the minimal value change within those who experience our religious educational or pastoral setting.

Yet these questions can still be raised: How can a climate for learning be changed or directed? How is a climate established at all? Does one listen to the rumors in the constituency or to the natives within the compound in trying to evaluate it?

The climate for value learning is easily assessed. When the climate is positive, identity issues may be more easily understood. Some methods which emphasize life purpose and mission can include the following: 1) *Informal discussions* with students, parents, and individuals involved about specific goals for the mission of religious organizations. 2) *Retreats* with the sole function of establishing a God-given direction and reassessing the directions in the past, sharpening the religious focus on the real issues of mission. This method has come to be understood as *strategic planning* in the secular workplace and *future planning* for religious entities. 3) *Values orientation* among various disciplines within our churches and schools, noticing the relationship of each one's function with the other fields of study. This helps integrate religion into real life. This also helps to broaden the base for value learning, taking the sole responsibility away from the clergy and distributing it equally to the saints. If we are a priesthood of all the believers, this is an essential ingredient in assisting change in the local church, school, or home. 4) A conscious *meeting for direction*, with all the individuals involved in worship, where God can minister to the school by the Spirit. 5) Any *dialogue* whereby the focus of the religious educational institution can be appointed its function in the light of its mission will assist the climate and therefore raise the value-transmitting potential. In addition such classic values formation activities as ranking, valuing, continuums, voting, clarification, case studies, and dialogue are important if identity issues are ever to surface and conversion is to result.

Another factor to consider in this issue is the nature of learning values themselves. For, like the learning process, values must be meaningful to be retained. The data about values cannot precede the knowledge that they are meaningful. If their meaning comes later in the learning experience, questions such as "so what" crop up. Values must be seen to be of worth to the lives of value-minded instructors, pastoral facilitators, and religious workers with internalized goals. The philosophical discussion about where values reside—in the mind or in the act—does not need a resolution as it relates to value learning. For people simply do receive values, and those giving them must live them. The problem of personal dedication to religious principles rears its head here. The teacher who instructs in high moral worth must himself or herself be exemplary of the value or it is not transmitted. By extension any group, institution, or individual must learn to live the values proposed if any change is to come. Focus on the identity issues in one's religious life helps point the church or school toward the specific value goal, and the recognition that this identity focus may assist in religious conversion makes that focus all the more important to facilitate.

If the experience of learning conflicts with the words that are uttered, youth has the tendency to distrust the experience and mistrust the words, and a negative identity is formed. For example, when children first hear from their concerned parents as they brace themselves for a spanking, "This will hurt me more than it does you," the children know this for the lie that it is.[30] But more illustrative is the story John Westerhoff tells in his book *Values for Tomorrow's Children* of the teacher who, becoming frustrated because of the lack of discipline and attention, goes off into a shouting tirade so that he may maintain order and then teach about the unconditional love of God.

If values also change under the direction of the personal magnitude of sensitive teachers, then the challenge is to evaluate our own motivations for teaching and to cultivate the types of personality characteristics that tend toward sensitivity. For in value learning as it relates to identity progress, being aware of the inclinations, feelings, world view, and frustrations of each student allows sensitivity to be more readily demonstrated. Yet the characteristic of sensitivity is not one simply decided upon and then lived out; rather, sensitivity comes as one sees in others worth and potential.

Lewis Sherrill, late religious educator, suggested an appropriate term for use here. It is to be the goal of pastors, religious workers, religious education, and religious educators. He described the word "wholth." This word points to the potential within each student for health of the entire self, plus the concepts of holiness and God. The power to become this way is the *dunamis* of God.[31] This is a worthy concept for students, yet more noble for religious educators. For, like "wholth," sensitivity is a gift of God that stems from knowing the worth of others as objects of love, and knowing oneself in the process of sanctification. Every individual in religious education needs religion in his own heart by faith and needs to possess a true self-denying, self-sacrificing spirit.

With these concepts, the potential for value-change and identity becoming crystalized increases, since values are more clearly perceived, and values are important in the actual functioning of identity. Using methods like these do not make positive values overnight. What does occur is that the potential for change increases when we get closer to our goal of reaching youth with real values for life and establishing a personal identity within their return for God. A person within this type of learning experience might express his or her feelings about teachers as do the lines of this haiku:

---

30. John M. Larson, "The Individual and the Learning Community," *Religious Education* (July-August 1972), p. 274.

31. Sherrill, *The Gift of Power*, p. 22.

> She opened life's God
> full, knowing the choice my own
> yet holding my weak hand.[32]

Value learning becomes a real instructional concern for those interested in identity formation in its religious setting. Religious conversion and the return of God is made easier when the deep meaning of the return is seen. Its deep meaning is manifested best in the values of the people who prescribe the return to God.

Scripture

A most vital content for religious instruction is the use of scriptures themselves. Since religious education and pastoral work is not designed to produce a product, per se, but rather is oriented to supply what is needed for the process of growth, scripture is to be viewed as a major resource for God's revelation of divine purpose. The use of scripture becomes crucial in light of the religious conversion-identity issue. The Bible as a revelation of God's disclosure to humankind can confront us with the existential questions which are the issues of identity. Youth in the midst of identity formation and at the crossroads of deciding for or against God in their lives are being confronted through scripture not with the historical "call" of God but with the present "call" of God. This calling forth is seen in the declaration of God's kingdom in the Old and New Testaments, and is typified in the "discipling" concept of the New Testament, specifically.

God's people have always been challenged to *become*. Scriptural passages which invite response become most useful in understanding the beckoning of God. Such stories as the exodus (Ex 12-16), the passover (Ex 12-13), Mt. Sinai (Ex 20), the Widow of Zarephath (1 Kgs 17:7-24), Daniel's stand in Babylon (Dn 4,5), the Queen of Sheba visits Solomon (1 Kgs 10:1-13), the temptation of Jesus (Mt 4), the healings of Christ, especially blind Bartimaeus (Mk 10), the confession of Peter (Mt 16), Mary and Martha's acceptance of Christ (Lk 10:38-42), Dorcas and her work (Acts 9:32-43), the widow's offering (Mt 12:41-44), Mary Magdalene sees Jesus in the Garden (Mk 16:9-11), the Revelation's churches (Rv 2-3), etc., all invite youth to respond to the historical setting, yet include the invitation for their personal response. Both focusing on identity (belonging) and conversion (return), these passages invite response and fit. The very language of the New Testament is rich with the paradigm for conversion. The death and resurrection of Jesus implies renewal. The story of Christ is to be experienced both as a historical event and

---

32. V. Bailey Gillespie, "Values Are for People," *Journal of Adventist Education* (December-January 1973-1974), p. 31.

as the personal power which enables us to follow him. Happel and Walter describe conversion as that experience in which "the self, the world, and God are reshaped. The self leaves behind the baggage of sin and self-inflicted suffering; the world becomes a place in which God dwells; and God turns toward humanity with a renewed sense of care."[33] This model can be personalized in each life when return is complete.

Scripture used only to inform and clarify becomes dry and cold. But such passages as invitations to disciple, to find one's sense of history, to commit, and to change lifestyle, are most useful in a ministry to those concerned with the identity issues of youth. The pastor or religious worker's responsibility to foster religious return through conversion as an identity function is taken seriously only when church men and women, pastoral facilitators, and religious educators themselves recognize the invitational nature of scripture. In commenting on a religious community's use of Luke 4:1-13 (Jesus' temptations), Irwin suggests, "In the intimacy of the small sharing group they were free to identify and to examine—even if only superficially at first—their values and lifestyles. The existential thinking of such a class session is continuous with the growth experience."[34] Perhaps the use of action-reflection models of exegesis, biblical simulations, or creative story-telling would enhance the existential understanding of the text.

The material used in scripture should enable youth to face inner conflicts that they will find in growing up in the community of believers. If the material of the Bible is used in order to manipulate youth or adults through crisis resolution, fear, or coercion, genuine religious conversion as we have defined it will not occur. The return to God will not be personal and volitional.

Genuine religious change is positive in outcome, resolves identity issues, and can only be conversion in its deepest sense if it is not preprogramed; it comes as the person works through his needs and encounters his conceptions of God and identifies with them.

A warning is perhaps in order here. The leaders of the church, pastoral facilitators, religious workers, and the institutions they represent must be careful not to supply an environment too conductive to change based on the obvious observable phenomena such as crying, stress, emotionalism, manipulation, etc. Change within in this context is coercive and denies freedom and individuality which real religious conversion and identity experience demand. The goal is to see changed lives because of an encounter with the God who is holy—motivated by God and not by humankind.

Scriptural material, and in fact all curricular materials and methodologies, should attempt to establish the basic ego strengths which reflect religious values—faith, trust, and love. Since personal identity is found within value-

---

33. Happel and Walter, *Conversion and Discipleship*, p. 13.
34. Irwin, *The Care and Counseling of Youth in the Church*, pp. 63,64.

laden experiences and choices, it is important that the instruction used in these kinds of encounters generate these supreme values and beckon us to become religious rather than force us into a mold which we will later wish to demolish.

Conversion, Identity, and Learning Theory

Explanations of learning theories are legion. In practice, they simply reflect attitudes which the religious educator holds. The concept of religious conversion as identity, function, however, hints at methodologies which inform what one does in a learning setting. For example, teachers of religion must avoid the use of fear and threat for learning. This serves as external psychosocial conflicts for the learner and aids in a possible negative sense of identity and may move one toward counter–conversion. Any approach which encourages anxiety should be avoided if that anxiety produces superficial changes and does not lead to a grappling with the existential questions of life. Some people never make changes except in the midst of stress, and as we have mentioned, crisis is a key context for identity decisions itself, but anxiety for the sake of anxiety and in order to derive an obvious result is simply manipulation and must be avoided.

The teacher should view some intense anxiety experiences, however, as normal during various age periods and plan so that his or her approach and philosophy permit them to occur. The teacher should provide a means for his or her own faith to serve in a guiding, modeling way to guarantee to the youth what faith does in personal life. Faith and hope in God can resolve anxiety and crises. Beliefs then become basic strength for others. This aspect of the teacher as facilitator and mentor, guide if you would, is implicit in the foregoing understanding of the close relationship of these two conversion and identity experiences as seen above.

In addition, thoughtful planning of experiences to challenge individuals to deal with and provide answers to those "big" value-laden questions about life should be targeted. Resolution of these issues through traditional religious approaches, doctrinal clarification, ritual, celebrations, and so on, aids in the identity/conversion quest. Wayne Oates suggests as possible enrichers of the identity confirmation in youth, for example, exploring activities such as the following: moratorium, striving, and taming.[35] The learning theory here suggests that people should feel free to select answers which have been guaranteed by adults who live these values.

Mary Boys suggests more significant things for those interested in the relationship between conversion and the practice of teaching. She correctly

---

35. Wayne E. Oates, *On Becoming Children of God* (Philadelphia: Westminster, 1969), p. 110.

claims, "Conversion and education share a fundamental starting point: the world is much larger and reality more complex than we think. Education is a catalyst for conversion. Without education our religious and moral conversion may all too easily become sentimental and simplistic."[36] In her call for religious educators to become converted, she identifies specific areas which would impact the religious instruction being carried out in parishes and schools. We need to balance readiness for learning with "an awareness of our own readiness for teaching," she declares, and along with this we are to rise to new levels of conversion "amidst the crisis of our lives, especially in these turbulent times which demand that we pass through an ordeal of a new interpretation of faith." She suggests consideration of three types of conversions that could renew the educational enterprise. Pastors, religious educators, and religious workers are to make a "lifelong commitment to learning, to expand our images of God and God's kingdom; to manifest a profound respect for the mystery of human development."[37] She correctly notes that the task we are called to do and the instruction we are asked to bring to the learner is a terribly painful and freeing task. The "movement of grace" on which conversion draws becomes the motivation for religious change.

Another point to make in this discussion is the fact that identity and conversion force us to deal with persons rather than institutions or religion in general. Both experiences are personal in nature and draw attention to the individual as chief learner in this schema. We are privileged to enter the lives, culture, and experiences of others through these experiences. "It is an invitation to transcend ourselves."[38]

The Christian church in its march through history with its revivals, its new age approaches, and its staid denominations, seeks the one thing that God brings. A new life, a new start, a change to make something out of the nothing which many lives evidence is the essence of religion. For Christians it is the knowledge of Jesus Christ in the consciousness of each individual who believes that brings this peace. The order that religion brings in life brings that peace, as well. Justification by grace and sanctification brought through the life of Christ and his death on the cross move us to an outlook on life which is redemptive in nature, communal by definition, and self-integrating through identity with God. The early church thrived on the celebration of the presence of God with humankind through the Eucharist while baptism initiated a person into close identification of being with God. The Christian realities of the Lord's Supper, ordinance of service, baptism, confirmation, prayer, worship, celebration, fellowship, all point to a close association of the presence of God with us as we struggle in the saga of life. As we repeat them in com-

---

36. Mary C. Boys, "Conversion as a Foundation of Christian Education," *Religious Education* 77 (March-April 1982), p. 223.

37. Ibid.

38. Ibid., p. 213.

munity they become identity experiences. The Old Testament images of pilgrimage, calling, covenant, promise, and redemption serve as identity hooks for the church to move individuals toward religious conversion by means of their identity function. They provide the philosophical hooks on which a learning theory can rest. Religious conversion as an identity experience and the converse, identity experiences as means whereby individuals may move to consider religious conversion as a means of changing, form the basis of the theory. Religious conversion and identity provide the experience whereby questors for wholeness sort out the real meaning of life. Experiences like religious conversion and identity provide the background for the infusion of Christianity into all the world and provide a basis for motivation in the religious mission.

Chapter 9

Religious Conversion:
Identity and Pastoral Counseling

"Well, you know, I'm very sensitive about trying to interpret that, because I think that many people have been driven from the church by seeking some classical form that their conversion took. You know, 'I remember the day! I remember the hour! I felt the power! I fell off a horse and woke up on a certain street!' I think people have been locked into a certain cataclysmic event, and people who may not have felt that way after trying often have felt that they haven't been called or that they haven't been converted. I really think that one can have high moments, but one in my judgment should never associate a convolution with a conversion."

Jesse Jackson

The search for identity has an impact on the interaction people have with pastors, religious educators, curriculum designers, and pastoral counselors. In addition to this identity quest, the religious counterpart, conversion-identity, becomes the object of an unwritten agenda for church educators, pastoral facilitators and pastoral counselors. Each of us involved with religious nurture and change, I believe, would like to be successful. We would like to look back over a year's ministry and see some type of progress. In workshops focusing on religious development and nurture and in seven years of teaching courses in this area, I have regularly used a questionnaire to initiate discussion regarding the goal of ministry. I ask students, "At the end of one year of ministry what would you like to see happen?" After some content analysis the answers group naturally into the following descriptions of people: 1) individuals who are loving and caring; 2) people that have a clear concept of themselves and mission; 3) church members who are deeply committed to the gospel; 4) lives that reflect the nature of Christ. It is rare, upon reflection, that anyone talks of clarity of theology or ideology, or understanding of the Word of God. While some of these cognitive areas—like prayer, Bible study, and devotional activities—are sometimes down on the list, they seldom surface when ranking is suggested. Usually, these four float to the top. We would generally all like to see people who, having been exposed and guided by our ministry, find God and follow the ethical demands of the "better way."

The relationship with God here suggested goes beyond beliefs, dogmas, and traditions to accept God's sovereignty as the *modus operandi*. This is the important task of religious education and the aim to which all of religious education is directed. This could succinctly be stated as its primary goal. After all, the kingdom of God in the biblical sense reflects a dual understanding, a quality of the present life which is to be lived daily by people involved with God who understand God's kingdom as a possible future reality.

How do you know when someone is mature and has a stable religious identity? This is one of those questions with many answers. Peter Benson of Search Institute has tried to identify aspects of mature Christianity which could aid in the formulation of questionnaires. His research team has identified eight areas in which mature faith interacts. In completing the statement, "The person with mature Christian faith . . ." his research suggests that such a one trusts and believes, experiences the fruits of faith, integrates faith and life, seeks spiritual growth, experiences and nurtures faith in community, holds life-affirming values, embraces a public theology, and acts and serves. Under each of these headings he suggests clarifications which provide at least thirty-eight different aspects of these eight headings.[1] Counselors, pastoral facilitators, and religious workers could benefit if their counseling moved people toward these objectives. However in his research with mainline denominations less than 19 percent have what he refers to as an integrated faith—one that has both vertical and horizontal dimensions.

A more difficult question can be asked as well. How do you know when someone has achieved identity? What are the elements of maturity which individuals need to develop? As we have seen, Erik Erikson has spent most of his professional life examining that question. Paul Roaszen abstracted Erikson's description of the mature adult as a person who 1) is tolerant to those who interact with them, 2) has the capacity to make informed choices, 3) has the courage to stand alone, 4) is able to achieve mastery in the tasks undertaken, 5) has the vision to open up new realities, 6) is able to weather the conflicts faced, 7) has the capacity to do well, according to the standards of those

---

1. Peter Benson, "The Person with Mature Christian Faith . . ." Research document based on the *Effective Christian Education* and *Valuegenesis* research study reports (Minneapolis: Search Institute, 1988).

who are significant to him or her, 8) elaborates dominant abilities into a full-time occupation, and 9) is able to be childlike and human when he or she is at play.[2] Earl Wilson commenting on this reconstruction of Erikson suggests that two other areas must be added to this identity schema for maturity to be complete; 10) awareness of oneself as a sexual being, and 11) awareness of oneself as a spiritual being.[3] The pastoral counselor has many of these same goals. While the context may be of crisis or questioning, many of these goals are the same goals of the caring person leading others to return to God and personal identity.

H. Richard Niebuhr suggests that the goal of religion in the life is a movement toward the "-ings" of life, the process of believing, confessing, and committing one's self to the lifestyle of Christianity.[4] This being the case, the role of others in guaranteeing faith in the growth of religious people is vital. The concerns of identity formation and its crisis process and the quest for a religious identity out of which religious conversion as an identity event comes, provide rich ground for those who counsel individuals in the midst of their quest, whether they are in the pastorate or without.

We might wish that the answers to the religious identity quest or even personal identity problems would come in an easily formulated axiom or traditional dogma. When a person goes on a pilgrimage, a quest, a clarification of his identity, that person finds identity does not come in the "form of a rose-trellised cottage, with wife and child waiting in certainty of schedule as he returns from the kind of work his father and grandfather did before him. No. His identity comes as a cloud by day and a pillar of fire by night. He goes out not knowing where he goes, not knowing when or whether he will come back."[5] Just giving out advice to those who are in the midst of their quest, giving prepackaged programs which provide shallow answers, will not fulfill the expectations of those whom we counsel during these questing years. Therefore, one principle objective of the counseling process is to help people understand the struggles and challenges of living by faith and to witness to that reality "through acts of clarification, liberation, and reconciliation."[6] Through these goals, personal identity flourishes.

Counseling Theory and Conversion

Counseling is a form of helping service that often uses "dialogue to guide

2. P. Roazen, *Erik H. Erikson* (New York: Free Press, 1976), pp. 65-66.

3. Earl Wilson, *Try Being a Teenager: A Challenge to Parents to Stay in Touch* (Portland, Ore.: Multnomah Press, 1982), p. 64.

4. H. Richard Niebuhr, *The Meaning of Revelation* (New York: Macmillan, 1962), pp. 63-65.

5. Ibid., p. 113.

6. Melvin Blanchette, "Facilitating Growth in Faith through Pastoral Counseling and Spiritual Direction," in *Handbook of Faith*, ed. James Michael Lee (Birmingham,

a person in dealing with a problem of self, situation, or both."[7] When counseling is practiced responsibly it addresses in a trustful way decisions that impact the course of one's life. Religious decisions are core to direction in life, and therefore, conversion and identity along with counseling are important. Pastoral care and counseling has often ignored the interior changes that people attempt. Most pastoral counseling has turned to the psychological or to spiritual formation techniques or meditation programs which lead people to God. Charles Kemp identifies nine types of pastoral counseling methods: diagnostic techniques, supportive techniques, insight-achieving techniques, behavior-change techniques, cognitive theories, educative techniques, growth-counseling models, religious disciplines, and supplementary techniques. Some of his categories are especially relevant to our discussion of identity and conversion. He suggests that most counseling theory falls into these broad areas.[8]

His identification of *diagnostic techniques* which include pastoral evaluation methods directly relate to our conceptualization. This history-taking procedure is like those used by psychologists and social workers. Learning family backgrounds is often an important first step in the therapeutic procedure. Individuals using these approaches often rely on the Minnesota Multiphasic Personality Inventory (MMPI) or the Taylor-Johnson Temperament Survey (TJ) to identify problems and explore options. This method includes history-taking or asking questions about one's identity, sense of fit, and relationship with God. This method can be useful for those interested in spiritual growth and conversion.

Paul Pruyser contends that the pastor should diagnose peoples' concerns in terms of theological categories when doing diagnostic analysis. Such questions should be asked as, "What is your relationship to the holy?" and "Do you have an experience of faith?" All questions about vocation and relationship to God are identity questions and should be explored. Positive answers to these diagnostic approaches could yield a rich harvest of information about one's feelings of identity and be helpful in exploring the concept of change (conversion). Through these questions a clearer understanding of the causes and "triggers" at work in change might be identified.

Kemp identifies *insight-achieving techniques* as particularly useful when thinking of identity issues and conversional change. We agree that "insight" is a primary goal of any counseling technique. While "insight" often moves people beyond themselves, it is not a total cure-all. "Insight is the capacity to understand ourselves, both intellectually and emotionally, to understand

Ala.: Religious Education Press, 1990), p. 243.

7. "Counseling," Iris V. Cully and Kendig Brubaker Cully, eds., *Encyclopedia of Religious Education* (New York: Harper & Row, 1990), p. 165.

8. Charles Kemp, *The Caring Pastor: An Introduction to Pastoral Counseling in the Local Church* (Nashville: Abingdon, 1985), pp. 58-64.

others, or to understand a situation."[9] In counseling approaches, especially those that have identity and self-awareness as their goal, insight moves people to understand their underlying motives and clarify some of the deep-seated reasons for feelings, behaviors, and problems. Change is possible when clarity and purpose come to a person's life. We are aware, however, that change comes slowly. We have seen this in our understanding of conversion. Long-term impact rarely happens as a result of one brief encounter with a pastor or counselor. Long-term change happens over time in the counseling situation. The key for the counselor, pastor, or youth minister working with members is to realize that through their ministry they can point out God's subtle activity, highlight it, and bring it to consciousness and then affirm it. As Marshall Shelley suggests, "It means asking, 'what is God doing with you?' It's a process of helping resistant people discover the reasons they are in their present situation, then convincing them things can be better, and then training them in a new way of life. This process usually takes years, not months."[10]

Another aspect of the counseling dynamic is the occasion by which people feel needed and become objects of care. When religious persons identify with God they enter into a covenant relationship of redemption. The Bible claims in 1 Peter 2:9-10 that they become "a chosen race, a royal priesthood, a holy nation, God's own people, that you may declare the wonderful deeds of him who called you out of darkness into his marvelous light. Once you were no people but now you are God's people." The caring community helps create an identity for others. A community of concern, of "faith, and free of pretense is needed,"[11] Counselors, pastors, and youth ministers would do well to recognize the power of identity relationships on the well-being of their troubled members. Any approach which provides a basis of identity will be helpful in establishing introspective self-awareness. This concept will be explored later.

On the other hand, when looking at the conversion experience and its help in the counseling situation we note that when the sense of God's presence is felt, clarification of one's life may be the result. Counselors who are sensitive to the inbreaking presence of God in the therapy session will find that their work will be rewarded. Wayne Oates suggests such an approach in his book, *The Presence of God in Pastoral Counseling*. He believes that God surprises both counselor and counselee with joy, understanding, and awe. "Often God prepares us for the mystic vision of his glory through the hungering darkness of our awareness of the absence of God."[12] Oates suggests

---

9. Ibid., p. 61.

10. Marshall Shelley, *Helping Those Who Don't Want Help*, 7 (Waco, Tex.: Word Books, 1986), p. 87.

11. Wayne E. Oates, *The Presence of God in Pastoral Counseling* (Waco, Tex.: Word Books, 1986), p. 18.

that over the many years of his ministry in counseling he has come to realize that some of his most significant memories in pastoral counseling have been in those moments of spiritual breakthrough when the presence of God became intensely evident without contrivance or technique on his part. The impact was awe-struck amazement for both the counselee and counselor. He claims, "An eternal 'centering' happens. As Thomas Merton says, the relationship 'is centered entirely on attention to the presence of God and to his will and his love.'"[13] Oates' work indicates that there are three presences in any counseling trialogue—the counselor, the counselee, and the third presence (God). One cannot eliminate or ignore the possibility of this presence when doing counseling. Those involved in conversional change, or in the identity struggle out of which may emerge conversion, must take this presence into account.

In addition to these concerns, what might be suggested for the benefit of the church and its members is a more inductive approach or attitude in counseling. Nelson Thayer argues that we should spend our time recapturing the realm of interiority as it recovers the realm of transcendence. Counseling using this model would necessitate developing the capacity of paying attention to one's own experience in its particularity and richness. This involves understanding the role of symbol. Being "attentive" is the term usually used here. The aim of this introspective approach is "not the eliciting of any specific feelings. Rather, there is the submitting of oneself to engagement with the symbolic forms and acts of the tradition, and paying attention to what happens 'within.'"[14]

As the pastoral counselor attempts to nurture the people, his or her practice will be informed by these perspectives in this inductive approach. The members would be taught to become aware of the types of experiences which are "beyond" the normal. Here conversion experience is especially useful. Thayer suggests,

> The pastor will help develop in the people a capacity for paying attention to those moments in which the structure of our ordinary everyday reality-oriented consciousness is modified by apprehensions of transcendence. These are moments (perhaps extended moments) marked by one or more of a diversity of qualities or characteristics. But the common element is the awareness that our ordinary everyday taken-for-granted reality is not the totality of reality.

One result of this "introspection" is greater self-awareness, which can be concurrent with the deepened experience of acceptance. Focusing on

---

12. Ibid., p. 32.

13. From ibid., pp. 32, 33., as quoted by Michael Mott, *The Seven Mountains of Thomas Merton* (Boston: Houghton Mifflin, 1984), p. 433.

14. Nelson S. T. Thayer, *Spirituality and Pastoral Care* (Philadelphia: Fortress, 1985), pp. 25,26.

one's spiritual condition in the counseling mode allows one to contemplate one's motives. Using therapeutic methods as introspective prayer, meditation, spiritual visualization provides the structure for this approach. This introspective reflection in the counseling situation may lead some people to explore themselves, their relationships, and their aims in relationship to God. "Our relationship to God inevitably includes the transference onto God of the expectations for personal identity, reward, and punishment by which we know ourselves in interaction with others."[15]

Crisis provides another excellent opportunity for the counseling situation to occur. Since ministers often deal with the broad spectrum of human situations in counseling, those that have uniquely religious contexts often open up a unique opportunity. Ellis Nelson argues that one of the roles of faith is in recreating beliefs. This aspect of faith functions best in times of crisis. "In times of crisis, conventional answers may be unsatisfactory. When anxiety erupts in acts of destruction or when a person's passions get out of control, former beliefs may not apply. Under these conditions a person may be forced to review his or her relation with God and seek an understanding that was not there before."[16]

Bruce Baldwin has suggested a number of crisis categories: 1) *dispositional*—anxiety felt due to anger, hopelessness or as a result of an external problematic situations; 2) *anticipated life transitions*—normal situations over which a person may or may not have control such as a move, job transfer, etc.; 3) *sudden traumatic stress*—where specific external events trigger a rapid reaction of distress involving anxiety or depression. Breakdown may result. Such things as the loss of a job, or death of a family member may precipitate this crisis; 4) *maturational/developmental crisis*—as life goes on a person makes adjustments with various degrees of success. Here identity issues are a primary factor; 5) *psychopathological crisis*—those which result from the reactivation of unresolved earlier failures in maturation or through critical losses; 6) *psychiatric emergencies*—suicidal or psychotic breaks with reality are included here.[17] Through crisis there is a more rapid modification of perception of one's self and one's world. These crisis situations provide excellent counseling moments. Since identity crisis and conversional crisis can be included here, one can readily see the opportunity for counseling during moments of transition and change. It is part of the church's theology to be concerned with others during times of extreme

15. Ibid., p. 99.

16. C. Ellis Nelson, *How Faith Matures* (Philadelphia: Westminster, 1989), p. 148.

17. From Bruce A. Baldwin, "A Paradigm for the Classification of Emotional Crises: Implications for Crisis Intervention," *American Journal of Orthopsychiatry* 48 (1978), pp. 538-551. Quoted in David K. Switzer, *The Minister as Crisis Counselor* (Nashville: Abingdon, 1987), pp. 32-33.

18. See Thomas C. Oden, *Pastoral Counseling* (New York: Crossroad, 1989)

change and transition.[18] Being aware of the nature of the dynamics involved in conversion and identity change can make counseling more effective and timely.

Counseling theory is filled with approaches and techniques which work when given specific situations and specific needs. Rather than to identify approaches which seem to work with those in the midst of identity crisis or conversional anxiety, it would be more helpful to identify characteristics which assist any theory to be more effective.

There are approaches which are desirable and helpful to the counseling process. William Miller and Kathleen Jackson have identified five.

1. *Flexible:* a thinking style that is open to new information rather than assumption-bound, seeking the paradigm to fit the individual rather than forcing all individuals to fit into a single mold.
2. *Eclectic:* in the best sense, willing to consider perspectives and intervention approaches from a broad range of sources.
3. *Practical:* helping you to know what to do next.
4. *Pragmatic:* choosing on the basis of helpfulness, interested in information and research on the relative effectiveness of different approaches.
5. *Differential:* changing with the individual's needs, rather than having a single perspective or intervention approach for everyone.[19]

Any counseling situation needs to incorporate these concepts. Those working with people who are experiencing anxiety about their religious change and personal identity may find help in adapting them to their counseling needs.

Counseling and Conversion

Pastors, counselors, and parents often interact with others in moments of psychological or religious stress during normal growth through adolescence to adulthood. During these moments, adolescents stand at a crossroad. Choices must be made which may determine the direction of the life for decades. At times of religious conversion the crossroads analogy is particularly significant. Usually, ongoing growth brings individuals to regular developmental steps, situational landmarks, and growth in the journey of life. During moments of identity crisis or religious conversion we have a particularly rich personal situation which the counselor or pastor can use that may alter

---

for a complete discussion of the history of pastoral caring from this excellent series as seen from the classical literature of the early church.

19. William R. Miller and Kathleen A. Jackson, *Practical Psychology for Pastors* (Englewood Cliffs, N.J.: Prentice-Hall, 1985), p. 69.

one's destiny.[20] Joseph Kelley suggests that these times are when Bernard Lonergan's views on conversion are particularly helpful for the pastoral counselor. Those undergoing intellectual, ethical or moral, and spiritual or religious conversion provide unique challenges for the therapist. He notes that, "In some sense the therapist walks with the client to the very center of the crossroad, stays there a while looking with the client as far as they could, and then assists him or her in the first halting steps down the new road."[21] The Lonergan definitions of religious conversion, Kelley suggests, can provide themes for change and provide the catalyst for authentic religious experience.

The therapist is not alone, however, in the identity or conversion quest. The therapist may be undergoing conversional shift, too. Theological themes like conversion "can speak directly to the therapist as well. We are no less a client of the ongoing conversion process. The client's difficulties and sufferings can be an occasion of grace calling the therapist to new, unexpected, and unhoped for transformation in thought, ethic, or spiritual life."[22]

Conversion has been related to psychosis in some instances because of the characteristic onset of the identifiable stages of both. The initiating condition or conditions of the two processes may be similar or even identical, and the stages in the process of religious conversion have been noted to correspond to the early stages of decompensation.[23] Johnson and Malony have identified various stages or changes which occur during the course of psychotherapy. Level 1 is a change in which a person is taught basic life skills, while Level 2 is an advance on level 1 and involves symptom alleviation using techniques such as rational emotional therapy. The next level of help, Level 3 sees changes at a deeper level of the personality. It is called the analytic phase, or the search for a new identity and meaning. It is a form of self-actualization. It may be a preliminary trigger for religious conversion, while Level 4 seems to be beyond the scope of secular psychotherapy according to Johnson and Malony. It is the change that comes from without, the conversion to the Christian faith.[24]

Pastoral counseling is, then, a unique challenge, and it has undergone over the years a great deal of change. Early in the history of pastoral counseling, determinism was the basic philosophical construct around which most counseling revolved. Most early pastoral counseling was deterministic

---

20. Joseph T. Kelley, "Some Implications of Lonergan's View of Conversion," *Journal of Pastoral Care* 40:4 (1986), p. 361.

21. Ibid., p. 364.

22. Ibid., p. 365.

23. Raymond J. Wooten and David F. Allen, "Dramatic Religious Conversion and Schizophrenic Decompensation," *Journal of Religion and Health* 22:3 (1983), p. 220.

24. Cedric B. Johnson and H. Newton Malony, *Christian Conversion: Biblical and Psychological Perspectives* (Grand Rapids, Mich.: Zondervan, 1982), p. 147.

in that the client was viewed as an object to be manipulated by the counselor who had the knowledge and know-how not possessed by the client. Thus, people receiving counseling were seen reacting from the direction of an outside force in determining life direction.[25] Humans were viewed as an object to be used, and counselors simply provided the choices and opinions regarding them.

In addition, the counseling process is not always easy to initiate. Kenneth Stokes' work on adult faith development suggests "that people are as likely to work through a crisis on their own as to share it with close friends. Most of them (60 percent) would likely *not* seek help from a religious counselor."[26] And to get adults to work on issues that are aimed at the purpose of life may prove difficult and to do that in a nonjudgmental or directive way is certainly a challenge.

It is true that the religious counselor does bring personal theological presuppositions to the counseling situation; however, such strict determinism has yielded to a more reasoned approach which includes a sensitivity to the unique personal situation. More existential methods are currently being used which I believe form the basis of a style of identity counseling I am suggesting.

When one takes an existential position in counseling, the counselor does not eliminate his basic assumptions about humanity and God's interest and requirements, but the counselor now no longer is so concerned with a system or technique as with an underlying attitude and understanding of the uniqueness of the human situation. This existential approach to counseling reinforces humanness as it is—as the counselee is becoming.

The pastor-counselor, then, needs to be asking the "when" and "why" questions to encourage discussion about the quest the growing person is undertaking. Paul Irwin suggests the use of questions which respect the individual's identity search. He gives hints to counselors in the discussion and suggests that: 1) the counselor ask questions which reflect youth's inner world and pose questions about personal interpretations of the symbolic meaning in youth's life; 2) the counselor should probe into the important relationships in which identity is formed; 3) the counselor should ask questions about the feelings and attitudes of the young person and should ask himself or herself as a counselor if he or she is picking up any sensitivity for these questions in the inner world of youth which reflect feelings about himself or herself; and 4) the counselor must, as well, be sensitive to what stage in this life pilgrimage the questor has progressed.[27] Using such techniques makes the

25. Dugald S. Arbuckle, *Counseling: Philosophy, Theory and Practice* (Boston, Mass.: Allyn & Bacon, 1967), p. 24.

26. Kenneth Stokes, *Dynamics of Adult Faith Development: Faith is a Verb* (Mystic, Conn.: Twenty-Third Publications, 1989), p. 75.

27. Paul Irwin, *The Care and Counseling of Youth in the Church* (Philadelphia:

counselor sensitive to the ongoing identity quest and its possibility to direct religious change as an option or outcome of the counseling process.

Provocative questions which amplify the quest for identity are the most helpful instrument in the pastor-counselor's tool kit. Those undergoing return to God through religious conversion are also aided by questions which provide clarity during their search for God. Questions such as, "What have you learned from this about your life with God?" and "How do you see yourself understanding your relationship with God?" and "What do you see happening to your life that indicates God's concern?" become the crucial ones during this time. Questions which probe human destiny, such as, "How do you see God working in your life?" and "In what ways do you hear God's voice in your life?" aid in the search for a clear picture of his or her own life in God's hands. Remember, theology speaks to the process of conversion and counseling deals with how people make changes.[28]

Since religion is a system that gives order to one's world, it seems logical that when one works through his or her identity questions and finds resolution in finding God those results may be therapeutic. When you examine the vocabulary used to define one's personal faith this is even more evident. For example, "Beliefs are cherished." People often say that "God, Jesus, Muhammad, and the Patriarchs are loved, feared, and revered."[29] Lovinger suggests that

> all these images are experienced within the person in ways quite similar to the experience(s) of important people in the individual's personal history. In essence then, what we obtain psychologically from significant people in our personal odysseys parallels what we can secure from religious ideas and figures: love, values, aid in regulating our wishes and activities, a personal tradition, ethical/moral guidance, a sense of ourselves, and approval or disapproval for our thoughts and behaviors. In other words, identity.[30]

Counselors agree that this search for meaning and destiny is a basic personality hunger. The sense of belonging and fit, whether it is sensed in the anxiety of not being at home in one's heart with God, or whether it is experienced in the crisis of personal identity, not knowing where one belongs at all, is not experienced in an abstract way in the lives of young people. We've seen its presence in the life as a "deep 'gut-level' conviction that life is trustworthy and worth the struggle in spite of its cruelty, agony, and contradictions."[31] The

---

Fortress, 1975), p. 56.

28. Johnson and Malony, *Christian Conversion*, p. 141.

29. Robert J. Lovinger, *Religion and Counseling: The Psychological Impact of Religious Belief* (New York: Continuum, 1990), p. 103.

30. Ibid.

31. Howard J. Clinebell Jr., *Basic Types of Pastoral Counseling* (Nashville.: Abingdon, 1966), p. 19.

counselor's role must be that of helping guide and assist in the struggle, rather than giving out information in pat answers. Youth, if they hear this kind of response, will soon leave and find their own quest in a different ideology or with a different series of caring people, perhaps without the benefit of religion and the ultimate answers it can provide.

Anyone who goes on a quest to determine his or her own sense of worth in others' and God's sight will not only be aided by suggesting clarification and movement in growth but will be nudged along the path to God as a way of ultimate worth. Perhaps this is why most agree that humanity is basically religious. If you leave men or women alone, they will seem to construct a basic fabric of meaning. In isolation humans will create their own secular gods. If a religious framework which is guided and directed toward God is provided, the chances of finding answers in God are greatly increased.

Twentieth-century humanity is no less religious than were their predecessors. St. Augustine's familiar lines are still true: "Thou has made us for thyself and our souls are restless till they rest in thee."[32] Whether the gods we create are so-called secular ones or whether they are religious ones, we order our religious life and devote attention to the things which seem to have personal worth and meaning.

The *questions,* then, are crucial in the counseling relationship. They must reflect and respect a sense of worth in the sight of God. Couple with the appropriate questions the concept that the pastor who counsels has a deep, contagious, and continuous knowledge of his or her conversion and identity with God, then the relationship between the one searching and the counselor will be therapeutic and beneficial. The questions which deal with life's destiny and one's relationship with the omnipotent God can be near the surface of our listening.

Below is a journal entry by a student in her late teens, posting her religious growth. Journal entries are excellent means of understanding a person's identity quest because the conflicts are easily described and the experience often is marked by such events. This journal was kept for ten weeks, and the daily entries evidence a growing sense of clarity about purpose in life. Notice the content of the discussion centers on personal, ultimate concerns.

> I do a lot of things that I hate. Being a hypocrite is not what I want to be and not what I want to do, unfortunately. There are some days when I catch myself. I really try not to gossip, complain, and put people down. I have a terrible inferiority complex. I have no means of taking my aggressions out, so I displace them and have to put the blame on something that is not guilty. I'm still having doubts as to whether I can really believe in religion.
>
> As a whole, there are so many things that you have to have blind feelings about if you believe in the Bible, Jesus, and the end of the world. Then there are facts that are supposed to be true about evolution and everything like that. I'm not

32. Quoted in ibid.

really sure what I believe. Church classes have not been any big help. I don't
like religion classes.

Last Friday night, Robin made the comment that if I went to church for once
in my life, maybe I could find a male. (We were on the subject of boyfriends at
the time.) That's another one of my basic problems—I want a boyfriend. I can't
understand why this is so foremost in my goals. I have a lot of friends and my family that all love me, but I still feel so lonely. I was with all my friends two weeks
ago, and I am lonely still. I am waiting for the right one to come along. It's been
hard to be patient. I'm not the flirting type, and I'm like my Dad—I am definitely not a little social butterfly. I don't meet people and talk to strangers very
openly and easily. I don't feel very secure with myself. I feel fat and ugly always
and I don't think I'm a total blast to be around. I want to cure myself of these major
trivias, and I feel that I can't trust people with my problems, and if I do, they'll
think I'm dumb, so they won't listen.

I know there is a God, but where? If I can't see him, then how am I supposed
to know if he's going to help me; and if he will, then how am I going to know and
understand that this is what's best for me?

Even though this entry deals with the real world of a nineteen-year-old girl,
it is interesting to watch the slow evolution of identity and "fit" questions.
Topics like irrelevant church classes, boys, theological belief problems like
Jesus, Bible, and eschatology were important. Note, however, the questing
quality of the questions at the end of the journal entry. The questions are
deeply theological ones in the midst of surface relevance. Often youth's
quest comes to us in the way of belief problems or social problems. For
example, "Tell me, Pastor, what do you think of premarital sex?" Or questions
about problems in the social sphere. The preacher in all of us sees a chance
to jump and make a dictum or dogma of clarification in the young child's life.
Caution, however, must overrule intellect, here. Wait and listen, see if the
questions are only shallow manifestations of deep identity concerns.

Using journal entries as a means to begin counseling can provide insight
into spiritual growth as well. I often ask students to describe their conversion
experience. The journals reflect traditional understandings of the event. In
reviewing over 250 such responses young adults indicated that their conversion experience was related to: 1) personal achievement, 2) influence of
significant others, 3) fellowship and friends, 4) experiences of finding oneself, 5) parental expectation, 6) traditional church expectations, and/or 8)
personal crisis. One can easily see the relationship to identity issues here.

A typical conversion story related to personal achievement was:

Another significant factor for my change was when I ran, and was elected, for student body religious vice-president. I feel it was an educational experience because
I began to notice things I'd never seen before. I was more aware of the spiritual
atmosphere of our campus and also the motives of the students. This had a profound impact on my religious life.

Often conversion dialogue centers about significant others and their influence on life-direction.

> I remember that I envied him [a friend]. I could see that he had something I didn't have. He was fulfilled but I was empty. I had been baptized at twelve but there I was sixteen and that baptism didn't really have much part of my life. I remember I told him I wanted that peace he had in his heart. I wanted Jesus to be my king and best friend. And we kneeled down in prayer. After that my friend left, but he had touched me so deeply that I stood after [that] alone in my house and cried. And I invited Jesus to be the ruler of my life from that moment.

Often personal crisis causes focus to change. Perception of self shifts and the individual is forced to make immediate choices which alter self-perception and identity. For example:

> For some people conversion comes by way of a tragic experience. An almost fatal experience. It is unfortunate that it takes something like this to jolt them into realizing that they could have died and they weren't ready. That is how it was for me. It took an almost fatal car accident for me to realize that I've been taking too many things for granted. I wasn't doing anything to prepare myself for Christ's second coming. Up to that point, I had been living a very selfish life. My one and only concern was me. I wanted to have a lot of fun, I wanted to make lots of money, I wanted to have a new car. After the accident, I took a long look at my life. There was nothing to be proud of. I started to change the way I lived and I tried to think of other people's needs rather than my own. I looked at Christ in a different manner. Now, I thank him every day for life, family, friends, and a chance to live.

And, there are those dramatic moments where the presence of God seems to break in. "I believe I had a religious conversion just this quarter. I've always believed in God and prayed to him somewhat occasionally, but being in my religion class and writing my journal has made me see just how important God is to me in my life. I cried when I heard about God; now I am touched when I hear songs about God and feel terrible for the extreme sinful behavior of mine. . . . Now, God and I have become 'one.' I don't feel distant anymore."[33]

The Church as Counselor

There is more to the counseling situation than the patient/client/pastor relationships. Pastoral counseling must be done in the context of the total church. Larry Richards suggests, "Christian education then can never deal

---

33. These responses are from quarterly journal entries regarding religious experience and conversion in the course Dynamics of Personal Religion. Journal entries often become the means whereby the counselor may enter into the story of the student and discover those significant things which make for personal religion and identity.

with individual life alone. Christian education has to concern itself with the processes within the body which nurture corporate and individual growth in Christ. Any Christian educational approach which focuses on either the individual or the group in exclusion of the other is bound to fall short."[34]

The attitude of caring and the character of a church is shaped by the members within it. Not only is the counselor's relationship supportive while aiding those in search of themselves and God, but also the member's attitudes in the local parish are equally as significant if healing, growth, and change are to take place. Since the people in the church project their expectations to others, and those in times of crisis look for expectations to be fulfilled, a church's close look at the message it is projecting may clarify the actual role performance in the questor's life. Reuel Howe suggests, "[God] speaks and acts through us, and we become the fellowship of the redeemed and the redeeming, the fellowship of the reconciled and the reconciling."[35] What the pastor or religious educator provides in theory and theology, the church—the members as faith community and religious workers—lives in truth. What the guarantor of faith can only personally witness to, the people of God enact.

The church is entirely too loveless. It exists often solely for its own sake and provides programs which only nurture selfish introspection. The members could fill their social needs elsewhere, but since the church is convenient, either by location or by association, its membership lives in a kind of selfish vacuum. The church I see, however, is one whose vision reaches into very practice itself. Randolph Crump Miller describes it: "Such a community is educationally viable, for education by one definition is what happens to a person in community. There is a nurturing process that occurs through what might be called osmosis where a sense of belonging is a powerful influence."[36]

The church, then, is a type of counselor itself. The pastor or religious educator who encourages this concern will, I believe, have congregational members involved with each other and have little time for theological arguments. The congregation which recognizes its role in the passages of identity will be providing the identity tags so necessary for acceptable growth toward God. For it is the church which organizes itself for nurture, support, evangelism, and mission. Those activities and programs which focus on personal meaning and identity have a better chance to nurture personal transformation. What are those events, programs, and special moments which

---

34. Larry Richards, *A Theology of Christian Education* (Grand Rapids, Mich.: Zondervan, 1976), p. 16.

35. Reuel Howe, *Man's Need and God's Action* (Greenwich, Conn.: Seabury, 1953), p. 141.

36. Randolph Crump Miller, in *The Religious Education We Need*, ed. James Michael Lee (Birmingham, Ala.: Religious Education Press, 1977), p. 34.

encourage identity and thus transformation?

1) *Regularized status passages.* For youth, these moments are rarely recognized by the church. Baptism is a primary event for the Christian. Entry into membership or union with Christ is often commemorated by celebration by the Body of Christ. However, entry into a "spiritual birthday," so to speak, in the conversional shift is seldom celebrated after the first event of membership or confirmation takes place. Regularized remembrance is important, especially to youth, because it reaffirms the group's interest in the quest for personhood and identity with God in religious growth. The church must pattern, then, in a tutoring relationship the necessary steps to God and reinforce by its celebration each member's acceptance and development in their growth. Along this line is the pastoral facilitator or religious worker's responsibility to provide information regarding vocation and direction. For youth this may include graduations, regular adult passages. For adults, it may include job transfers, marriages, etc.

2) *Vocational guidance.* One neglected area in church responsibility is in aiding this important identity tag—the life job or vocation. Youth seeking role identity can have the crisis resolved early if the church takes this clearly theological task to heart. The word vocation implies a calling by God. What clearer identity focus is there than in one's life work? This calling implies a God-concern for the life choices of its membership. If vocational counseling is not part of the church's responsibility, the questor may be so involved with a role crisis that a genuine return to God can't even be considered. Early in the history of the church the offices held within the body were called vocations and implied a calling by God to a task that only they could do. When the church fails to provide role identifications and meaningful moratoria for youth, confusion often results. A congregation's conscious effort to provide reassessment of the tags for identity formation will encourage resolution of the identity crisis in a positive way.

3) *Ideological formation.* The church's community testifies to ideology as well, which has meaning and elicits commitment. The church's role in developing personal ideological formation is vital. The church as tutor and counselor, or the pastor or religious educator as symbolic of the ideology manifest, will, through the "style of life" of the congregation and his or her own person, either validate and call forth positive response or offend the budding ideologist in his or her personal identity quest.

Since religious conversion is usually accompanied by an ideological commitment, what the church does after it learns of its members' commitment to mission becomes the major challenge. In workshops in Europe during the summer months, North American pastoral types were reminded of the subtle ideological differences in the political sphere and their influence in forming solid foundations in religion. Secularism and a definite movement away from a God-minded society were replacing a church's mission because youth could not see a vitality and focus and direction within the church's ideology. Ideology was more theological than practical. But good theology always moves one to practice and ethics.

Theological thought has always been a microcosm of the human search for God. As theology was irrelevant, humankind in concert with the need for meaning sought a God that was real. Through orthodoxy and traditionalism, liberalism, neo-orthodoxy, existentialism, and theology of liberation, hope and joy, we can encapsulate the human search for a meaningful ideology. When the redemptive fellowship of the saints fails to provide a climate which shows meaningful ideology, people in search of congruity in their lives, and of course in their religious commitments, will seek elsewhere. The church as comforter or the pastoral facilitator or religious worker as counselor must attempt to build relevance into the theological quest with a life response in the church members and a personal life of the leaders which orders properly the response that we wish to occur in the ones we guide to God.

The task of guiding others' ideologies implies respect for the personal responses being made by those we counsel or guide. What methods work best? Respect may very well be the greatest attribute counselors, religious educators, pastoral workers, and parents could have when dealing with identity issues. A basic theological tenet of God's relationship with the world is free response and respect. God allows free response, and those who follow after God must be equally open to encourage freedom of response. Religious conversion is only really understood in the context of one's free, uncoerced response to God's invitation to return. Someone who is told what he or she is to be like, who is urged to accept someone else's constructs ideologically, who is pushed before being ready will only encourage a new crisis of identity when coercion becomes evident. For, "as he 'casts about' restlessly through infancy, childhood, and early adolescence, he comes to feel most at ease when he knows clearly what he means to others. He or she has an identity, a place, and estimate for others . . . finding out for oneself who one is by choice is the search upon which the adolescent is thrust."[37]

Adolescence is one particular time when this larger task of formulating an ideology and interpreting the world and life becomes consequential. This time period is important because of some qualitative changes that occur. One qualitative change includes the development of a higher form of thought, often called "formal" thinking. This type does not develop automatically. Teachers of youth have the responsibility to encourage formal thinking by using those methods which foster openness and flexibility. "Adolescents must be challenged to explore questions and problems, to search out contradictory views, and to make appropriate distinctions between what is crit-

---

37. Niebuhr, *Meaning of Revelation*, pp. 107-110.

ical and what is not. Contradictions can be catalysts for new understandings of and commitment to a position, a value, a moral system, or a faith stance."[38]

4) *Crisis resolution.* Religious development is often viewed as a series of situations, stages, or spirals.[39] It is by moving through these life cycle passages that the person may encounter various crises which challenge decision and encourage faith commitment. Erikson's model is an example of this type of progression. Even though these theories have been criticized and need reconsideration when it comes to women's development, which is formed mainly through relationships, not just through autonomy, the fact that there are natural transition points can be helpful in understanding the church's ministry to people in change.[40] Iris Ford asks, "How do concerns about relationships affect growth in faith? Relationships form the embeddedness out of which a person reaches for growth. Supportive people call a person out of self to respond and thereby grow."[41] In moments when relationships are tense, and the pressures to resolve them seem strong, the church can minister best. According to Kenneth Stokes, "There is a relationship between periods of transition, change, and crisis in one's life and one's faith development."[42] He also suggests that it is apparent that "faith development is more likely to occur during those periods when one's life is in some degree of disequilibrium. The result may be a 'stronger' faith, a 'weaker' faith, or perhaps just a 'different' faith, but the individual's perspective is changed because of ferment at some of life's turning points."[43] These moments can be turned into positive growth and change when the church becomes sensitive to them. When the church recognizes these moments of opportunity for change and becomes alert to those transition moments and the crises that often bring them, growth will begin and personal commitment and direction may be the result.

There are some specific areas which come to the front in this type of counseling and support given by the parish and the pastoral worker or religious educator, specifically. They are 1) issues involving accepting religion as a personal faith, 2) issues involving maturity and belonging, and 3) issues focusing in on religious change as a key factor.

---

38. A. Roger Gobbel, Gertrude G. Gobbel, and Thomas E. Ridenhour Sr., *Helping Youth Interpret the Bible* (Atlanta: John Knox Press, 1984), p. 31.

39. See Iris M. Ford, *Life Spirals: The Faith Journey* (Burlington, Canada: Welch Publishing Company, 1988), pp. 89-97.

40. See Carol Gilligan, *In a Different Voice: Psychological Theory and Women's Development* (Cambridge: Harvard University Press, 1982). and Robert Kegan, *The Evolving Self: Problem and Process in Development* (Cambridge: Harvard University Press, 1982), p. 165.

41. Ibid., p. 96.

42. Stokes, *Dynamics of Adult Faith Development, Faith Is a Verb*, p. 61.

43. Ibid.

Personal Faith

A key focus during the time of identity crisis during the stress and anxiety of the religious return in conversion is the personalizing nature of the faith response itself. Faith is not an entity to be obtained; it is simply a word that describes one's response and relationship to God and the resultant trustworthiness of God which can be relied upon. For the religious person to be fully equipped to function in relation to the sovereignty of God in life and to feel at home with his or her relationship with God, a time of personal, individual response or reflection must be provided.

Individuals who come during the anxiety of a religious identity crisis need direction toward the leveling influence that a deep abiding trust in the consistency of God will provide. Often individuals come for help, but our discussions center in the theological clarification that well-trained scholars can provide, and yes, even enjoy providing. However, the person on a slow return to God, or even in an abrupt response to God's call, needs time for personal faith to be individualized and internalized. How can the counseling relationship provide help? What the counseling relationship should provide is a safe place to hide. The concept of God in scriptures implies this. God is seen as a rock, as a place to hide in the Old Testament. We think of a rock and we imagine a great mass of granite; our God would not be content to be anything less than El Capitan in Yosemite, or the Grand Canyon. However, this concept misses the point provided by the beauty of the Old Testament poetry. God's nature is described in the Old Testament as a rock that has holes in it. God is so close to us that a place for shelter is provided, a place in which we can hide, a place that proves God cares, and a place where humankind can be nurtured. In addition, scripture teaches that we are only complete while we are in relationship with God. People become perfect in the Old Testament sense only in relationship with God. Genesis suggests this closeness in the phrase, "Walk before me, and be perfect."[44]

Meaningful relationships with God become such only as God is seen interested in troubled lives. Counselors, religious workers, religious educators, and parents who fail to see the need for individual responses to God during reflective sessions with young or old searchers fail in their task as religious leaders.

What methods can help? Reflective methods which provide a moratorium and rebirth are the most helpful here.

1) *Retreats* are an excellent means to focus on this personal caring of God, and they form an important link with identity search, getting one away from the press of society and life itself and enhancing the change for personal faith.

---

44. Genesis 17:1.

2) *Journal keeping* is another method which can provide startling insight during religious quest. As specific events are remembered and significance is attached to them the person in reflection notes movement and growth. As journaling identifies those personal problems and meaningful ideological issues, the person grows in self-understanding and purpose. Change is begun and conversional response initiated.

3) *Meditation and prayer* become therapeutic methods of personalizing religion. Through deep reflection one may come to understand a relationship to ultimate reality as in the conversion experience which brings new meaning. "This in turn can lead to the removal of the symptom" which causes the problem. This process is noted by Johnson and Malony in an analysis of Viktor Frankl's work. Frankl pointed out that the etiology of a neurosis may be based on the existential frustration that comes from an experience which has no meaning in personal life. When the person discovers meaning, Frankl found, phobias disappear and creative growth may begin.[45]

4) *Celebrations and creative projects* enrich the environment of worship and nurture the chance for God to touch personal life. If we are in creative action, the mind symbolizes and organizes the meanings of life and religion in very personal terms. The symbols are drawn from the mind's concepts and because of that, provide a creative means of explaining God.

5) Theologians are trying *biblical rewriting and storytelling* as specific creative means for personal insight into the community of faith. Developing a little story, like the journal writing suggested, can provide a unique chance for personal reflection. For, "to engage in telling one's 'little story' can be helpful in fitting it into the 'big story.' This enables a person to see his or her existence with an enhanced measure of coherent, historical meaning."[46] The obvious product of such activities suggested and guided by the counselor will enrich the reflection necessary for faith to have meaning. It will be a personal faith, then, and not someone else's faith which sustains through turmoil and brokenness.

While all the above methods are not traditional therapeutic ones, they allow the client to become engaged with personal identity issues as a means to focus on change. According to Johnson and Malony there are at least two levels of change suggested when one compares conversion with clinical counseling or psychotherapy. The first comes in learning life's skills. The symptoms which are alleviated make deeper change at the level of meaning and self-realization. "The change that has ultimate ramifications in terms of destiny and realization of personhood comes with conversion." The second level of change is a circumstantial relatedness between conversion and psychotherapy. One may impact the other, but conversion may cause a sense

45. Johnson and Malony, *Christian Conversion*, p. 153. Or see Viktor Frankl, *The Will to Meaning* (New York: World, 1969).
46. Irwin, *Care and Counseling of Youth*, p. 67.

of identity.[47] Any method which focuses on peak experiences or meaningful clarification provides counseling direction and may move the individual to consider religious change as a possible solution to the anxiety and stress that may come from a sense of sin or distance from God.

Maturity and Belonging

This issue of maturity and belonging which a counselor or pastoral facilitator must face in dealing with youth in identity passage is especially important. Since personal identity formation as well as conversion's response as an identity function are age-related in part, it is necessary to encourage growth and movement in times of identity confusion for resolution to take place. This can be best done by envisioning a better way.

Humans have the capacity to see, if only in the mind's eye, how we "ought" to be. We can envision the future, we can make it live—if only in our imagination, it is so. This capacity for reaching beyond forms the basis for symbolizing and creativity in humankind. The religious worker or pastoral counselor's responsibility here is to aid the individual in envisioning possibilities for life. Growth and maturity are products of striving and stretching.

The Bible's use is significant here. Text after text can be presented as potential ways that one, in relationship to God, becomes whole. We must use the Bible to provide a relationship between those portions of scripture which invite identity discussion and which correspond with some aspect of our own individual life experience. Counselors can use the Bible to invoke personal life progress.[48] Suggestions to rewrite portions of scripture which stretch human values have a significant effect in the identity quest by providing the goals in religious life. For example, the discussion in 1 Corinthians 13 on love is excellent, far above the normal way men and women love. Love is here described as never rude and always long-suffering, and so on. The possibilities are beyond the mortal realm, except through a gift from God. Through the envisioning and stretching process, using written and dialogical material, questors can find direction for their lives. The goals become clarified because the target is clear. The goals in scripture are somewhat idealistic, but, no one will ever mature if they are not stretched. What might occur when this style of nurture is initiated? The result of this type of counseling and pastoral methodology will be a sense of belonging (identity).

The sense of fit comes through counselors, significant others, religious

---

47. Johnson and Malony, *Christian Conversion*, p. 155.

48. For a complete discussion of a method which invites this kind of deep, personal introspection and interaction with the Old Testament see Conrad E. L'Heureux, *Life Journey and the Old Testament: An Experiential Approach to the Bible and Personal Transformation* (New York: Paulist, 1989).

workers, parents, and communities also striving to mature. The person then learns that all are on a journey. No one has yet reached the end. The race is not over, nor the prize on the mantlepiece. Everyone, too, has friends who are striving, and all need the stretching and visioning that religious faith provides. The counseling relationship, then, is not designed to produce a type of product, but rather to equip a person to grow toward maturity in religious experience and to sense a spirit to fit.

Religious Change

This last area of concern for the pastoral worker or counselor comes when he or she is confronted with someone in the midst of making choices which will affect the religious life specifically. Those who come to us sensing the "call" of God in their lives are the ones I am now talking about and those who perhaps have never before sensed the presence of God in their lives, but who now feel this nudging and desire some clarification as to this gentle pressure.

It has been suggested that one of the most essential ingredients for a happy and satisfying life is understanding one's sense of purpose and meaning.[49] When one looks at the Old Testament figures we note that their sense of conviction was often based on their understanding of their *calling*. Conrad L'Heureux proposes that a profitable focus for Bible study would be on what he identifies as "call narratives." Stories of biblical call narratives "can be a highly effective way for us to get in touch with our own inner experience of how we too each have a unique call. Because of this call, our life journeys become something more than aimless wandering. They take on direction and significance."[50]

It is during these times of anxiety and often guilt that the religious worker, pastoral facilitator, or counselor can provide a most necessary service and insight. Discussions which show God's deep care for the questor and illustrations regarding biblical individuals who were accepted by God, but yet still seemed to struggle to maintain a relationship, are important. Jonah, Abraham, Moses, Daniel, Mary, Martha, and even the New Testament Peter are all excellent examples of people coming to know God yet having not quite resolved all of the issues and problems of their own lives and identity. The prophet Elijah's own experience with the still, small voice reflects moments of quiet meditation when new concepts and insights of God are most apt to occur, rather than in the hustle and bustle of fire and lightning.

Guilt is often the motivator for religious change, however, and it is this factor that sends many depressed people to religious people or pastoral counselors for help. Guilt is caused by the perception of a demand that cannot be met,

49. Ibid., p. 41.
50. Ibid.

or through the condemnation—real or perceived—of another that their lives are out of harmony with that will of God. Often we superimpose guilt because we want people to do it our way. When this guilt is perceived, it is more or less real, and the anxiety is just as great, even though it has been produced by the wrong means.

The message religion has to provide the world is one of freedom from guilt and one of salvation and fit. Implicit within this message is the concept of forgiveness and hope and the experience of celebration, joy, and peace. It is here that the community (church) as counselor can be of great help in providing the reality of acceptance and identity.

The way the counselor and community handle their own anxiety and guilt may provide a clue to understand how anxious seekers after God may find rest. This "living theology" becomes important. God must be presented as a God with whom we can be identified. The themes of scripture which reinforce this can be good starting points for inductive study. The religious counselor may guide, sustain, reconcile, and assist the person undergoing conviction for change through the use of such passages and by modeling a life of acceptance, forgiveness, hope, and joy.

We all carry guilt for a number of reasons. Often the guilt is the product of our own doing, and (a sense of) forgiveness is harder to obtain if the guilt is not deserved. Guidance to identity in God, and with that the peaceful assurance of forgiveness, is essential if we are ever to survive in a relational world.

The individual who can rest in the assurance of God's forgiveness and grow to know the will of God will be better able to cope with a life of stress and anxiety about his or her identity. It is this sense of basic acceptance and oneness with God's will that is the essence of conversional change and return to God.

The religious message to people who feel themselves misplaced and out of touch with reality is that there is a newness of mind available in religious return. The answers to the identity quest, the acceptance and at-homeness available, and that belonging and stability all reside in the community of those who believe in God. It is experienced in the acceptance of the community, and it is sensed personally in a knowledge of belonging and fit. What must be made clear is that life with God is a present reality and a real possibility, for with return to God comes peace—not just the presence of tranquility in the life, but a sense of reconciliation and personal belonging and a sense of history.

There are other implications that have not been mentioned which have significance for those who make it their profession to guide, nurture, and aid the religious development of others.

Implications for the practice of preaching include concern for the development of specific age-related, needs-based, identity issues which find their roots in careful biblical exegesis.

There are broader implications for pastoral care, too. First, church leaders should be alert to the fact that individuals are in movement and no one is static. This dynamic nature of religious growth makes care multitextured, nonjudgmental, varied, and person-centered. Next, special times have a different significance. Moments of identity questing, personal crisis, stress, and pain are especially important times for ministry to occur at every level of the pastorate or school. These moments may be triggers for movement toward or away from God.

And last, knowing other's needs makes us better prepared to help ourselves move to God when we suffer problems, anxiety, or pain.[51]

With inner peace comes surety and direction, and with a new direction, anxiety is obviously eliminated. Faith communities provide not only powerful potential forces for mental health, but also equally unique contexts out of which people seek and grow toward completeness and wholeness. Through counseling that is sensitive to identity issues and conversional moments of crisis, value is placed on the individual uniqueness of God's creations. There results a profound sense of acceptance within the healthy faith community. Miller and Jackson have concluded concisely:

> In part this acceptance comes of the recognition that each person is an individual and unique creation of the same God. In part it emanates from the faith's teaching regarding God's love, forgiveness, and acceptance of people in spite of their shortcomings. But perhaps the most tangible manifestation is to be found in the community itself—in this group of seekers taking an active interest in each other's welfare in the course of a long and constant journey. There is an open belongingness to many faith communities that welcomes in the stranger and fosters in its members a sense of strength and support that enables the taking of new risks and actions.[52]

The religious conversion experience with its identity implications as well as the process of the identity quest itself provides potential for the church's mission, an invitation to reorder ministry in ways which enhance personal development, and new insights into pastoral care.

---

51. For an excellent discussion of the implications for religious educators and pastors of the developmental growth of persons, see James F. Cobble, *Faith and Crisis in the Stages of Life* (Peabody, Mass.: Hendrickson Publishers, 1985), pp. 150-156.

52. Miller and Jackson, *Practical Psychology for Pastors*, p. 405.

Chapter 10

Religious Conversion and Identity: Implications for Nurture and Ministry

"You gotta pray for something to get the spirit. An' when Ah prayed Ah wasn't near the church. You know the quarters on the plantation, well, the church is way aroun' on the front, an', of course, it was too far, an' Ah just prayed in my house. Ah didn't sing no hymn when the Spirit hit me, Ah jest shouted. Ah screamed an' hollared, an Ah sho' cried. You jest get so sorry you cry an' cry an' cry. The Spirit of God makes you jump benches, an' they never hurts themselves. Ah never jumps, Ah jests runs an' shouts an' hollars. But now, Ah stop runnin'."

Henrietta Gant

Some tourists were exploring New Mexico's Carlsbad Caverns. While they were in the depths of the caves, the lights went off. Among those trapped in frightening darkness were two children. Suddenly, the young child began to cry. The older one was heard to say tenderly: "Don't cry! There is one up there who knows how to turn the lights on again."

Determining what causes and contributes to personal change is an illusive endeavor. The insights revealed through research are helpful but can never entirely explain the phenomenon. However, one thing stands out. Conversion and discovering personal identity both are profound experiences. These experiences have historically and individually provided personal clarity and vision, such as described by Henrietta Gant, an African-American slave, who was interviewed in 1939 about her religious conversion (see above).[1]

---

1. Hugh T. Kerr and John M. Mulder, *Conversions* (Grand Rapids, Mich.: Eerdmans, 1983), p. 158.

When searching for answers, I found myself wandering down paths which led through various disciplines—sociology, psychology, theology, and practical theology. So much of religious experience is explained by various disciplines in religion. Through all of this I have been amazed by those persistent personal stories of change brought on by all kinds of events and situations. There have been times when God seems to come, and the impact of that experience is felt.

> My conversion is when I did my first communion. My sisters and I were prepared for this new step in our lives. We learned about God and how He created the world. We learned how to pray and were told not to sin. Every weekend we met at church and we listened to our catechist. We answered questions, drew pictures of God and the angels, and we had some homework, too. We were so excited to hear about God. We always were told that if we behave bad, God would be mad. So we always behaved good. Finally, the day came to do our first communion. We had to do it, and I was nervous. It was my turn, I went in, the room was dark, I knelt down and saw this little window and the priest opened it and all I could hear was his voice. I told him it was my first confession and then I confessed all my sins. He blessed me and I felt clean for the first time and I knew I was ready to receive the body of Christ. We were all dressed like brides in our own dresses and the church was crowded with people. Finally it was time, we put our hands together, the priest gave us the Eucharist and I received the body of Christ and responded "amen." When I received it my heart was pounding so fast and I felt so happy and new inside because I had Christ. This was my conversion and first beautiful step in my religious life. (Maria, age 17)[2]

These moments when God breaks into life and we identify personally with God happen anytime, anywhere. They are coupled with significant experiences that open up possibilities for reflection, introspection, and decisions. They happen in relationships with others, through "triggers," and can even come with psychological explanations. The domino effect plays well here: One event impacts another, and so on to illumination when the whole is viewed. Stories of personal change often reflect such growth.

> What is unique about my experience is that I had to reject all the religious passivity and tradition that I grew up in, because it had no meaning to me. One does not inherit faith. One must find it alone. I had to start with no beliefs, and then work up from there. Meeting people, finding God's will, developing my own approach to God, finding out what I wanted. I believe that my experience is unique and constantly growing. It is yet impossible for me to find a specific denomination that I completely agree with, so I attend the church that satisfies my fellowship needs, and I can identify with. I don't want to become a clone—I want to become a child of God, full of his joy. (Wendy, age 19)[3]

Studies of conversion and identity have their practical side, too. It is in this

---

2. Interview from a freshman student at La Sierra University, Riverside, California during 1989 in the course Dynamics of Personal Religion.
3. Ibid.

area that one of my colleagues, Charles Teel Jr., argues "the rubber meets the road" and "we give arms and legs to what otherwise would be a dry theory." Conversion and identity experience are both ways in which people find meaning in life, identify with ultimates, and sense acceptance and belonging. Conversion at its best is an identity experience with God. What then are the implications of these facts for ministry and nurture?

How do you build ministry which takes into account conversion as a means of identifying with God? How do you build a ministry that moves people toward personal identity in relationship with God?

All ministry is people-centered. All identity has an ideological component. The interrelationship between the role of others and the formation of a belief system is essential in our understanding of our own experience with God.

> What ideologies afford youth is a cognitive tool by which to get a handle on life and to solidify their identity. A crucial element of identity formation is finding a match between how you perceive yourself and the ways in which others view you. Being able to maintain a consistent conception of oneself as well as maintaining a consistent impression on others requires the possession of an ideological outlook that not only tells one who he or she is, but also what action and commitments are expected.[4]

Erikson suggests ideology is an attitude which finds its roots in a general need for a worldview that pulls together one's commitments and levels out the "upsetting swings" in mood and opinion which are often evident in what he has called identity confusion.[5] So establishing an ideology is a task for which religious traditions are well-suited.

Ideology Building

Religious faith provides an identity for believers through ideology. People's perspectives are influenced by their worldview or ideology. People see themselves in relationship with God, and their actions and lifestyle choices stem from that reality. Biblical doctrines are often the agency in which that ideology of God is explained. They enable people to make decisions based on confidence in what they believe to be God's will. Religious faith also, as Fuller suggests, "frees individuals from being at the total mercy of events in the outer world. Instead of being subjected to every new external influence, they are prepared to bring their own set of values and goals to bear upon the interpretation of everyday life."[6]

---

4. Robert C. Fuller, *Religion and the Life Cycle* (Philadelphia: Fortress, 1988), p. 38.

5. See Erik Erikson, *Young Man Luther* (New York: Norton, 1962) and History and the Historical Moment (New York: Norton, 1975), p. 257-58.

6. Robert Fuller, *Religion and the Life Cycle*, p. 39.

One aspect of ministry interested in identity issues is providing opportunity for careful commitment to personal ideology through study of objective revelation which governs and directs most choices for Christians. Often when young adults try to make decisions of their own regarding doctrinal or ideological perimeters, they have grave doubts about their religious life. They have commitment through personal experience, but have limited resources out of which to formulate personal doctrine. Here the church can minister in a substantial way. Opportunities for study, support, exploration, and dialogue can open up the world of commitment.

The style of presentation is often more important than the content. Research has shown that congenial relationships are necessary if positive attitudes toward religion are to be developed. "When a congenial relationship exists between an adult and a young person, the youth tend to adopt the values of the adult."[7] In addition to this, gentle reasoning or induction are effective methods in assisting young people toward solid values.

Merton Strommen argues that one's theological orientation is crucial in determining whether or not one will learn significant values. A grace orientation with a focus on love, promise and presence of Jesus Christ inspires people to accept the lifestyle and ideology of Christ.[8] Modeling of grace by adults is important if the church is to have committed young members. In contrast to this approach, a legalistic orientation may make people reject the very values the institution was hoping to communicate. The church's manner in communicating values and doctrinal commitment is an important concern in establishing solid religious identity and encouraging change.

After religious commitment through conversion, the church must find a way to begin to build ideology (doctrine) and maintain the first-hand encounter with God through that investigation by a method that draws people to God rather than repulses them. Fuller suggests:

> Whatever the individual's particular manner of achieving a firm ideological outlook on life, the demands of identity formation tend to prompt youth to examine the intellectual aspects of religion; it also compels them to subject religion to what might be called ideological critique. To be worthy of their devotion it must be tested by the standards of logic and reason, and weighed on the scales of scientific knowledge. During such inquiry and critical examination secondhand faith quickly breaks down. The process of individualizing the ready-made faith handed to one at an earlier stage in life accelerates under the impetus of intellectual doubt.

Conversion provides identification with God. Identification is necessary for religious certainty. Even though this experience is often subjective, it

---

7. Merton P. Strommen, "How Values are Communicated," report to Project Affirmation, North American Division of Seventh-Day Adventists, Silver Springs, Md., p. 1.

8. Ibid., p. 5.

provides the motivation for study, formulation of ideology, attitude building, and life choices.[9] Church workers, pastoral counselors, and religious facilitators can be a significant help in establishing ideological commitment and therefore in encouraging identification with God if they design appropriate curriculum and assist ideological clarification. James Heady shares a conversation with a young wife who finds God's directions through in-depth instructions which shape her understanding of the church and God's will.

> From the day I started taking instructions, I felt much more at peace. There was a feeling of security comfort and belonging that I could never remember feeling before. All my formative years in the Congregational church, and all the Bible schools plus Sunday school had taught me about God and the Bible, but until now something was missing. . . . But after years of turmoil, the church eventually straightened out without setting up a number of competing Catholic religions. The continuity from Christ to the present day remains unbroken. This strongly appeals to my sense of order.[10]

Religious experience does not happen in isolation. As we have seen, religious conversion is always in context, and the impact of others in experience is well-documented. The role of dynamic people and their influence on commitment and change is clear. I mentioned earlier in this book the study for the Seventh-Day Adventist denomination coordinated by Search Institute called *Valuegenesis,* where over 20,000 sixth- to twelfth-grade students, their parents, their pastors, and their teachers were interviewed. It was clear that a church climate which is warm, encourages question-asking, is caring and is permeated with a grace orientation rather than a legalistic approach to rules and standards is the most conducive to spiritual growth and church loyalty. Church climate is a product of relationships and interactions. People do make a difference in the religious experience of others, and that impacts religious change. This research is validated by recent studies by major denominations in Search Institute's work on effective Christian education.

This research (*Valuegenesis*) reveals an approach to God which is love-based, accepting, and open and is more successful in helping children and youth develop faith in Christ and in internalizing values than an approach which is motivated by or promotes an attitude of legalism (judgment, fear). The research indicates that six out of ten Seventh-Day Adventist youth are worried over the fact that they do not feel ready for Christ's return. A sense of assurance does not seem to exist regarding this aspect of their religious

---

9. Merton P. Strommen, *Five Cries of Youth* (San Francisco: Harper & Row, 1988), pp. 122,123.

10. James F. Heady, "A Wife's Example," in *Spiritual Journeys: Toward the Fullness of Faith,* ed. Robert Baram (Boston: St. Paul Books & Media, 1988), p. 124.

experience. Most want help in dealing with this issue. They covet a deeper and more certain relationship with God. Seven in ten declare interest in school programs that focus on this subject. There is a challenge for church workers and leaders here.

Most (72 percent) reject the idea that there is nothing one can do to earn salvation. Responses such as these indicate that the majority of Adventist youth are law-oriented. This is consistent with what has been discovered in national norms established by studies of various denominations. This may be explained by developmental understanding, but it certainly provides a moment of pause in those responsible for helping youth find assurance in their walk with God. Youth most often believe salvation depends on what they do rather than realizing that what they elect to do is a by-product or result of the saving activity of Christ.[11] Adult Adventists, while somewhat less legalistic, have a similar bent, the research reveals.

With research like that, what should a congregation do? The answer is to be found in curriculum as well as in relationships. The curriculum should encourage the seeker to distinguish between a gospel that focuses on God's promises and will, and a stance based on observing a required set of behaviors. The more positive view of God's love is powerful in creating change and building relationships.

Teaching methods, including the communication of lifestyle practices and appropriate church standards, should be utilized which are founded upon a grace orientation. Pastors and youth workers have a responsibility to increase the number of youth who await Christ's return with confidence, joy, and hope. Teachers must burn with a personal concern that each of their students comes to know Christ. Programs of personal conversations with youth should be developed that help adults (teachers, parents, youth leaders, pastors) lead youth into a faith relationship with Christ. And because we recognize the importance of others in helping people find God and embarking on their return home (conversion), these programs should encourage individual spiritual development through a dialogical approach which would use open, thoughtful, and challenging approaches to change.

Personal Religious Development

An attitude of tolerance is the mandate for ministry to youth. When I am asked to help people understand the faith-life of young people, I usually

---

11. V. Bailey Gillespie, "Faith, Values, and Commitment in the '90s—Report and Recommendations, Draft I," *Valuegenesis*, Project Affirmation, 1990, p. 8. For a complete discussion of *Valuegenesis* research see: V. Bailey Gillespie, "Passing the Torch of Faith: A Special Report," *Adventist Review* (January 3, 1991), pp. 5-11, and V. Bailey Gillespie, "Risk and Promises for Adventist Education: An Agenda for Action," *Adventist Review* (January 10, 1991), pp. 16-19.

take a clue from Michael Warren, who suggests that we keep in mind that in order to help others find God and identify with eternal things, it is important to think about one's own personal religious development. We must keep in mind the fact that religious development is like all other kinds of development; it takes years![12]

There are rapid movements and shifts in belief and latent periods where not much seems to be happening. There are reflective moments when the God concept is vague and other times when religion is the most important thing ever considered. These shifts in personal development reflect the movements in the life cycle, sexual differences, maturation, and influence. There is no "typical" religious person. The church (or faith community) will be well served if it envisions itself as a "romper room," equipped with buffers and safe havens for the sometimes rambunctious, sometimes melancholy, "children" as they grow in faith. People who struggle finding their place with God, who have difficulty attempting to locate God in their world, who find that their commitments often shift, and who find stability in the faith of a community which is living out the calling and mission of its faith decisions.

Becoming trustworthy guides and guarantors of faith is a challenging task. Since people learn best by experience rather than by observation, the quality of actual faith in the church may be the best teacher of what it means to be accepted, loved, and identified with God. Since conversion as an identity experience brings understanding of God's will, the actual living out that will in life and community will go a long way toward making the subjective experience of God real and significant.

Young people are especially vulnerable to inconsistent community. Since their learning is primarily through first-hand experience rather than through reflective cognition, a key factor in developing personal faith is how the church lives out identity with God. One can ask interesting questions which probe this issue. Can the church move people to change when little change is taking place in its own congregation? Can being identified with God be all that important when young adults seldom see people living their lives as if God had accepted and forgiven them? Do church workers who organize and plan programs of ministry realize the importance their approach and modeling of faith has to those trying to make decisions and come home to God in conversion?

What is imperative is that you spend time getting to know the people for whom you minister. Get to know some young people. Get to know their gifts and possibilities. Get to know the needs of those attempting to find God. Nevil Harner enumerates needs of youth that must be kept in mind by any youth minister: 1) the need to discover the overarching principle (God)

---

12. Michael Warren, *Youth and the Future of the Church: Ministry with Youth and Young Adults* (Minneapolis: Seabury, 1982), pp. 61-63.

in life; 2) the need to find themselves; 3) the need to focus on some sort of life goals; 4) the need to find intimacy and a mate; 5) the need to find society's desire for their lives—the questions of identity and meaning; 6) the need to discover the nature of community.[13] These needs, while especially focused on youth, are those of all believers. The need to find one's self and the need to find a life goal, along with the need to understand personal meaning, are all identity issues that commitment to God fulfills. After you get to know people, you can call them to be better than they are. You can show options for their choices; you can share what has given meaning to your life. This is helpful not only with young people, but with all members of the congregation. Any congregation which wants to be more effective in encouraging identity and conversion in their members would do well to begin to schedule programs, workshops, and discussions which focus on life goals and personal spiritual experience.

Programing or People

Most church workers resent having to follow a "program" because these are often packaged approaches sent down from the institutional church which are supposed to be a panacea for the ills of the local congregation. If there are people who do not know God or cannot find themselves, you order that special package from the district office and use it properly so all problems can be solved. Churches have waited for years for just the right program; regional administrators have hoped for the packaged correct answer to the church's problems; and God is waiting for *people* to change rather than for *programs* to be delivered. Anyone who has worked in the area of change knows that one of the most powerful and enduring influences that exists to help people shift their beliefs or behaviors is that of the presence of dynamic individuals who are excited about what they believe. Many youth and adults have been turned on in school by the influence of a teacher who loved his or her subject matter so much that every day class became an adventure. Thousands have tried diets, bought athletic equipment, or purchased land because of a powerful witness by a dynamic person. While these types of people are rare, their impact cannot be underrated.

In the area of religious change specifically, dynamic people have amazing influence. But dynamism and charisma are not the only qualities that draw young people. The quiet, gentle listener and supportive guarantor tenderly moves a young person to God as effectively as the pull of enthusiasm. This dynamism is of a different type. The overriding emphasis is interest in others. As you attend to others' histories and interests, you assist them toward a spirituality that is Christian and suited to the present day and their

13. See the classic treatment of youth's need by Nevil C. Harner, *The Educational Work of the Church* (Nashville: Abingdon, 1939).

own level of development. Your involvement in others' lives triggers commitments which may yield a conversion as an identity-forming experience.

Certainly you plan programs which move people to touch the numinous, but as you provide experience-rich encounters with religious themes, you get involved in others' lives. This attending to others in a personal way is the most important thing anyone can do for another's spiritual journey. As you attend to the moments of crisis which create opportunities for religious change and for God to break into life you learn patience as well as a sensitivity to others' needs. And these flower into a personal outlook blooming with possibilities.

> There is a way of living in which nature becomes transparent and starts teaching us about our life and our death, about the flow of our existence. It teaches about suffering and it teaches about joy for those who pray and for those who are constantly willing to see that life is a gift of God, when life becomes no longer *chronos* but becomes *kairos*—that's a Greek word for opportunity—the opportunity to change your heart and your mind. That's the great conversion, when I no longer see the interruptions as disturbances but as the great chance, as the moment in which God is molding me and giving shape to my life. I have to start listening very carefully. "Why did that illness come in my life? Why is war going on? Why are all those things happening to me?" We must wait and watch for that moment of crisis, for change, for opportunity. I believe we are heard best when we respond rather than when we initiate. When we wait rather than rush ahead.[14]

We must think of these moments of listening as moments of chance. A chance to change, to truly hear what is going on in the individual's life and heart. Too often religious change has only been cognitive conversion. True conversion involves the process of clarification of life and the chance to form a new worldview with God as the center and others as equals. No "program" can be that involved. No packaged approach, printed tracts, brochures, advertising, or evangelism can become that centered in the lives of others. But if religious change is to grip us at the core of our selves, then we must learn to love others and listen to their needs. This influence models the good Samaritan, points us to Jesus as he was with the woman at the well at the foot of Mount Gerizim, and reminds us of the attention that Mary gave Jesus in spite of Martha's insistence to get on with life. As Warren said, "Youth [all people] are looking for the signs of transformation in the very persons and communities that would call them to transformation."[15]

Research such as that found in Merton Strommen's *Five Cries of Youth* is showing us that we must minister to the whole of people and not to what we perceive them to be.[16] When individuals in the church recognize that the

---

14. Quoted in Warren, Youth and the Future of the Church, p. 64-65. Or see Henri J.M. Nouwen, "More People, More Love" *National Catholic Reporter* (October 13, 1979), p. 134.

15. Warren, *Youth and the Future of the Church*, pp. 63-67.

16. Strommen, *Five Cries*, pp. 144-157.

church is interested in them as complete people, then progress will be made in influencing them to participate and make commitment. Sadly, the church would often rather be right than loving. Building relationships is a low priority, while budget concerns and promotion tend to surface to the top. Only as the institution (church) is broken down to its subparts (individual members) does the sense of community of faith and "romper room" haven transcend the corporate priorities.

Symbols of Change

As a means of cementing a feeling of community with the life of the church, religious workers, pastors, and youth ministers can use symbols of religious faith that invoke identification with God. Although this is a rather subjective use of symbols, still, religious people need to constantly be acquainted with those rich representations of ultimate reality which have an evocative aspect to them. "Triggers" for conversion come in many ways. Often change comes when we are invited to be different, to reinterpret the ordinary, or to imagine God in a new and personal way. Such religious happenings as liturgical ritual, drama, art, personal sharing, and worship draw one to be different and to imagine one's life anew. They are also a means of establishing a common language of faith which facilitates a sense of community.

Through such symbols one identifies with God (one who is both caring and personal). Participations in the symbolic representations of God move one beyond simple statements to affirming an experienced reality. Involvement in symbolic understandings helps us declare something intensely personal. Those people identify with God as their own God. And that God is one who recognizes them as in need of forgiveness and acceptance. When one comes close to ultimate reality one senses that things can never be the same again. The world must now be seen in relationship to that reality, and all of life's choices and understandings must now be focused through that prism. Considering God's will becomes a way of relating to life.

What are the experiences which invoke this reality? What are the experiences which invite conversion and identity? They include intense caring and fellowship, liturgical experiences, communion, Eucharist, mission involvement, and the involvement of leading others to find God. For women in the church, it might include ministries which touch their unique sensitivities and religious experience, for men it could include traditional leadership experiences in the church, yet equally personal involvements. While the church does not want to fall into any role patterning, sensitivity to unique needs must be included in all the decisions of the church regarding programing change. Those involved in planning such experiences need to recognize the evocative nature of symbolic representations of God. They need to realize that understanding symbols provides stretching which often moves us beyond ourselves to the realm of the transcendent.

Change and the Church

One question concerning conversion that needs to be addressed is that of readiness. Is it possible to nurture others to a position where "conversion" might happen? Or as Thomas Groome says, "Is our task as religious educators to nurture, to convert, or to do both to our students?" and, "Can a religious educator, whatever his/her particular tradition may be, sponsor others toward such critical consciousness?"[17] Groome argues "no." One answer might be to focus on the religious facilitator him/herself. "My basic thesis is that central to all of the above questions is the educator's own 'conversion.' That shapes the kind of nurturing conversion he/she will do in the religious educational moment and the form of faith activity toward which he/she can sponsor others."[18] Additional answers to these questions include: 1) structuring situations in which people are confronted with the potential and possibilities they have with God in their life—this draws people out of themselves and into spiritual possibilities; 2) developing relationships which are open, attentive, and caring—this encourages thoughtful modeling and appreciation of others' conversion; 3) providing options for members to study various curricula in the church which are needs-oriented and evocative of change. People learn best when they are interested and motivated to understand, and change is easier when interest is heightened; 4) and finally, enriching church climates—to enhance the potential for personal decision making in a warm, open, and exciting community.

While attention to one's own attitudes toward God is crucial, as Groome suggests, it is equally important that the church, its members, staff, educators, pastoral counselors, and youth ministers develop an attitude of openness to probe the personal questions about identity and to explore those aspects of church life which promote identification with God and encourage careful, thoughtful, and reflective change.

Conclusion—Conversion and Identity

On the basis of our understanding of conversion as an identity-forming experience, the biblical understanding of the term, research regarding the experience, and developmental psychology's input regarding identity formation, I have proposed a model of conversion as deep change with personal identity-forming qualities brought on by and through the impact of

17. Thomas H. Groome, "Conversion, Nurture and Educators," *Religious Education* 76 (September-October 1981), p. 484.

18. Ibid., p. 485.

others, environments, and the transcendent nature of the experience of God. I have suggested that conversion transforms both the perspective of an individual toward his or her world with regard to values, purpose, and direction as well as transforming one's personal understanding of his or her role in it. As Walter Conn suggests, conversion takes place as a shift in "structure (in contrast to a horizontal change of content) from a spontaneously instinctive or a reflectively personal orientation toward truth, value, and love."[19] It includes moral, cognitive, and affective domains and the shifts which occur are often age-related, gender differentiated, or environmentally triggered. Both identity and conversion reorient the individual to new purpose and direction. In that sense, conversion is an identity experience of the deepest kind.

David Wells ends his discussion about conversion this way:

> The test of conversion, then, is whether a sinner continues to see sin as displeasing to God and continues to turn from it, continues to seek Christ and trust him for life, forgiveness, grace, and guidance. It is whether believing in Christ leads to following him by denying ourselves and daily taking up our cross and following him, seeking his kingdom above our interests, loving and serving his people because of his love for us. It is whether the graces of Christian character begin to appear. It is whether we begin to learn how to live in God's world on his terms, recognizing him as the sovereign creator and sustainer of all, thankfully accepting from him the good gifts and experiences he gives us and accepting the disappointments with the kind of submission that can come only from a deep sense of his abiding goodness. When conversion leads to a love of God and his glory and a commitment to serve and honor him in all that we do, then the conversion is genuine. It is in these ways, the ways of the life of faith, that we are given the only evidence of the reality of a person's profession of faith.[20]

Even though Wells' discussion is in specifically Christian terms and reflects a distinctively masculine view of God's personhood, his stress on God's interest in changing us in every area of our life is powerful.

The church worker, pastoral facilitator, youth worker, and pastoral counselor can make a contribution in the lives of others as they become sensitive to the dynamics of these experiences—identity and conversion—and through them move the person to deeper commitment and direction in life. Conversion and identity both provide a way to change—direction and clarity in the midst of personal darkness.

> Two roads seemed to diverge from this point, as I saw it from the one I had chosen. One was rather dark and very smooth, broad and ever broadening until it debouched in a dark desert and ceased to be a road. The other was brilliantly lighted, almost too light for comfort, I felt, though light was needed, for the road

---

19. Walter Conn, *Christian Conversion: A Developmental Interpretation of Autonomy and Surrender* (New York: Paulist, 1986), p. 267.

20. Wells, *Turning to God*, p. 148.

was rough and horribly steep and ever narrowing. This, the lighted road, was the one I had chosen, though I was only at the beginning: the obstacles and the wearying steepness and the dangerous narrowness, all lay ahead. Still, I could see where I was going, and that seemed to me to be the great thing.[21]

---

21. Sheldon Vanauken, "Encounter with Light," in *Spiritual Journeys: Toward the Fullness of Faith*, ed. Robert Baram, p. 353.

Index of Names

Index of Subjects